MARTIN SABO

MARTIN SABO

THE MAKING OF THE MODERN LEGISLATURE

LORI STURDEVANT

mnhspress.org   @mnhspress

The Minnesota Historical Society Press is a member of the Association of University Presses.

Manufactured in the United States of America

10 9 8 7 6 5 4 3 2 1

∞ The paper used in this publication meets the minimum requirements of the American National Standard for Information Sciences—Permanence for Printed Library Materials, ANSI Z39.48-1984.

ISBN: 978-1-68134-325-9 (paper)
ISBN: 978-1-68134-326-6 (e-book)

Library of Congress Control Number: 2025934517

for William Kelly
1939–2023
who badly wanted more leaders
like Martin Sabo

"Martin's thinking always was,
'I'm going to be part of a larger effort
to make things better for the world.'"

WILLIAM "BILL" KELLY, MARCH 2, 2023

CONTENTS

Introduction . . . 1

CHAPTER ONE

Alkabo's Son . . . 3

CHAPTER TWO

Pivot to the City . . . 21

CHAPTER THREE

A Torch Passes, Slowly . . . 37

CHAPTER FOUR

Minority Leader . . . 59

CHAPTER FIVE

It's a Miracle! . . . 75

CHAPTER SIX

The Key Turns . . . 94

CHAPTER SEVEN

In Charge . . . 110

CHAPTER EIGHT

A Speaker for Everyone . . . 132

CHAPTER NINE

Dominoes Fall . . . 157

CHAPTER TEN

The Way to Washington . . . 179

CHAPTER ELEVEN

Congressman Sabo . . . 199

CHAPTER TWELVE

The Liberal Decentralist . . . 223

Acknowledgments . . . 233 / Notes . . . 237
Bibliography . . . 259 / Image Credits . . . 262
Index . . . 263

MARTIN SABO

INTRODUCTION

FROM THE VANTAGE OF 2025, THERE'S SOMETHING QUAINT about the political style of Martin Olav Sabo. A leading Minnesota legislator and congressman of the late twentieth century, Sabo was a shoe-leather, door-to-door candidate who never aired an attack ad or publicly slung a demeaning epithet at an opponent. He was a student of the "inside baseball" of the legislative branch of government—calendars, committee assignments, fiscal notes, office space. (And yes, he also studied baseball.) He cared not just about what government did but also about how it performed and which level of government was best suited to the task at hand. He didn't just refuse to demonize members of the opposite party. He befriended them and encouraged their participation in decision-making.

Those characteristics may sound like the practices of an earlier time. But that does not mean they should be dismissed or forgotten. This book was born of a conviction that the Sabo story is worth telling amid the cutthroat partisanship that characterizes twenty-first-century American politics. The anxiety many Americans feel about their system of government makes now an apt time to examine the life and work of someone who showed that it is indeed possible to make that system work "for the better."

Martin Sabo was an institutionalist. But immutable preservation of the Minnesota or the United States houses of representatives was never his goal. He sought those bodies' improvement (he was too modest—and realistic—to claim that he sought their perfection) for the sake of making them better able to deliver the public services he believed Americans deserved. When he concluded that institutional rules and norms needed to change to better meet society's needs, he willingly led the charge to make those changes. But when critics denigrated those institutions or sought to make them dysfunctional—particularly for personal or partisan gain—he rose to their defense. Despite his lifelong attachment to those two elective bodies, he understood that they belonged not to him but to the people and that his role was one of stewardship.

While this book describes the entire seventy-eight-year span of Sabo's life, it concentrates on the period 1969–78, the last ten of the eighteen years he spent in the Minnesota Legislature. Those years saw momentous change in both state policy and institutional operations, and Sabo was in the thick of it. Remarkably, most of what Sabo and his colleagues accomplished in that era has stood the test of time. It has also been emulated around the country—and in that spread, too, Sabo played a role, by giving Minnesota a prominent place in the National Conference of State Legislatures. Sabo helped engineer that organization's creation. When he reflected on his whole career in interviews at the end of his life, he evinced particular pride when describing the Minnesota Legislature of the 1970s.

In these pages, I invite readers to discover, as I did, that the relevance of Sabo's story is not confined to one state or one time. As many examples both ancient and modern attest, representative democracy isn't easy. The leadership required to make that system of government effective is not typically in abundant supply—and when such leaders arise, they are not always appreciated by voters. But this book asserts that when someone of keen mind and good heart, someone like Martin Sabo, chooses to make representative democracy his life's work, an admirable result can ensue. That kind of career politician deserves citizens' respect—and their votes.

CHAPTER ONE

ALKABO'S SON

EVEN IN ITS HEYDAY, ALKABO, NORTH DAKOTA, WAS AN unlikely incubator of American state or national leadership. At its population peak, sometime in the 1920s, the tiny town on North Dakota's windswept northwestern prairie was home to about a hundred people, mostly immigrants or children of immigrants from Norway. Though the Soo Line railroad served the town, bringing a lifeline of goods, news, and connection to the outside world, a sense of isolation pervaded the place. By the time Martin Olav Sabo was born on February 28, 1938, the little town had been battered by more than a decade of economic depression and was struggling to survive. It was a struggle the town would eventually lose. Alkabo's population in 2016 was said to be "between seven and nine people, depending on the time of year."[1]

Yet, unassuming Alkabo and its inhabitants were particularly suited to instill democratic values and leadership skills in their children. It was a place where children learned early that their families' well-being was linked to that of the community. Lives there were rich in relationships, and interdependence was taught to the young as a survival skill. It was a place where adults not only talked about the importance of education but demonstrated it through personal sacrifice. It was a place where citizenship was taught by example and where the American Dream of a better life for the next generation was so palpable it could practically be felt in the soil.

It was a place where a boy could quickly become a man, one deeply connected to his community.

From Norway to North Dakota

The first European settlers in North Dakota's northwesternmost outpost arrived in 1905 and called the place Spring Valley. That same year, a twenty-two-year-old Elling Sæbo left Hjelmeland, Norway, in search of something he had little chance of ever acquiring in his homeland—a farm of his own. He was one of several children born to Maria Jonsdottir Riskedal during her second marriage, to Ola Ellingson Fister. (Their children took the name Sæbo, Americanized to Sabo, which was associated with a church and parish south of Hjelmeland on Norway's jagged southwestern coast.) Maria's first marriage had already produced a son. Under Norway's ancient primogeniture code of intergenerational land transfer, her first son would inherit their small farm. Elling and his younger brother Bjorn were obliged to pursue other occupations or to find land elsewhere if they wished to make their living as farmers.[2]

By the turn of the twentieth century, the pattern of northern Europeans leaving home and searching for opportunity in the United States was well established. Norwegians began settling in the upper midwestern states of Wisconsin, Iowa, and Minnesota even before the Homestead Act of 1862 lured them with the powerful magnet of free land—160 acres to any citizen or aspiring citizen willing to live on and cultivate that land for five years. The Homestead Act was intended to encourage western-state settlement and food production by people exactly like Elling and Bjorn Sabo—eager young people focused on making a lifelong attachment to their new homes. The land giveaway also drew an ample share of charlatans and land speculators. It was said that of some 500 million acres dispersed by the General Land Office between 1862 and 1904, only eighty million acres went to actual homesteaders. Despite those small homesteaders' diligent

HR 125

Thirty-seventh

Congress of the United States,

At the Second Session

BEGUN AND HELD AT THE CITY OF WASHINGTON

in the District of Columbia

on Monday the second day of December one thousand eight hundred and sixty-one

AN ACT to secure homesteads to actual settlers on the public domain.

Be It Enacted by the Senate and House of Representatives of the United States of America in Congress assembled,

That any person who is the head of a family, or who has arrived at the age of twenty-one years, and is a citizen of the United States, or who shall have filed his declaration of intention to become such, as required by the naturalization laws of the United States, and who has never borne arms against the United States government or given aid and comfort to its enemies, shall from and after the first January, eighteen hundred and sixty-three be entitled to enter one quarter section or a less quantity of unappropriated public lands, upon which said person may have filed a pre-emption claim, or which may, at the time an application is made, be subject to pre-emption at one dollar and twenty-five cents, or less, per acre; or eighty acres or less of such unappropriated lands, at two dollars and fifty cents per acre; to be located in a body, in conformity to the legal subdivisions of the public lands, and after the same shall have been surveyed: Provided, That any person owning and residing on land may, under the provisions of this act, enter other land lying contiguous to his or her said land, which shall not, with the land so already owned and occupied, exceed in the aggregate, one hundred and sixty acres.

Sec. 2. And be it further enacted, That the person applying

Text of the Homestead Act of 1862.

labor, many of them remained ensnared in poverty—especially those who filed claims after choice parcels were taken and all that remained was the agriculturally marginal soil of the Great Plains. Places like northwestern North Dakota.[3]

Elling Sabo started his American life in Iowa, presumably working as a hired farmhand, likely among Norwegian immigrants with whom he was acquainted. He was a quiet man and a diligent worker who enjoyed playing cards and swapping stories with other men, but he never took a wife. In 1910, he filed a homestead claim on 160 acres southeast of the hamlet by then called Alkabo, a mash-up of the words "alkali" and "gumbo," which described the area's poor soil.

Little brother Bjorn Andreas—who took an American-sounding nickname, Ben—had followed Elling to America in 1908 but was ahead of him in North Dakota. Two years before Elling moved west, Ben—at age twenty-one—filed a homestead claim in Elkhorn Township north of Alkabo in what was described as "a remote area with high hills." Five years later, after meeting the Homestead Act's "proving up" requirement and paying the modest fee it required, Ben crossed the international border and tried his hand at farming in Canada. It

Postage stamp commemorating the centennial of the Homestead Act of 1862.

evidently was not a satisfactory experience. By 1914, a year after the railroad came to town, Ben was back in Alkabo—twenty-seven years old, still a bachelor, and financially able to buy land that had been homesteaded a decade earlier by one of the first Norwegian immigrants to the region, Peder Bredevin. Peder and his wife and daughter had decided to give up prairie isolation, move to town, and open a livery shop. As their example attested, family life on the harsh and lonely prairie was hard to sustain.[4]

The weather figured prominently among the Sabo brothers' many challenges. In July 1916 a tornado ripped through the region and destroyed Ben's house and barn—a major disaster anywhere, but particularly so on the mostly treeless prairie, where building supplies were not readily at hand. Ben "never trusted the weather after that," a local historian recorded. But he decided that while "he couldn't control the weather, he could do something to protect himself against it." He dug a storm cellar, covered all but its entrance with earth, and made it a permanent and often-used fixture on his farm. Later, he would instill in his children a deep respect for the weather. "We grew up watching the clouds," his daughter recalled.[5]

It may have seemed to the locals that the Sabo brothers were destined to spend all their days as Norwegian bachelor farmers, a midwestern rural archetype caricatured by Minnesota humorist Garrison Keillor decades later. The description seemed to fit quiet Elling. But Ben, a more outgoing chap, grew restless with only his brother for company during North Dakota's long winters. He rented Peder Bredevin's by then vacant house in Alkabo in the winter of 1924–25, and before long it was a regular gathering spot for other bachelors and even, on one occasion, the local Lutheran church's Ladies Aid Club.

When the snows of the following winter commenced, Ben decided he could finally afford to visit his parents. He had not seen his mother and ailing father for seventeen years. He left on December 4, 1925, expecting to return in the spring. Ola's death while Ben was in Hjelmeland prolonged his stay. So did a rapidly developing relationship with an attractive young woman who was employed at a nearby hotel.

Klara Haga was fifteen years Ben's junior and acquainted with Ben's family. She was bright, strong, full of energy, and possessed of a hearty sense of humor. Ben was quickly smitten. They were married in Norway on April 17, 1926, and made plans to travel to North Dakota—Ben returning in July, Klara joining him a month later after a stop to visit her brother Magnus and his family in Granite Falls, Minnesota. Less than two years later, on March 18, 1928, the couple welcomed their only daughter, Anna Marie.

Isolation and grinding physical labor took a toll on many farm wives on the Dakota prairies during those years. The locals in Alkabo were likely watching for signs of distress in young Klara, who had been accustomed to electricity, modern appliances, and indoor plumbing in Norway and had nothing of the sort in the tiny two-bedroom farmhouse that was her new home. What they saw, local historian Elaine Leininger records, was that "she adapted well to life on the prairie. . . . She carried in coal or wood for the stoves, caught water in barrels when it rained, and sewed, cooked and did whatever else she saw that needed doing." Rainwater was used for washing; drinking water was obtained from the town pump in Alkabo, two miles away, and hauled home in ten-gallon cream cans. The farmstead was home to horses, a few dairy cows, and small flocks of chickens and turkeys—all providing sustenance while demanding daily attention.[6]

While Anna Marie was still a toddler, Klara arranged for childcare so she could enroll in the local elementary school and learn English alongside the village's youngest children, many of whom spoke Norwegian at home. Decades later, villagers remembered their teacher reminding them not to speak Norwegian to Klara as they did to their parents. They were charged with helping their eldest classmate learn. She took classes for three weeks. "Before long, she was reading the newspaper in English at home," her daughter related.

Serving Alkabo

Ten years elapsed between the births of Anna Marie and Martin Olav, the couple's only other child. For Ben and Klara they were years of maturation and deepening community involvement. Ben was elected township justice of the peace and served on the school board; Klara was immersed in activities at the Alkabo School and Writing Rock Lutheran Church, the clapboard church near the Sabo farm that Ben helped build. It was named for ancient thunderbird petroglyphs carved on two granite boulders nearby. Klara encouraged her husband's service in elective office. Her father, Martin Haga, and his brothers had done as much in Norway.[7]

But the 1930s were also times of hardship as the Great Depression depleted incomes on the nation's farms. The three-room Sabo house was damaged by fire in May 1929. It was hastily repaired and remained so spartan that a few years later, when Klara's mother, Kari Velde Haga, visited her daughter, she voiced alarm about the house's primitive state.

Family lore tells that Klara responded with offended pride: "She said, 'You can leave right now with that attitude. This is my home,'" Klara's granddaughter Julie Sabo related. "Her clear standard was that you do not complain. You're not poor. You hold your head high and you make do with what you've got."

Disaster struck Alkabo on Halloween 1932 when the little town's only school, built in 1916, was destroyed by fire. Classes moved to a nearby building that also housed a newspaper. Schools in neighboring towns donated books and supplies. Despite the deepening depression and the area's meager population, no one questioned whether the school should be rebuilt. The only question considered by Ben Sabo and his fellow school board members was the size of the new school. They opted to go big. They undertook a community fundraising drive that fostered a variety of events, including a women's basketball game in which Klara Sabo was among the players on the court.

The result, ready for the start of classes in September 1934, was a building that would long stand as a testament to the lofty value Alkabo's pioneers attached to public education. The split-level Alkabo School, built in Italian Renaissance style, served children in all twelve grades and included a gymnasium large enough for basketball with a theater stage at one end, a kitchen, two bathrooms, and

Gravel road intersection in Alkabo, North Dakota, in 2022.

three classrooms with ample space for books and supplies. A point of community pride from the outset, its dedication ceremony drew state as well as local dignitaries and provided Ben Sabo with a high point in his service to his community.

The building ceased operation as a school in 1963, but in 2025 it still stands on the edge of the nearly abandoned town, protected by both its status on the National Register of Historic Places and the fond memories of the people who were educated there. It houses a small museum that is open by appointment.[8]

Martin Arrives

What the school lacked was a school bus to deliver farm children to its door in the morning and take them home at night. As a result, farm parents like the Sabos were obliged to make extraordinary efforts to get children to and from school each day. Neighbors pitched in with what today would be called carpools or "sleigh pools" when snow was too deep for motor vehicles. Some families arranged for their children to stay in town with friends or relatives during the school week, returning to their parents' homes on weekends.

For the Sabos, the struggle to get Anna Marie to school each day must have been keenly felt in the winter of 1938 and thereafter. Martin Olav was born on February 28 in Crosby, a town thirty miles east of Alkabo that was large enough to have a small hospital. Klara, then thirty-six years old, had rented a room in Crosby during the final weeks of her pregnancy at the urging of her husband so that her birth could be attended by medical professionals. He was anxious about the prospect of a home birth in the dead of winter, far from any help that might be required. Anna Marie remembers long quiet weeks that winter with her kindly father, their happiness when Klara came home briefly to celebrate Ben's fifty-first birthday on January 27, and their glee when Klara and baby Martin came home to stay in March. Before they did, Ben sat his nine-year-old daughter down for a serious talk. "He said, 'You have to stay in and help your mother now,'" she related. Ben would see to it that his daughter could safely traverse the mile-long driveway from the Sabo farm to the main county road to get to and from school. When she got home, new chores would await her. Long hours of outdoor play after school were over. "My life changed tremendously," she said.

A new arrangement was made in the winter of 1940–41 as Martin turned three. Klara and her two children joined another farm wife, Ingeborg Norby, and the school-aged Norby children at a house in town owned by an older Norby son, Julius. The two women created a temporary household during the week, taking turns at childcare and seeing that the children got to school. Sometimes Klara and little Martin would visit school during the day, giving both of them a chance to improve their English while still speaking Norwegian at home. Martin had one other linguistic aid that Anna Marie had lacked as a young child—a radio. The Sabo household got its first radio, a large battery-powered model, soon after Martin was born. The result: by age five, Martin was fully bilingual.

Experiencing the advantages of living near the school likely helped to persuade Ben and Klara to seek a permanent change of address. Martin was deemed ready to start first grade as a five-year-old in 1943—a year earlier than expected. His mother timed his school start to coincide with that of another girl in the community, "to make sure I had some competition in the classes," he explained late in life. He joined a class with a total enrollment of four students.[9]

The need for one so young to get to school and back each day led the family to decide they would abandon their farmhouse and find year-round lodging in Alkabo. Building a new house was prohibitively expensive. But moving an existing house to a vacant lot near the school was doable, they decided. The couple found a suitable property in the late fall of 1943, moved the house the next spring, and worked with a local carpenter to adapt it to their needs. By the time Martin started second grade, the family was settled in an in-town house with a yard suited for a garden, a shed, and accommodations for a few cows and chickens. Martin's trip to school had been reduced to just one block. A few years later, Klara joined him at the school as its "lunch lady." Martin was never far from loving, watchful adult eyes.

Though the Sabos now lived in town, Ben continued to farm the small holding he had owned for more than thirty years. But increasingly, his main occupation was that of assessor for government farm programs, a position of considerable trust and responsibility as farm subsidy programs emerged with the New Deal. Ben's measurements determined the size of both government subsidy payments and local property tax bills. As assessor, he visited every house and farm in the area, deepening his relationships with his neighbors.

Church and School

Family life in 1944 changed in one other way. Alkabo School did not offer a full high school curriculum during World War II. Only grades nine and ten were taught. Some of the area's children ended their education at that point—but not Anna Marie Sabo. She aimed to become a teacher. It was a goal shared by her parents, even though it meant she would need to leave home and finish high school elsewhere. For her junior year, they chose Crosby High School, just thirty miles east of Alkabo and a short, regularly scheduled train ride away. Weekends at home were thus a possibility. For her senior year, the family opted instead for Oak Grove Seminary, a boarding high school established in 1906 by the Lutheran Free Church, their denomination. It was in Fargo, on the eastern edge of the state, four hundred miles from home. Anna Marie graduated in 1946.

The decision to send Anna Marie to Oak Grove says much about the large influence of the Lutheran Free Church in the Sabo family's lives. That small but regionally significant denomination had deep Norwegian roots but was purely American. It came into being on the campus of Augsburg Seminary (now Augsburg University) in Minneapolis in 1897 at the impetus of two Augsburg professors, Georg Sverdrup and Sven Oftedal. They broke away from the United Norwegian Lutheran Church in America as the result of a doctrinal dispute over how much freedom should be afforded individual church members and congregations. Sverdrup and Oftedal identified with a revival movement launched earlier in the nineteenth century by Norwegian lay evangelist Hans Nielsen Hauge. It emphasized personal piety and Bible study and maintained that congregations should operate independently of church hierarchy. "A free church in a free land" was their rallying cry, carried to the North Dakota prairie by immigrants like the Sabos.[10]

The congregation at Writing Rock Lutheran Church, near the Sabo farm, was too small during Martin's youth to support a pastor of its own. It partnered with three other Lutheran Free Church congregations in the region to hire a single pastor who conducted two services per Sunday, alternating the locations. That biweekly worship arrangement seems not to have diminished the attachment the Sabos and other congregants had to their parish. Klara was said by her family to be especially devout. After leaving the farm, she and several other neighbors established a regular Bible study class that was an important part of their lives for many years. Ben was a regular churchgoer and could be called upon to deliver lay sermons when pastors were unavailable. But his family remembers him as less pious than his wife. "He played cards, and he probably had a beer now and then," his granddaughter Julie related. Both practices were discouraged by the church.

As Martin put it late in life, "church and school melded together" in Alkabo. Church meant more than religion. It provided social life, entertainment, and a link to the larger world. As a young teen, Martin and several of his peers were allowed to attend summer Bible camps at a Lutheran Free Church retreat on Lake Metigoshe, nearly two hundred miles east of Alkabo on the Canadian border. It was a place where young people could enjoy nature, learn water sports, and meet other youth from around the state while they deepened their attachment to their church. The water sports didn't take with Martin. He never learned to swim. And his singing voice was such that he was often invited to read scripture rather than join a choir. But by the time he was in high school, Martin could speak about his faith with ease and sincerity.[11]

With few peers in his hometown, Martin was drawn to adult interests and companionship. When Anna Marie was home from college or teaching, the family of four would gather for games of cards, dominoes, or Monopoly. When she was teaching at nearby Hillside School, a one-room schoolhouse where she instructed five students in four grades, Martin would help her grade papers. When Ben headed to the village pool parlor for a card game, Martin would tag along. Anna Marie remembers that Ben resisted when young Martin begged to accompany their father to the farm for work in the barn and fields. Klara intervened on her son's behalf.

"Mom said, 'If you want Martin to grow up to help you, you have to let him come with you now,'" Anna Marie recalled. The father-son teamwork they established when Martin was small endured. A few years later, Ben welcomed Martin's help both on the farm and as his assistant assessor. When Ben took a job as the Alkabo School's janitor, Martin functioned as his unpaid aide during his high school years.

Working together gave Ben ample time to convey his hopes for his son's future. He made clear that he didn't want Martin to scratch out a living on a Great Plains farm. He wanted his son to pursue a college education and become a professor. Klara had a different but similarly ambitious idea. She envisioned her only son as a clergyman. But she also wanted him to be no stranger to hard physical labor. Since her daughter had begun milking cows at age eight, Klara insisted Martin should assume that responsibility at the same age. "Mom didn't want Martin to be denied any advantage that I had," Anna Marie said.

Politics of the Prairie

As they labored side by side, Ben and Martin had what his sister called "prime time to visit" about one of Ben's favorite topics, politics. Ben Sabo was a staunch Democrat who unabashedly shared his political thinking when given the opportunity. That made him a typical Norwegian, according to a 1949 academic treatise on Norwegian immigration to North Dakota. "The Norwegian, of all the Scandinavian peoples, has the strongest liking for politics and has the most thorough political training at home," it asserted. "It may be said that he brought with him to America a fairly clear understanding of republicanism: elections, representation, local self-government and constitutions."[12]

The origin of Ben's political preferences is not clear, but it's likely no coincidence that he became a Democrat while still a new American in the late 1910s, years when the leftist Nonpartisan League was sweeping the North Dakota prairie. The league flourished in that state from 1915 until the early 1920s, then dissipated, only to see some of its ideas emerge a decade later in the Democratic Party and President Franklin D. Roosevelt's New Deal—and in Minnesota's Farmer-Labor Party, which had its heyday in the 1930s. The Nonpartisan League advocated for state ownership of banks, grain elevators and mills, and insurance providers—and for full suffrage for women. The aim was to give the people, through their government, a viable, lower-cost alternative to the business services available to them via the private sector. At its peak, the Nonpartisan League boasted 100,000 members, including North Dakota's governor Lynn J. Frazier. By the time Martin Sabo came of age, the league was a faded political memory for many North Dakotans. But in the Sabo household, many of the league's ideas were still current and still appreciated.[13]

In the 1940s—first as war raged in Europe and the Pacific, then as tension heightened between the United States and the Soviet Union—Ben was an avid newspaper reader and radio news listener. His son followed his lead. Before long, others in Alkabo were aware that young Martin Sabo could discuss politics as knowledgably and eagerly as his father. During the 1952 presidential campaign, Martin submitted a letter to the editor of the county newspaper endorsing Democrat Adlai Stevenson over Republican Dwight Eisenhower. Seemingly in response, on Halloween night, just days before the election, pranksters painted "I LIKE IKE" on a Sabo barn. It wasn't clear whether the intention was to tease Ben, Martin, or both about their presidential preference, but the joke was taken in stride by both Sabos. The pro-Eisenhower message on the barn "weathered the elements through both of the Eisenhower administrations," local historian Elaine Leininger recorded.[14]

Martin's middle-grades teacher, Myrtle Skabo, encouraged his interest in government and politics. She arranged for the seventh-grade boy and two other students to attend the state Young Citizens League convention in Bismarck, the state capital, in the spring of 1949. The league, a civics-oriented network of young people's clubs, flourished in North and South Dakota in the 1940s as a wholesome and educational social activity for older children and young teens. In the years before television arrived to divert students' attention, the Young Citizens League was particularly popular in schools too small to offer many extracurricular options. North Dakota boasted of 2,500 YCL chapters by 1950, engaging youth in activities including tree planting on school grounds, raising money for the Junior Red Cross, and studying local and state history. Their state conventions included tours of the state capitol, the governor's mansion, and other state facilities. Martin's trip to the 1949 convention was his first to his state's seat of government. It fired his imagination.[15]

One other event in the late 1940s had a lasting impact on Martin Sabo's thinking about government. In 1948, electrical service came to Alkabo. It was the long-awaited result of the Rural Electrification Act championed by President Roosevelt and enacted by Congress in 1935. For the first time, homes could be outfitted with electric lights and appliances such as refrigerators and vacuum cleaners. Lives were made easier overnight, and the gap between rural and urban American lifestyles quickly narrowed. Like many rural dwellers, Martin Sabo would always remember the day his home was wired for electricity. Though he was only ten, "he knew where it came from," his daughter Julie attested. "It showed him the great impact that government could have in improving people's lives."

Baseball and Belonging

Young Martin developed one more fascination that would prove enduring. He was crazy about baseball. With few playmates nearby and adults not always on hand, Martin loved to twist the radio dial during long summer twilights until he could hear the distinctive sounds of a professional baseball game that was being played far, far away. Skillful sports announcers brought the game to life in his mind's eye. On clear nights he might have been able to hear the broadcasts of WDAY in Fargo, KLPM in Minot, or even WCCO in Minneapolis, all stations established in the 1920s. His radio reception got a lot better in 1948, when KWBM (today's KEYZ) came to Williston, sixty miles away. He would remember hearing radio broadcasts of basketball and hockey games as well. But neither winter sport captivated him the way baseball did. With few if any playmates, he spent hours tossing a baseball into the air to hit it or throwing it against the house to catch it, his sister said.[16]

Martin's baseball fixation may have struck his neighbors as odd, since neither he nor they had ever seen a professional game played. Television would not come to northwestern North Dakota until the late 1950s. The nearest major league teams in the 1940s were based in Chicago, and the Cubs and White Sox were not the teams Martin favored. From a young age, he was a New York Yankees fan. "I had to be a Dodgers fan, just to be different," remembers Gary Rust, an Alkabo boy who was seven years Martin's junior and who learned the game of baseball from his older friend. He listened in awe as Martin recited players' names and batting averages.

"Martin would play with me like a big brother," Rust, who grew up to be the longtime mayor of Fortuna, North Dakota, said in 2023 about his friend. On warm summer Saturday nights when the adults in the area came to town to meet and shop, Martin would recruit boys his own age, Gary's age, and those in between for an impromptu game of baseball in the pasture behind the Sabo house. "We'd use cow chips for bases," Rust said. "He'd tell us all of the ins and outs of the game."

The only school sport Martin played was basketball, and that activity was not available to him each year. In some years, Alkabo School didn't have enough boys to put a team on the court. When it did, Martin suited up. It was expected. His team rarely won a game, but winning wasn't the point. Similarly, Martin joined the school choir, though he was such a poor singer that he often just mouthed the words. And he participated in the school play, which was chosen carefully each year with the number of cast members in mind. The aim was that every student would play a role.

That was the civics lesson of Alkabo, Gary Rust said. "Everybody worked together. Everybody played a part. The sense was that you had to work together—that your whole town was watching you and depending on you. That made us very close knit." Alkabo's adults, including Ben and Klara, were stern and kind of rugged, according to Rust, but "they would be the first to offer help. . . . Every time there was a gathering or the community needed something, everybody showed up." That sense reached far into the surrounding region, he added. Alkabo may have had fewer than a hundred residents. But when the school had its annual lutefisk dinner to raise money, seven hundred meals were served.

Top of the Class

Small classes meant that Martin knew his teachers well, and they knew him. In high school he had one teacher for three years who taught all subjects, a first-time teacher named Dave Baglien. He and Martin developed a close bond. Martin remembered him as "exceptionally good" at encouraging "kids to be thinking. He tried to do whatever he could to get kids to quarrel with him and ask questions," Sabo recalled. Baglien's strong suit was social studies—Martin's favorite subject. He acknowledged later in life that Alkabo School did not offer good preparation in math and the sciences. He took algebra by correspondence during his senior year, learning in his last year of high school a mathematical discipline generally taught to eighth or ninth graders in larger schools. Martin's daughters recall their father joking that he learned more math by playing whist and dominoes at home than he did in school. But Martin and his two classmates found a way to take courses in international relations and psychology, topics many American high school kids never encountered. Mr. Baglien encouraged Martin to enter a state history competition. He did. He won first place.[17]

In Alkabo, a young person who proved himself to be responsible was readily given more responsibility. When Martin was twelve, his parents deemed him mature enough to live without them for a few months. Ben and Klara made a much-anticipated trip to Norway in 1950 to reconnect with family members Klara had not seen since her marriage twenty-four years earlier. They left young Martin under the watchful eyes of nearby Uncle Elling and Anna Marie, then twenty-two, who was teaching at a country school and commuting by car from her parents' home. Martin was left in charge of the family's chickens and cows, including one that would give birth to a calf while his parents were away. They would be gone for six months. Martin was told that the egg money earned while he managed the chickens was his to keep.

Somewhat surreptitiously, to avoid Uncle Elling's possible objection, the younger Sabos set out to teach Martin to drive. They would get into the car with Anna Marie behind the wheel as they drove past Elling's house, a block from their own. When they were safely out of Elling's sight, they would switch positions. Martin learned how to drive that summer—illegally. North Dakota began requiring drivers' licenses in 1935 and drivers' examinations as a licensure requirement in 1947. Martin had neither. Nevertheless, when the younger Sabos confessed to their parents that Martin had acquired a new skill while the elders were away, Anna Marie recalls that Ben was delighted. The lad could now assume more responsibilities on the farm and drive himself to Luther League meetings at Writing Rock Church. They would catch up with the licensure requirement in due time.[18]

Anna Marie was an increasingly intermittent presence in Martin's life as he approached high school graduation in 1955. She had taken a teaching job thirty miles away in Crosby and was home less frequently. While there she met Lloyd Huesers, a fellow teacher; they married in 1959. But the Sabo siblings had forged a tight bond—one that went far beyond driving lessons—that made her a source of lasting influence on her brother. Notably, she had spent one satisfying academic year at the Lutheran Free Church's Augsburg College in Minneapolis and would have stayed longer had Augsburg offered the elementary education preparation she sought. In those years, the Minneapolis college only offered training for high school teachers, so eventually she obtained a degree from Minot State Teachers College. But she spoke positively of Augsburg, as did Lutheran Free Church clergy and leaders that Martin had met through church activities. He paid heed. "I don't think I even applied any place else," Sabo would say about his decision to enroll in Augsburg College after high school graduation.[19]

Martin Sabo was valedictorian of his class—a class of three. Those small numbers did not relieve Martin of valedictory responsibility. Education-minded Alkabo made much of high school graduations. Martin was expected to deliver a speech. He took the assignment seriously, his sister recalls, practicing in advance in the school's combined gymnasium/auditorium to make sure his voice would carry throughout the large space.

Meanwhile, a teacher assigned him to take charge of activities for younger children at the school's year-end picnic. Much to Martin's satisfaction, the plan was for a softball game. He was to mark the field behind the school for that purpose and round up the necessary supplies. "He got a hilarious response from the other students when he arrived with a gunny sack full of cow pies" to serve as bases. "His teacher probably wasn't as amused," local historian Leininger remarked. Martin might have been surprised by the response. As an Alkabo son, he had learned to shoulder community responsibility and to make do with what he had.[20]

CHAPTER TWO

PIVOT TO THE CITY

ENROLLING IN AUGSBURG COLLEGE WAS SUCH A NATURAL NEXT step for seventeen-year-old Martin Sabo that he didn't seriously consider any other post-high school option, academic or otherwise. Yet it had to have been no small matter in the late summer of 1955 for him to say goodbye to all that was familiar and board a train bound 650 miles east, to live in a big city he had never seen among people whom, with only a handful of exceptions, he did not know. His willingness to get on that train says much about the young man's courage, ambition, and—perhaps most of all—his attachment to the Lutheran Free Church.[1]

To a contemporary observer, today's Augsburg University might appear to be a typical liberal arts college with a few graduate programs, not unlike many other small private higher education institutions scattered across the American Midwest. But Augsburg's story is distinctive. And many of the events and ideas that made Augsburg stand apart in the mid-twentieth century also made it a fitting training ground for a rural young man on his way to a life of public service in Minnesota and Washington, DC.

The contrast between sparsely populated Alkabo and Minneapolis in the mid-1950s could hardly have been greater. Martin was bound for the largest city in the region, then occupied by more than a half million people (with another 300,000 across the Mississippi River in

St. Paul). While overwhelmingly white, the city had well-established African American neighborhoods, one north and one south of downtown, and a small but growing Native American enclave not far from campus. Just upriver from campus, the city's renowned flour milling district straddled the Falls of St. Anthony. Once the largest producer of flour in the nation, the mills were in decline at mid-century. The neighborhood between the mills and the Augsburg campus, long a landing spot for Scandinavians and other working-class immigrants, was also deteriorating, offering ample urban temptation to college students.[2]

When Martin arrived on campus, he found an eighty-six-year-old institution in transition. For most of its history, Augsburg had been a church-oriented school, training students for careers in the parishes of a small, mostly rural branch of Norwegian American Lutheranism. But spurred by postwar enrollment growth, visionary presidential leadership, and a quest for accreditation, Augsburg had gradually embraced an expanded liberal arts curriculum and a mission of service beyond the church. During Martin's student years, the school was moving from what Augsburg history professor Carl Chrislock called its "colonial period" to "the mainstream of American higher education." Martin experienced and benefitted from features of both institutional types.[3]

The Augsburg Evolution

Founded in Marshall, Wisconsin, in 1869 as an all-male clergy training school, Augsburg relocated in 1872 to a plot that was then on Minneapolis's southeast edge. Today that site is near the city's core, adjacent to Interstate 94. (This history is aptly captured in the title of Chrislock's 1969 Augsburg centennial volume, *From Fjord to Freeway*.) Two years later, two young theology professors arrived from Norway to give the school its defining character for the next half century. Sven Oftedal and Georg Sverdrup brought with them fixed ideas about how best to prepare clergy for service in congregations of Norwegian immigrants in the Upper Midwest. They emphasized personal piety, individual responsibility, rigorous Bible study, and congregational autonomy ("a free church in a free land"). But, unlike leaders of some other Christian sects, they did not teach that believers should separate themselves from the larger world. Rather, they aimed to prepare students for civic leadership in the largely rural parishes they would serve. Under their direction—both Sverdrup and Oftedal would serve stints as Augsburg's president, as would Sverdrup's son George—Augsburg offered students an uncommon mix of piety and populism.

Its early name, Augsburg Seminary, did not fully describe its academic scope. From the start, the school offered instruction that began at the preparatory (or, if needed, even elementary) level and continued through college and graduate study. Theology and the Norwegian language were woven throughout the original curriculum. The seamlessness of that program was Augsburg's pride and professed distinction. Its competition from a wider-ranging "humanistic" educational approach at another Norwegian American Lutheran college forty-five miles to the south, St. Olaf College in Northfield, was a source of tension within the two schools' mother church, the Norwegian-Danish Evangelical Lutheran Church in America. The desire of Augsburg professors to protect and preserve their version of clergy preparation was a major driver of the wedge that splintered that denomination in the 1890s. Sverdrup and Oftedal are credited as founders of the breakaway Lutheran Free Church, which emerged as an independent organization in 1897. It might be said that the Lutheran Free Church was a creature of Augsburg, not the other way around. The relationship was so close that well into the twentieth century the hiring of Augsburg's presidents and professors required a vote by annual Lutheran Free Church conferences.[4]

Change came slowly to the little school, and when it did, financial exigency was often the propelling force. At about the time Sverdrup's son George became president in 1911, the need to boost tuition revenue led to declarations in school catalogs that students who did not plan to become ministers were nevertheless welcome to attend. Shortly before World War I, science courses were added, English language classes were beefed up, and a Greek language requirement was waived for students not preparing for the ministry. The Norwegian language requirement was dropped in 1921, the same year in which women were finally admitted as students. Soon thereafter, intercollegiate athletics arrived: first basketball, then baseball and football. Augsburg's prep school closed in 1933, a victim of the Great Depression. That year, professors' annual salaries fell to a paltry $1,215.[5]

Those lean years also put an end to a plan that had been in the offing for more than a decade to relocate the campus to comparatively rural Richfield, ten miles to the south. At the time, the decision to remain near the urban core was lamented by some at Augsburg who craved more distance from the gritty city. But by the time Martin came to campus, a different idea was taking hold. The school's location was an asset to the preparation of young people for careers that would benefit society, argued forward-thinking president Bernhard Christensen. He embraced the city and wanted Augsburg students to do so too.

When Sabo arrived in 1955, Christensen had already been Augsburg's president for seventeen years; he would remain in the post through 1962. He proved remarkably adept at nudging the institution into its modern urban frame without losing the support of the college's mostly rural constituency. It was a feat Christensen was well prepared to perform. A son of Danish immigrants, Christensen was born in 1901 in tiny Porterfield, in sparsely populated northeastern Wisconsin. After grade school, he was dispatched to Augsburg for prep school, college, and seminary, but he was never ordained as a Lutheran Free Church clergyman. Rather, he pursued advanced theological study far from the Midwest, in Europe and at Princeton University, Columbia University, and the Hartford Seminary in Connecticut, where he was awarded a doctorate in 1929. He returned to Augsburg in 1934 to teach theology and philosophy, eager to expose students to the idea that they had a Christian duty to "explore the world of learning freely." Four years later, he succeeded George Sverdrup as president.[6]

Slowly but persistently, Christensen shifted Augsburg's academic emphasis away from strict Lutheran dogma toward intellectual freedom and the personal development of each student. A name change signaled the shift: in 1942 the school's official name became Augsburg College and Theological Seminary. The seminary would continue, graduating a few dozen clergymen each year, until it merged with Luther Seminary in 1963 and left the campus. But the college program was now paramount.

"Personal growth was very much what Augsburg emphasized" in the 1950s, attested Joanne Stiles Laird, one of Martin Sabo's Augsburg contemporaries and, like him, a native of North Dakota raised in the Lutheran Free Church. Religious instruction and worship were still expected of students, she recalled. Attendance at a minimum of three chapel services per week was required; students were directed to sign in to record their attendance. One religion class, two hours per week, was mandatory for each student, each term; a Bible class required of all freshmen, both terms. The rigor and content of those classes varied considerably. One older professor's classes were notoriously "just like Sunday school," Laird recalled. The 1957 yearbook boasted that the college offered "religious activities of every kind including two spiritual emphasis weeks during every school year."[7]

Nevertheless, Laird stressed, the Augsburg she and Sabo attended "was not a Bible school. They weren't there to make Christians out of you. They expected you were Christian when you got there." Religion classes were more likely to be academic than evangelical, she said. "Augsburg was an intellectual center. It was there to encourage personal growth as a predicate to a life of service. We were taught that in order to love and serve others, you must know and love yourself. It was your responsibility to be the best you could possibly be." Laird said the college's motto in those years might have been: "Be yourself. Be strong. Make an impact." It was a message befitting democracy.

The freedom of inquiry that Augsburg increasingly prized in the 1950s did not yet extend to freedom for students from strict rules about behavior. Alcohol consumption was forbidden on campus though it happened, Laird said. "We had our share of drinkers, of kids with problems." Students were strictly segregated by gender in dormitories. Card playing was banned. Dancing that involved bodily contact was punishable by expulsion—an archaic rule that students had for several decades found particularly confining. Augsburg historian Chrislock noted that students in the 1950s did not just quietly flout such rules, as their predecessors had. In a harbinger of 1960s student activism, students in Sabo's era openly campaigned to change rules they opposed. They found allies in that effort among the school's younger and more liberal professors.[8]

A Mentor for Martin

After World War II, as student numbers swelled, Christensen recruited a cohort of young faculty who, unlike their predecessors, did not all have a Norwegian Lutheran background or an Augsburg degree on their résumé. "They lifted the college's academic level and gave life to [Christensen's] vision of a dialogue between Christian faith and all the disciplines," a former Augsburg student would write years later. Their caliber helped win long-sought, much-coveted accreditation for the college from the North Central Association of Colleges and Schools in 1954.[9]

Among these faculty were several to whom Martin Sabo gravitated and one who became a mentor and lifelong friend. Carl Chrislock, the history professor who would tell Augsburg's story in *From Fjord to Freeway: 100 years, Augsburg College*, was such a guiding force that Martin would later say that he had not majored in history; rather, "I majored in Chrislock."[10]

At a larger school at which professors and students did not readily become acquainted, a quiet, unassuming underclassman like Martin Sabo likely would not have come to the attention of a busy scholar and lecturer like Chrislock. But at Augsburg, where Martin was one of only seven hundred undergraduates and close student-faculty relationships were encouraged, they found each other and learned that they had much in common. Like Sabo, Chrislock had grown up in a small Norwegian-dominated farming community, Wanamingo, Minnesota. Both had grown up speaking Norwegian as well as English. Both came to Augsburg before the customary age of eighteen; Chrislock graduated from Augsburg with a history degree at age twenty, in 1937. Both admired the prairie populist movements of the early twentieth century. Chrislock's scholarly focus was the pre–World War I progressive era in Minnesota and the Dakotas, a topic that would have appealed to the son of early twentieth-century Norwegian immigrants. His book *The Progressive Era in Minnesota, 1899–1918* was published in 1971.[11]

Sabo was eager to study both history and political science. Chrislock, who had arrived on campus in 1952, was teaching both subjects and working to establish a political science department at Augsburg. That effort would not come to full fruition until the mid-1960s. "Most of [Chrislock's] classes were history, some were political science. In those days professors taught lots of different classes," Sabo recalled decades later. "I had every class he taught . . . I thought of him as much as a friend as a professor."[12]

Martin likely was seeking friends, or at least familiar faces, as he settled into the men's dormitory that first fall. He wasn't a musician or a team-sport athlete. That meant he did not have a ready-made circle of friends waiting for him. While not deeply introverted, Martin was neither gregarious nor garrulous. "He was quiet, no nonsense, like his father," recalled Vicki Skor Pearson, a classmate from Williston, North Dakota, who was acquainted with the Sabo family.[13]

Another classmate, Grace Kemmer Sulerud, said that even though more than half of Augsburg students in the 1950s grew up in rural places outside the Twin Cities, Martin's extreme small-town background set him apart.

"He was in a psychology class with me, and the professor asked, 'How many of you were valedictorians or salutatorians in high school?' Martin's hand went up, along with a lot of others. But then he was obliged to confess that he was one of just three students in his high school class. That got a laugh" as he blushed, she said.[14]

A portion of Martin's nonacademic time was committed to working for financial support. Augsburg's $200-per-semester tuition was a financial stretch for the Sabos. Like a majority of his Augsburg peers, he was employed either on or off campus during all of his student years. Beginning in the 1930s the college's administrative offices included what amounted to a placement service to help students find off-campus work. Martin's initial work-study job did not require leaving campus. He worked in his dormitory's food service. Later he took a job as an orderly at nearby Fairview Hospital.[15]

Despite a work schedule that made extracurricular activities difficult, Sabo responded affirmatively when one student organization called. Junior political science major Harlan Christianson "came around looking for Democrats," Martin recalled late in life. Christianson, a future chief sergeant-at-arms for the Minnesota House of Representatives, was evidently so delighted to discover that the strapping freshman from North Dakota was a Democrat that he hurried to share the news with student body president Jim Pederson, a senior from Nye, Wisconsin, and the founder and leader of the students' Democratic club. Pederson headed to the men's dormitory to meet the potential recruit.[16]

"I found him in a hallway somewhere. I introduced myself and asked if he was Martin Sabo. He responded 'Yep,'" Pederson recalled. "'Do you want to get involved with the Democrats on campus?' I asked. 'Yep,' he replied. That was the whole conversation! I discovered that Martin Sabo was a man of very few words."[17]

Soon thereafter Martin was off to his first political meeting. He signed on with Students for Stevenson as former Illinois Governor Adlai Stevenson prepared for a second run for president against Dwight Eisenhower in 1956. Before long, he was heavily involved doing door-knocking and other things for candidates both on campus and in its surrounding neighborhood. He was elected president of the Augsburg Young Democrats club in his senior year.[18]

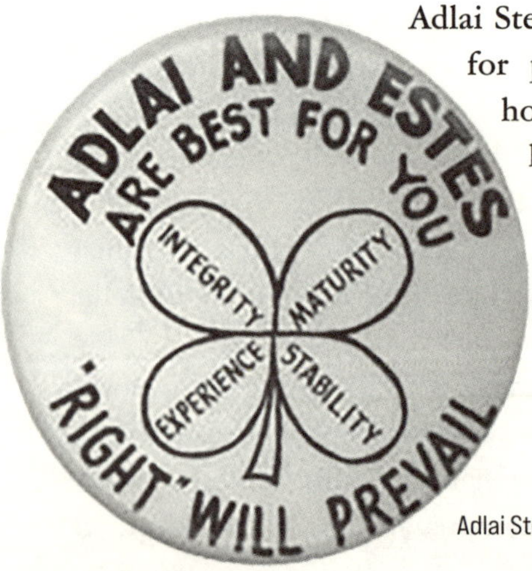

Adlai Stevenson 1956 presidential campaign pin.

After meetings and door-knocking outings, Augsburg's young Democrats often would debrief and unwind at the home of their favorite professor, Chrislock. In 1955–56 they came to an upper duplex the Chrislock family rented in south Minneapolis, but by the next year the family had become homeowners a few blocks away and less than two miles from the Augsburg campus. The professor's son Winston, two years younger than Martin, remembers those visits by what he called the "Augsburg mafia" as "almost like family gatherings. . . . They were all of the same type as my dad," said Winston. Martin was soon one of the four or five regular visitors who talked exclusively about politics as they relaxed with their professor. Winston, who would go on to a distinguished career as a history professor at the University of St. Thomas in St. Paul, said Martin was not as talkative as others in those household gatherings, but he had a "low-key, Scandinavian sense of humor." The youth discerned that Sabo was "not shy, but thoughtful. It always seemed as if he was observing you."[19]

Martin and Carl Chrislock had one more thing in common: both were heavy smokers. Tobacco use by men was tolerated by the Lutheran Free Church while other personal vices were condemned. Martin had acquired a tobacco habit before he left Alkabo. Winston described his father as a "terrible" smoker. The air was soon blue when the two of them settled in for a conversation. Both would be heavy tobacco consumers throughout their adult lives, and both would suffer ill health as a result.

The 1956 Augsburgian yearbook pictures a fresh-faced, crew cut Sabo in only one group photo—that of the Public Affairs Federation, the school's official political club. "The PAF—working not only in suborganizations [Republican and Democratic] but also as a unit—has been actively engaged in stirring up interest and excitement in political affairs throughout the year," the caption said. The 1957 book depicts him again with the Public Affairs Federation and its Democratic subgroup, which included four women and sixteen men. The larger PAF group photo shows only men. That year he is also photographed with the Future Teachers of America club—perhaps suggesting the future that Martin then believed was in store for him after college.[20]

The 1958 yearbook, documenting Sabo's junior year, hints at a different professional future. In this book, he no longer has the look of plaid-shirted, sunburned farm kid. Dressed in a sport coat and tie, he looks smart and even a bit sophisticated as the year's student body vice president. Martin won that post on his second bid for student government office. An earlier attempt for a student council seat had not been successful. He faced the same candidate but a larger electorate when he ran for student body vice president and won. "So that got me involved," Sabo would relate matter-of-factly near the end of his life. In that telling, he did not elaborate on the significance of the student council defeat. But its mention indicates that the memory of that singular rejection stayed with him. It was the only election Sabo ever lost.

The Call

The transformation of Martin Sabo from prairie teen to urban adult was nearly complete when he graduated from Augsburg in 1959. Sabo would never again return to Alkabo for more than brief visits. After graduation, he and four others in Chrislock's "Augsburg mafia" took up residence in an apartment above Bob Larson's Fairway Grocery at Twenty-Second and Riverside, across the street from the Augsburg campus. The group's de facto leader was Jim Pederson; Jim's younger brother Dwight, Harlan Christianson, and Dennis Peterson were also in the apartment. Sabo worked as an orderly at Fairview Hospital and enrolled in the history graduate program at the University of Minnesota, situated just across the river (and soon to become Augsburg's immediate neighbor as construction commenced in the early 1960s on the university's west bank campus). When he wasn't working, studying, or playing a little pick-up basketball with Winston Chrislock, Sabo stuffed envelopes or performed other chores for the Democratic-Farmer-Labor Party (DFL).

He was plunging into politics at a time when competition was keen between the DFL and Republican parties in Minneapolis. Hubert Humphrey, who engineered the 1944 merger of Minnesota's

Farmer-Labor and Democratic parties to help himself win the Minneapolis mayoral race in 1945, was elected to the US Senate in 1948. It was not until he ran for a second Senate term in 1954 that the DFL would capture the governorship for the first time, electing Orville Freeman, Humphrey's political lieutenant. That year, DFLers ("Liberals" in the era before party designation) also won a majority in the Minnesota House. But Republicans ("Conservatives") remained firmly in control of the state Senate. The DFL won its second US Senate seat in 1958, electing St. Paul's US Representative Eugene McCarthy as the state's junior senator. But a year earlier, the Minneapolis mayor's office had reverted to Republican control, with former state legislator and Republican State Party Chairman P. Kenneth Peterson elected to what would be two terms. Five of the state's nine congressional districts in 1959 were occupied by Republicans, including the Minneapolis-dominated Fifth District, where physician and former medical missionary Walter Judd had been in office since 1942.[21]

The burgeoning issue of the era, in Minneapolis and in the nation, was civil rights for non-white Americans. But in Minnesota, civil rights was not the partisan issue that it had been—and would remain—elsewhere. Both of Minnesota's political parties included strong advocates for equal justice and opportunity for African Americans and other people of color. Likewise, at predominantly white Augsburg College, students were witness to nonpartisan leadership on the issue. Augsburg's President Christensen was an early appointee to Mayor Humphrey's Council on Human Relations, a groundbreaking body established in an effort to end discrimination against the city's Jewish and African American populations. In 1948 Christensen succeeded another prominent Lutheran, the Rev. Reuben Youngdahl of Mount Olivet Lutheran Church (and the Republican governor's brother) as the council's chairman. Christensen held that post for several years, forging a link between Augsburg and civil rights in the city.[22]

The eldest member and most politically active of the Fairway apartment household, Jim Pederson, was by 1959 a salaried employee of the state DFL Party. Pederson had enrolled in Augsburg Seminary after graduating from college in 1956. After a year and a half of theological study, he took a job teaching at the Hennepin County Boys School, a correctional facility on Glen Lake in Minnetonka. He lived on the campus among a "rowdy bunch," he recalled, and struggled to maintain order among the seventh and eighth graders he taught. Going to meetings of the Fifth District Young Democrats organization was likely a welcome respite. At those meetings, Pederson became acquainted with state DFL Party Chairman Ray Hemenway. The founder of a building products company in Albert Lea, Minnesota, Hemenway was an outgoing and outspoken fellow closely allied with the state's dominant DFL personality, Hubert Humphrey.

"Ray called me at the school one day and said, 'Do you ever want to do something worthwhile in your life, or are you going to die in that place? I want to hire you for my staff,'" Pederson related years later. He took a field representative's job—a jack-of-all-political-trades position. Pederson raised money, organized local meetings, recruited speakers, and did the speaking himself if need be. Hemenway understood that by hiring Pederson, he also gained the volunteer services of his politically savvy young housemates.[23]

The Minnesota DFL Party, then and now, operates in each two-year election cycle with a series of successive caucuses and conventions that begin at the neighborhood, or precinct, level. Anyone eligible to vote in the coming election is eligible to participate in precinct caucuses, which are typically conducted in February or early March. At those meetings, delegates are elected to conventions at the legislative district level, which in turn elect delegates to congressional, state, and national conventions. Those meetings endorse candidates, compose and adopt platforms, elect party leaders, and organize for the campaign season.

One evening prior to the 1960 precinct caucuses, Sabo joined the Pederson brothers and a few other volunteers at the home of Don and Arvonne Fraser near the University of Minnesota campus. Their purpose: stuffing large envelopes with materials to be provided to precinct caucus participants a few days hence. Donald Fraser, an attorney and the son of longtime University of Minnesota law school dean Everett Fraser, had been a member of the state Senate since 1954. His wife Arvonne Skelton Fraser had been his political partner since they met in 1948 while working for Hubert Humphrey's first US Senate campaign. Don was a field representative in that campaign; Arvonne managed the campaign office. They were married in 1950. (Their coworker on that campaign was future US vice president and lifelong friend Walter Mondale.)[24]

Sabo may have been surprised that evening when Ray Hemenway walked in seeking a conversation with the Frasers. Jim Pederson likely was not. He knew that the Frasers' counsel was highly valued within the party and that their home, a large Victorian duplex, doubled as meeting space for DFL activity of all sorts, including high-level conversations about candidate recruitment. Early in the conversation, Sabo excused himself and left. Pederson was asked to stay and join the leaders' discussion. It was about their desire to find a DFLer willing to run against state Representative Carl Hagland, who had been elected to the state House from the near-south side of Minneapolis in every election since 1934 and—significantly—was a member of the Liberal caucus. Hemenway and Fraser were plotting to take out one of their own. The reason: Hagland was believed to be taking bribes.

"Freeman had a problem with Hagland," Pederson said years later, suggesting that the move to oust Hagland may have originated in the governor's office. "He was a crook," and as such, a potential embarrassment to a party that Humphrey and Freeman had worked hard to build. "Freeman was squeaky clean. So were Don and Ray," Pederson said. Hagland was someone on whose vote the governor could not rely, he added.

Fraser and Hemenway wanted Pederson to run against Hagland. Pederson demurred. "I wasn't so sure I wanted to be in the mess" that he feared a challenge to Hagland would entail. He countered with a different idea: "How about Sabo?" Martin had confided to Pederson that he hoped to run for elective office one day, though he had not spoken specifically about a bid for a legislative seat.

"Jesus Christ, is he even old enough to vote for himself?" Hemenway asked. Pederson assured his boss that Sabo was about to celebrate his twenty-second birthday. Voting age—and the age of eligibility for legislative service—was twenty-one.

"Okay, it's settled. You go home tonight and tell him he's going to be the candidate, then start teaching him what the Legislature does," Hemenway ordered. He punctuated those instructions in characteristically blunt fashion: "Either you find a candidate to run against Hagland, or you're fired."

Pederson did as directed.[25]

"I argued against it," Sabo would later relate. "I told Jim I was too young to run against someone in my own party." Pederson vowed to deliver the DFL endorsement to Sabo at the party's April 2 convention. He promised to take charge of fundraising. And he arranged for a few persuasive phone calls to Sabo by Fraser and Hemenway.

"I lost the argument," Sabo said.[26]

The Answer

Pederson delivered on his promise. At the April 2 Hennepin County DFL convention, Sabo was endorsed for one of two House seats allotted to Senate District 31, which included the Fifth and Sixth Wards in Minneapolis. (In those years, House members were elected at-large within Senate districts.) Hagland was not on hand and his name was not offered for endorsement. Rather, his supporters unsuccessfully sought a "no endorsement" outcome. The next day, Hagland told reporters that he intended to run for reelection regardless of the party's decision and that he expected organized labor to support him, not the upstart Sabo. He charged that the convention had been "rigged with a lot of students," a charge party officials denied.[27]

With party endorsement and the assurance of financial backing and the DFL sample-ballot inclusion that it brought, Sabo was off and running. Make that walking. He commenced a door-knocking regimen so rigorous that decades later it remained legendary among Minnesota political operatives. Sabo was applying the retail politics of a small prairie town to the big city. The *Minneapolis Star* credited him with knocking on 12,000 doors in a campaign that "was probably unrivaled in the state" in worn shoe leather.[28]

Sabo simply knocked on doors, and there were plenty of doors to visit in the district in 1960. That was before the city's Gateway redevelopment project had cleared flophouses from Washington Avenue and before the University of Minnesota's west bank expansion had removed the humble dwellings that had housed the city's early immigrant mill workers. No abode was too dilapidated for him to visit. In more than a few places along Cedar Avenue—once dubbed Snoose Boulevard because of its working-class Scandinavian population—he made his pitch in Norwegian to elderly voters.

"Martin made a point of visiting every resident, in person," remembered Winston Chrislock. Then a University of Minnesota undergrad, Chrislock had been assigned by political science professor Charles Backstrom to join a campaign and write a paper on the impact of party endorsement. That gave him academic permission to do what he wanted to do anyway—help his friend Martin campaign.

"He had these little cards with his full name—Martin Olav Sabo—on which he would sometimes write a few words," Chrislock remembered. The wholesome, crew cut twenty-two-year-old made a positive impression at the door. "People were always glad to see him and would always invite him in."[29]

But Sabo resolved early to politely decline offers of extended hospitality. His goal was to keep moving. "I wanted thirty seconds to tell them who I was and ask them for their votes, and say thank you," he said in 2015, describing his strategy. "I never wanted to ask somebody what's your opinion on this or that issue. I think you sort of embarrass people, putting them on the spot when you do that." In his rookie days on the trail, he said, he was drawn into a thirty-minute discussion with someone at the door only to discover he was speaking to someone from Iowa who was in Minnesota visiting his sister. "I decided that's not a very good strategy."[30]

Winning a House seat in 1960 required being one of the top four vote-getters in a nonpartisan primary and one of the top two vote-getters in November to fill one of the two at-large House seats assigned to each state Senate district. In the September 13 primary, Sabo came in second in a field of twelve candidates, behind incumbent Jim Adams, by only sixteen votes. Hagland was the fourth-place finisher, 252 votes behind Sabo but still politically alive.[31]

On November 8, Sabo again came in second to Adams, winning election and ending Hagland's political career. In January he became Minnesota state Representative Martin O. Sabo, the youngest member of the 1961 Legislature.

CHAPTER THREE

A TORCH PASSES, SLOWLY

THE INAUGURATION OF A YOUTHFUL NEW PRESIDENT IN 1961 conveyed a sense that America's government had entered a season of renewal. But when President John F. Kennedy proclaimed on January 20 that "the torch has been passed to a new generation of Americans," Minnesotans might have questioned whether that observation applied to their state's lawmaking body. Its 198 members included a half dozen thirtysomethings; a twenty-eight-year-old future governor, Representative Wendell Anderson; a twenty-nine-year-old future judge from south Minneapolis, Senator Jack Davies; and a very green twenty-two-year-old from Davies's district, Representative Martin Sabo. Downstairs from the House and Senate chambers, one of the Capitol's executive suites was occupied by youthful thirty-three-year-old Attorney General Walter F. Mondale, the nation's future vice president.

But those youngsters were far outnumbered by legislators born in the nineteenth century. The 1961 Minnesota Legislature was a club of gray-haired white men. Just two of the 1961 session's legislators were women; none were people of color. The newly elected governor was Elmer L. Andersen, a liberal Republican, business owner, and former state senator from St. Paul. He was fifty-one years old.

The rhythm and requirements of the lawmaking enterprise as it was practiced in 1961 were well suited to an older workforce. Since

1879, by state constitutional requirement, the Minnesota Legislature had met in regular sessions only during odd-numbered years—and then only for ninety "legislative days," that is, days excluding Sundays and legal holidays. Sessions typically commenced within a few days after the start of a new year and ended in late April, just in time for farmer-legislators to return to their fields and plant the year's crops. Meetings on Fridays and Saturdays were rare; on Sundays, they were verboten. A four-day work week was typical.[1]

When the workload exceeded the constitutionally allotted time, or when governors and legislators failed to come to agreement on measures essential to government operations, governors were obliged to call legislators back to St. Paul after adjournment for a special session. Such "extra innings" were rare in the state in the 1930s and 1940s. But special sessions had been required to complete legislative business in 1951, 1955, 1957, and 1959. An attempt in 1960 to change the state constitution to allow for longer regular sessions had failed despite winning nearly 260,000 more "yes" than "no" votes. The reason: In Minnesota, a constitutional amendment must be approved by a majority of those voting in an election. A blank response to the ballot question counts as "no." For that reason, the 1960 amendment for longer regular sessions fell about 25,000 votes short of adoption.[2]

The synchrony of the legislative calendar with Minnesota's agrarian schedule was no coincidence. Despite the explosive growth of the Twin Cities metropolitan area in the years after World War II, the 1961 Legislature remained a disproportionately rural institution. The reason: legislators had refused for nearly a half century to adjust district boundaries to equalize their population—an exercise known as redistricting.

As Minnesota's population swelled during the nineteenth century, increasing the size of the Legislature and drawing new district boundaries were frequent undertakings. It happened seven times between 1860 and 1913, enlarging the Legislature from 63 to 198 seats. But the 1913 map was the last revision that would be drawn until 1959, and the 1959 change did little more than add a few new districts in the metro area. It kept the Senate at 67 members, its size since 1915, and enlarged the House from 131 to 135 members beginning in 1963. Most district boundaries were unchanged. Sabo spent his first several terms representing a district whose map originated in 1913.[3]

The failure to draw new district lines was no mere oversight. Rural legislators were intent on avoiding redistricting. They knew well that any plan to equalize district populations would erode rural political clout. Residents of the metro area were catching on to that fact too. In 1945 Jay Smith of Minneapolis, a Republican who aimed to run for the Legislature in 1946, filed a lawsuit asking state courts to order new district maps. He argued that since his district was then the most populous in the state, with four times as many people as some of the state's rural districts, maintaining the current map amounted to discrimination. A hidebound Minnesota Supreme Court did not agree. A "mere change" in population was not sufficient to nullify a district map, the state's high court ruled. Only evidence of "an intention . . . to utterly ignore or disregard" the Constitution's requirement of equal districts "in order to promote some other object other than a constitutional apportionment" could do that, the court said.[4]

Federal courts were inclined to look more critically at population disparities. But they too seemed reluctant in the 1950s to order another branch of government to get with the constitutional program. The opinion rendered in a 1958 Minnesota case before a three-judge federal court panel noted that "substantial inequality" in population existed in the state's districts. "Substantial" was an understatement. The 1950 census had found that the state's smallest House district had 7,290 people while its largest had 107,246. But the judges weren't yet ready to compel action. "It seems to us that if there is to be a judicial disruption of the present legislative apportionment, it should not take place unless and until it can be shown that the Legislature meeting in January 1959 has advisedly and deliberately failed and refused to perform its constitutional duty to redistrict the state," the judges deferentially ruled. It would take several more years before Minnesota and the nation would get serious about redistricting. Thus, a new legislator from Minneapolis in 1961 was obliged to make rural friends and find rural votes for any measure he sought to enact.[5]

The Nonpartisan Legislature

For Sabo, rural relationship-building undoubtedly began with the leaders of the Liberal caucus, both of whom represented far-northern Minnesota. Majority leader Fred Cina, born in 1908, was an attorney from Aurora, a town on the Iron Range with 2,800 people in 1960—a metropolis compared with Alkabo, North Dakota. House Speaker Edwin J. Chilgren was from Littlefork, population 805 in 1960, in far-northern Koochiching County. Chilgren was born in 1897, forty-one years before Sabo. He had served in the House since 1927 and had seen plenty of rookies come and go. But he had reason to notice the new arrival from Minneapolis. Chilgren had been born in Jämtland, Sweden, and emigrated to northern Minnesota as a child. After high school he'd been a printer, a lumberjack, and a US Marine during World War I before using his service bonus money to buy the *Littlefork Times* newspaper in 1921. An ambitious son of Norwegian immigrants from a remote village in North Dakota would have been someone with whom Chilgren could identify.[6]

Chilgren and Cina headed a caucus that had been in the majority since DFLer Orville Freeman was elected governor in 1954. It was the longest run of House control they had enjoyed. Prior to the DFL sweep in 1954, Liberals had only controlled the House during two sessions, 1933 and 1937—years when a Farmer-Labor Party governor was in office and the Democratic Party was running third in statewide

House Speaker Edwin J. Chilgren in 1960.

elections. After the Democratic and Farmer-Labor parties merged in 1944, the new party gradually increased its competitiveness in the House, improving candidate recruitment and campaign support. Liberals were also able to lure more converts from the Conservative caucus. Conservatives defected to the Liberal caucus twenty-two times between 1945 and 1949, while during the same years only five Liberals made the opposite switch. But DFLers/Liberals were less successful in the state Senate, where longer terms (four years instead of two) and longer tenures made Conservative caucus members harder to dislodge. The Senate had been consistently in Republican/Conservative control since statehood was granted in 1858.[7]

Sabo's caucus had been called "Liberal" rather than using the name of a political party since 1913, when the Legislature moved itself to "the non-partisan class" on the state's ballots. That change erased party affiliation from candidates' names on ballots and allowed the top vote-getters in primary elections to advance to the general election, regardless of their party ties. The result was a greater likelihood that each seat would be contested in the general election, providing voters with more choice. But nonpartisan elections also provided legislative candidates with an opportunity to be less than forthright about their political loyalties. Candidates faced no requirement to declare their caucusing intention. If they chose to tell voters which caucus they planned to join, the declaration was not binding. In districts dominated by one party, the absence of party designation denied legislative candidates a chance to capitalize on their party's name or its endorsement.

For those reasons, unease about the Legislature's nonpartisan status was growing in the early 1960s. In 1964 the *Minneapolis Tribune*'s customary election-year Voters' Guide asked Hennepin County legislative candidates to respond with brief essays to two policy questions that the newspaper deemed relevant to the Legislature's work. One question was, "Please explain why you favor or oppose party designation for candidates for the state Legislature." Thirty-one of thirty-seven respondents—one of them Martin Sabo—expressed support for returning party designation to legislative ballots. Readers were likely left with the impression that an end to nonpartisan legislative elections was imminent. That impression would have been mistaken.[8]

The Freshman

By 1960 Minnesotans had evidently become disenchanted with DFL Governor Freeman. He lost to former state Senator Elmer Andersen by 23,000 votes. But the state's voters that year went for Democrat John Kennedy over Republican Richard Nixon for president and gave state House Liberals their largest majority in a generation—73 to 58.

A narrower margin would have shone a brighter spotlight on a rookie like Sabo and might have landed him plum positions as Chilgren doled out committee assignments. (That power was the speaker's sole prerogative, for both the majority and minority caucuses.) When every caucus member's vote is needed to enact legislation, even the lowliest freshman becomes the object of solicitude by legislative leaders and lobbyists. But the relatively comfortable margin Liberals enjoyed in 1961 eliminated any imperative to show Sabo special courtesies. "I started out with pretty bad committees," he would recall a half century later. The list: commercial transportation and communication, elections, state institutions, higher education, and welfare.[9]

Those committees typically did not command headlines. But their topical breadth supplied Sabo with a crash course that covered a considerable portion of state government. Those assignments also afforded him time to sit in on the meetings of other committees as a nonmember, especially the big three—taxes, appropriations, and K–12 education. It was a diversion he relished. He found listening in the back row of committee hearing rooms preferable to sitting at his desk on the House floor—the only personal desk then available to rank-and-file members—or in the often noisy "bull pen" room legislators shared. Sabo's quiet demeanor likely did not draw attention. But his recurring presence eventually did. A freshman legislator attending meetings simply to observe and learn was behavior deemed unusual by veteran legislators who held committee gavels.

Legislative committee chairs in the mid-twentieth century functioned as lords of their own fiefdoms, answerable only to the speaker who appointed them. They alone could decide what bills would be reviewed by their committees and in what sequence. They could decide which bills would be the subject of public testimony and for how long. Such hearings were not yet recorded in 1961. Committee minutes were often kept in less-than-fulsome detail, obscuring committee work from public review. As deadlines neared, committee chairs alone typically assembled major bills, the texts of which were in intentionally scarce supply. League of Women Voters lobbyist Pat Davies, wife of state Senator Jack Davies, remembers that during the 1960s lobbyists like her had to pay to obtain copies of bills—if they were available at all. It was not uncommon for rank-and-file committee members to be asked to vote on bills whose texts they had not seen. Newbies were expected to keep quiet and fall in line.

That expectation was not difficult for Sabo to meet—at least initially. He was not given to unnecessary chatter. But the more he learned, the more he was struck with ideas he thought should be part of bills and debates. His House floor desk was right behind that of Representative Robert Latz, a gregarious attorney and former assistant attorney general from north Minneapolis who had arrived in the House in 1959, one term before Sabo. That extra seniority and age—Latz was eight years older than Sabo—inclined Sabo to share his ideas with Latz and ask him to present them to the body. "I kept poking Bob to say, 'Bob, why don't you get up and say this or that,'" Sabo recalled years later. "He turned to me one day and said, 'Why the blank don't you get up and say it yourself?' So I did." After that, "I became a little more active in debates."[10]

The Young Turks

Several new metro districts were on the 1962 ballot as the 1959 redistricting plan went into effect. It brought little change to Sabo's district or his election outcome. He won a second term the same way he had won his first, by coming in second to Liberal caucus mate

Representative Jim Adams in an at-large contest in which the top two vote-getters were elected.[11]

Still, the 1962 election was noteworthy as a harbinger. It brought the first trickle in a series of changes that over the next dozen years would become a torrent, greatly altering the operations of the Minnesota Legislature.

Voters in 1962 likely did not think they were making a major move when they finally approved a constitutional change lengthening regular legislative sessions from 90 to 120 days. They likely thought they were simply adapting the Constitution to what had become customary practice. In 1961 as in four of the previous five regular sessions, one or more special sessions had been required to complete the Legislature's work. It was not the case that the proposal to allow longer sessions won more votes in 1962 than it did two years earlier. In fact, the number of "yes" votes in 1962 was some 20,000 fewer than it had been in 1960. But total turnout in the 1962 midterm election was smaller by more than 300,000 votes than it had been in the presidential election two years earlier. This time, the "yes" tally surpassed the "majority of those voting" threshold for amendment adoption by more than 65,000 votes.

That change still left the Legislature confined to regular sessions that met only in odd-numbered years. But four and a half precious weeks had been added to the calendar. Longer sessions permitted legislators to think more expansively about how best to respond to state needs and to adapt more fully to the new responsibilities the federal government would soon be sending to the states.

The 1962 election also ushered in a cadre of ambitious young Republicans who seized opportunity in the new suburban districts the 1959 redistricting plan had created. They were a well-organized group. Their first successful campaign, in 1960, had elected thirty-year-old Minneapolis attorney Douglas Head, a Yale graduate and future state attorney general. The volunteer-heavy, door-to-door strategy employed to win that seat—which unwittingly mirrored Sabo's door-knocking performance that same year—was studied and copied by a half dozen first-time Republican candidates two years later. Their explicit goal: regain Conservative caucus control of the state House.

The engineer of their coordinated effort was the thirty-one-year-old chairman of Hennepin County's Young Republican Club, Lyall Schwarzkopf. He was himself a successful candidate, winning a House seat in the district immediately south of Sabo's. That was not all the two had in common. Schwarzkopf was the son of a widow who owned a hardware store on Riverside Avenue across the street from the grocery store and apartment in which Sabo, Jim Pederson, and the other Augsburg recent grads lived. "I knew all those guys," Schwarzkopf attested decades later.

In 1958 Schwarzkopf married Augsburg student Inez Olson, the daughter of Augsburg theology professor Iver Olson. Inez Schwarzkopf was Martin Sabo's classmate. Lyall and Inez met while she was working at Messenger Press Bookstore at Twenty-Second and Riverside, a few doors away from the grocery and hardware stores. That neighborhood in the late 1950s was a nest of future political talent.[12]

Schwarzkopf won in District 35. The other House seat in that district went to Gary Flakne, a future Hennepin County attorney. Bill Frenzel, a future congressman, won in District 30; John Yngve, a future chair of the Metropolitan Transit Commission, and Salisbury Adams, a Harvard-trained lawyer, won in District 31; and Otto Bang won in District 33. Together with a few like-minded and similarly youthful allies from Greater Minnesota, including Paul Overgaard of Albert Lea and Arlen Erdahl of Blue Earth, these Republicans were dubbed "The Young Turks." They succeeded in wresting control of the House from the Liberals, capturing an 80–54 majority in 1963. Conservatives would reign in both the state House and Senate for the next ten years.

But Republicans would have to wait for their "trifecta"—that is, control of the governor's office as well as the two legislative chambers. After a four-month recount, DFLer Karl Rolvaag unseated Republican Governor Elmer L. Andersen. Rolvaag's margin of victory was ninety-one votes, making it the closest US gubernatorial election in the twentieth century. Rolvaag was the state's first governor elected to a four-year term, thanks to a constitutional change the state's voters had approved in 1958.[13]

Sabo the partisan was undoubtedly disappointed to find himself in the minority caucus in 1963. His hopes of chairing a committee or carrying a major bill anytime soon were dashed. But Sabo the political science student admired what Schwarzkopf had achieved. "They elected just an incredible group of talented people," Sabo said of the Young Turks years later. "They were very smart and talented legislators."[14]

Meeting Sylvia

Any sting Sabo felt upon landing in the minority undoubtedly was also eased by positive developments in his personal life. At a bonfire gathering of the young employees of Fairview Hospital in the fall of

Governor Karl F. Rolvaag in 1966.

1961, he met Sylvia Lee, a vivacious nurse who had graduated in 1959 from St. Olaf College in Northfield, Minnesota. He was smitten.

Those feelings deepened as he came to know her family's story. Sylvia Ann Lee was the daughter of Sylvan and Agnes Dahl Lee, a couple who shared Sabo's Norwegian and North Dakota heritage. Sylvan had been raised in Gwinner, North Dakota, a small town southwest of Fargo where his family owned a bank. That was a precarious occupation in North Dakota in the 1920s and 1930s. Sylvan went to work at the bank right after high school, only to watch it fail. He next tried his hand as the proprietor of a general store, then a grocery store, where he exhibited a dedication to hard work and community service that rubbed off on his three children.

All the while he was a shopkeeper, Sylvan Lee dreamed of becoming a Lutheran pastor. When he got serious about pursuing that goal, he had difficulty finding a seminary that would admit a man in his mid-thirties. Finally, Wartburg Seminary in Dubuque, Iowa, a school with German Lutheran roots, accepted him. After becoming a clergyman, he was called to St. John's Lutheran Church in Sioux Falls, South Dakota, a small but rapidly growing congregation founded in the 1940s. It was part of the American Lutheran Church, a denomination formed through a series of mergers that included the Norwegian Lutheran Church in America, the body from which Augsburg College's Lutheran Free Church had separated in the 1890s. Lee would be St. John's senior pastor for eighteen years; the three Lee children, with Sylvia the eldest, would come of age in Sioux Falls.[15]

Martin first proposed marriage in 1962. Sylvia said no. She wasn't ready to be tied to a politician and his district. She wanted to travel. With a friend who was also a nurse, she packed her Volkswagen Beetle for a yearlong road trip, to be financed by a series of brief gigs as traveling nurses. Her sojourn ended at Sioux Valley Hospital in Sioux Falls, where she landed a job as a nursing instructor. She also reconnected with Martin Sabo in Minneapolis. When he proposed marriage a second time, she said yes. They were married by her father at his church in the presence of Martin's mother—now a widow—and three hundred guests on June 30, 1963.[16]

Five months earlier, on February 1, 1963, after decades of division and many years of negotiation, the Lutheran Free Church and the American Lutheran Church officially combined. Augsburg and St. Olaf Colleges—and Martin Sabo and Sylvia Lee—had become part of one Lutheran family.

One Person, One Vote

One other development in 1962 would eventually be transformative for Minnesota's legislature and many others around the country. On March 26, the US Supreme Court handed down the first in a series of landmark decisions on legislative redistricting. The opinion in *Baker v. Carr* put the nation's legislatures on notice that the federal courts could and would apply the equal protection clause of the US Constitution's Fourteenth Amendment to lawsuits over unequal legislative district apportionment. No longer would courts bow to the argument that redistricting was essentially political and should be left to the purview of the legislative branch. Rather, the six to two court majority said, unequal districts were a violation of the US Constitution, and that made them subject to remedy by federal courts. Associate Justice William Brennan's majority opinion essentially invited citizens in states with malapportioned districts to come to the court for relief.[17]

By itself, *Baker v. Carr* did not move district lines in any state. But it started a cascade of lawsuits that two years later would produce an unmistakable Supreme Court directive: legislative districts must be approximately equal in population. Each new census must lead to an adjustment in district boundaries to equalize them. That word came in an eight to one ruling by the US Supreme Court in the case *Reynolds v. Sims*. Together with *Wesberry v. Sanders*, a companion case concerning districts in the US House of Representatives, the court had spelled out what came to be known as the "one person, one vote" principle: in the United States, the weight and worth of each citizen's vote for representation in the US House and state legislatures must be approximately the same.[18]

The Reynolds opinion was issued on June 15, 1964. Politically savvy plaintiffs in Minnesota were more than ready to act. Already on June 4, a group of nine metro-area residents led by Milton Honsey, the mayor of suburban New Hope, had filed a lawsuit in federal court asking that the 1959 legislative map be declared unconstitutional. A three-judge panel with a Minnesota pedigree seemed happy to oblige. On December 4, 1964, a panel led by future US Supreme Court Justice Harry Blackmun—a St. Paul native then residing in Rochester—said that the Minnesota Legislature had "an unmistakable duty to reapportion itself periodically in accordance with recent population changes." He noted that in the Minnesota Senate, one senator represented more than 100,000 people while another only 24,428—a situation he called "improperly discriminatory." If the 1965 Legislature did not do its duty, Blackmun wrote, the plaintiffs "may seek further relief from this court at any time." In other words: legislators could either draw districts with equal population, or the federal courts would do it for them—soon.[19]

Governor Karl Rolvaag had already assembled a seventeen-member bipartisan committee to begin drafting new maps to be introduced in the 1965 session. But with both the House and Senate in Conservative hands, the work of the DFL governor's committee and of a group of DFL legislators that included Martin Sabo was not destined to win the majority's respect. Instead, the Legislature sent Rolvaag a redistricting bill that he vetoed on May 24, 1965, the last day of the regular session. It kept the Legislature at 67 Senate and 135 House seats. Among the vetoed bill's flaws, Rolvaag said: DFL districts tended to be larger in population than Republican ones, "concentrating as many DFL voters as possible into as few districts as possible." For example, under the vetoed bill, three state Senate districts in DFL-dominated north and northeast Minneapolis averaged 58,455 people, while six districts in Republican-leaning south Minneapolis averaged 51,646. In both instances, Minneapolis districts were larger than the 50,953 that was the population target for Senate districts of equal size.[20]

Rolvaag signaled to legislators that he would give them one more crack at redistricting in time for the 1966 election—and before the federal courts stepped in to do the job for them. Election-year candidate selection efforts were already underway when he called legislators back to St. Paul on April 25, 1966. His initial directive: no new map would win his signature unless its district populations varied no more than 10 percent from the equal-population ideal—50,953 for Senate districts; 25,288 for House districts. The map legislators sent him on May 9 violated that guideline with some districts that were too large, particularly in fast-growing suburban areas—or so Rolvaag responded in his veto message on May 11.[21]

A second bill was assembled and sent to the governor on May 18. That one became law. Rolvaag yielded on his insistence of no more than a 10 percent deviation from the target population in any district. Several dozen districts breached that threshold. One House district in Swift and Kandiyohi Counties was off the mark by more than 25 percent. But time was running out. By mid-May, Rolvaag was embroiled in a sizzling intraparty fight to keep his job. He evidently was ready to close his term's redistricting chapter and move on.

While it may not have conformed precisely to "one person, one vote," the new scheme was a major change. It dramatically tilted legislative power toward the previously underrepresented metro area. Eleven new state House districts were created in the Twin Cities area, setting off a scramble in both political parties to seize the opportunities those new districts presented.

The new plan also began a transition in House elections from multi-member to single-member districts. After the 1966 election, about three-fourths of House districts were assigned defined territory within a Senate district. (Prior to that, only a few House districts had territory that was specified in statute, often to coincide with municipal boundaries.) The new House districts were labeled with the Senate district number plus either A or B. But in Hennepin, St. Louis, Olmsted, Washington, and Otter Tail Counties, the long-standing practice continued of at-large House elections within each Senate district, allowing the top two vote-getters to be elected. That arrangement lasted until the next redistricting in 1972. House candidates in those five counties who campaigned door-to-door—as Martin Sabo continued to do—had twice as many doors to visit as their counterparts in the rest of the state.

All that door-knocking continued to pay off for Sabo. In 1966 Sabo and Representative Jim Adams were again the DFL-endorsed candidates in a contest that would produce two winners. For the first time Sabo emerged as the top vote-getter, besting Adams by 594 votes.

The Metropolitan Council

Finally—and arguably for the first time in state history—the Twin Cities metropolitan area was fairly represented in the Legislature that convened in January 1967. For Sabo, awareness of that fact and the lawmaking potential it presented—even for a member of the minority caucus—must have been invigorating.

Sabo was no longer a rookie as he began his fourth term. He was soon to be twenty-nine years old, a husband, and the father of two daughters, Karin Margaret, born May 5, 1964, and Julie Ann, born March 18, 1966. With regret, he had given up on the idea of pursuing a graduate degree in political science at the University of Minnesota. Instead, he sold insurance for Aetna Life Insurance Company during legislative interims. He and Sylvia had become homeowners. Their modest four-bedroom house on East Twenty-Second Street was a few blocks from the Mississippi River and a short distance from the Augsburg campus.

His period of legislative apprenticeship had ended. No longer were his days filled with tedious hearings in obscure committees or back-row observations of the more important committees on which he did not serve. Already in his third term in 1965, Sabo had landed spots on two committees that offered both more lawmaking challenges and greater visibility—Health and Welfare and Metropolitan and Urban Affairs. In the latter committee, he found himself functioning as the de facto DFL leader on legislation to improve sewage disposal in the metropolitan area, a topic that had been neglected for so long that it had taken on more than a regional significance. Sabo and the DFLers opposed allowing three increasingly affluent suburbs—Bloomington,

Burnsville, and Eagan—to establish their own sanitary sewer/water treatment facility on the Minnesota River. They wanted the tax base of those communities tapped to serve a larger region. That idea did not prevail on the sewer question in 1965. But the idea of tax-base sharing among metro communities would not go away.[22]

The Citizens League, a homegrown, citizen-driven public policy think tank founded in 1952 and based in Minneapolis, took the lead in proposing tax-base sharing and metro-wide approaches to public services such as water treatment, transit, airports, and parks. Its visionary executive director in the mid-1960s was Verne Johnson, an attorney, former chief of staff to Republican US Representative Walter Judd, and a former one-term member of the Minnesota House who would go on to a career as an executive at General Mills. During the winter of 1966–67, Johnson hosted conversations on Sunday nights at his Edina home involving key players in the Citizens League's effort to create something new—a Metropolitan Council. It was conceived to be a regional planning agency with a reach spanning the seven counties of the Twin Cities area. Would it be elected or appointed, and if the latter, by whom? Would it be a provider of services as well as a planner? Would it have authority to make its plans stick? Would it have the ability to levy taxes? And could rural legislators be persuaded to support its creation without seeing it as a threat? These were among the questions that were up for debate in Johnson's basement among invitees that often included league activists Dick Fitzgerald, Charles Clay, Greer Lockhart, Leonard Ramberg, and James Hetland; journalists Ted Kolderie and Peter Vanderpoel; and legislators Bill Frenzel, Harmon Ogdahl—and Martin Sabo.[23]

Johnson's invitation to Sabo for those talks bears notice. Sabo was a twenty-eight-year-old member of the House minority at the start of the 1967 session who had no leadership title or responsibility. Unlike Republicans Frenzel in the House and Ogdahl in the Senate, Sabo was not positioned to sponsor a major bill. Yet Johnson wanted him in the room. The Citizens League executive director had undoubtedly watched Sabo's performance on the House Metropolitan and Urban Affairs committee in 1965 and saw something he liked. Johnson was keen to secure support for a Metropolitan Council from members of both parties, in the hope of ensuring its survival through future political power shifts. He judged—correctly—that Sabo was a quick study who would grasp the issues at hand, arrive at a sound position, and help sell that position to his colleagues.

Sabo was easily convinced that a regional planning council would be a plus for the Twin Cities. He indeed helped secure its creation by the 1967 Legislature, working closely with future US Representative Frenzel. However, his allies failed on one point. They wanted the fifteen members of the Metropolitan Council to be elected, not appointed by the governor. But more senior and rural legislators, including influential Conservative Senator Gordon Rosenmeier of Little Falls, strongly disagreed on that point. Sabo offered an amendment on the House floor to make the council an elective body. It failed on a 66 to 62 vote. In 2024—nearly sixty years later—a Minnesota legislative task force was assigned to debate again whether the Metropolitan Council's members should be elected. The task force deadlocked on the question. The issue remains unresolved in early 2025.[24]

A year after the Metropolitan Council bill was enacted, the Citizens League turned its attention to "fiscal disparities" in the metropolitan area. The topic might have been called "municipal government inequality," caused by uneven patterns of commercial/industrial development. A patchwork of winners and losers had developed that left some municipalities able to provide abundant amenities with low homeowner tax burdens, while others had to levy high property taxes on residential properties in order to afford only basic services. The remedy recommended by a Citizens League committee called for metro-wide sharing of 40 percent of the tax base associated with new nonresidential development. A key member of the Citizens League's tax-base-sharing committee was Martin Sabo. The legislation it generated was sponsored in the House by Republican state Representative Charles Weaver of Anoka and cosponsored by Representative Martin Sabo. Though it took two legislative sessions to enact, the so-called "fiscal disparities" bill was signed into law in July 1971; it remains in 2025 a policy achievement noted and admired in other parts of the country.[25]

A Chance to Lead

Sabo's years of quiet observation of the House's most important committees paid off in 1967. He graduated to both the K–12 Education and Taxes committees. His seat on the Taxes committee was granted through a bit of serendipity. Another Liberal caucus member, north Minneapolis attorney Ed Gearty (a future Minnesota Senate president), had been appointed to both Taxes and Appropriations by Conservative Speaker Lloyd Duxbury. The dual appointment was Duxbury's error, and a careless one at that, revealing his inattention to minority representation on key committees. The speaker surely knew that the heavy schedules and demands of the Taxes and the Appropriations committees did not allow a House member to serve on both. When Gearty pointed out the mistake, Duxbury offered Gearty a chance to choose on which of the two committees he would remain. Gearty chose Appropriations. That created an opening for one more minority member on Taxes. Sabo got the seat.[26]

He had landed on the committee at a time when state tax policy was in flux. Unlike most states, Minnesota did not yet collect a sales tax in 1967. Most other US states adopted a tax on retail (and sometimes wholesale) purchases to bolster government revenues during the Great Depression, when property tax receipts dropped dramatically throughout the country. Minnesota faced the same problem. But instead of a sales tax, it created a state income tax in 1933 which, in its initial years, was dedicated to spending on K–12 education. The tax was preferred by Governor Floyd B. Olson and his left-leaning Farmer-Labor Party because it was structured in a progressive fashion, sparing low-income earners and falling harder on high earners. During the worst days of the Depression, the state Senate's Conservative majority went along, acknowledging the political appeal of taxation "based on ability to pay." Together with the regressive property tax, the progressive income tax made Minnesota's tax structure among the most equitable in the nation.

But by 1967 a version of the property tax problem that had hobbled state and local governments thirty-five years earlier was back.

Property taxes had again risen to politically painful levels as local governments struggled to keep pace with a growing population's demand for services. The educational requirements of the large baby boom generation pushed school property taxes to uncomfortable heights. Lower-income homeowners, particularly seniors on fixed incomes, complained that high property taxes were pushing them out of their homes. Meanwhile, Minnesota's state income tax had become one of the nation's highest and was also triggering potent political resistance. Many Conservative legislators—and a few Liberals—believed the time had come to impose a state sales tax and use it in part to reduce either the property or the income tax, or both.

But the sales tax also had detractors in both parties. The same Farmer-Labor thinking that blocked the creation of a state sales tax in the 1930s persisted in much of the DFL of the 1960s. Liberal legislators were particularly keen to keep a sales tax off essentials such as food, clothing, and prescription medicines.

The new occupant of the governor's office was also unfriendly to a sales tax—at least, one enacted by the Legislature. Republican Governor Harold LeVander had vowed during his winning 1966 campaign against DFL Governor Karl Rolvaag that he would insist that any new sales tax be imposed by the state's voters via a referendum, not by the Legislature. It was a strange position for the governor of a state whose constitution did not allow for direct enactment of statutes via initiative and referendum. But LeVander wouldn't budge, even as a bill to create a state sales tax garnered public support from his fellow Republicans and gained momentum in the Legislature.[27]

The tax bill drama that ensued gave Sabo and every other lawmaker an object lesson in separation of powers between state government's legislative and executive branches. It also gave Sabo his first taste of a leadership role on major legislation.

Sabo approached service on the Taxes committee as if it were a university graduate seminar and he was preparing a doctoral thesis. He attended every meeting, examined every bill, and sought to understand the history, policy, and politics propelling every proposal. He was philosophically disposed to reject a sales tax because it would fall disproportionately on lower-income consumers. But he also detected a flaw in the $224 million tax reform bill that Conservatives were bringing to the House and Senate floor. It was not in fiscal balance. It overspent, he determined, and would leave the state with a $40–50 million budget deficit after two years. The need for higher taxes would recur in a short time, he predicted. Sabo brought that flaw to the attention of Liberal minority leader Fred Cina, who also served on the Taxes committee and took the lead for the caucus on tax bill floor debates. Cina encouraged Sabo to make that point public.

Then serendipity struck again. Cina's daughter fell ill. The Liberal leader needed to be absent from the floor debate on May 19–20. "He sort of asked me to lead the floor debate against the bill," Sabo remembered years later. It wasn't an obvious choice. Several other Liberals on the Taxes committee had more seniority. For example, the caucus's assistant leader, B. F. "Pat" DuBois, was a Taxes committee member, a bank executive from Sauk Centre—and twenty-three years older than Sabo. He might have been tapped to make the Liberal case against the bill.[28]

But Sabo was ready for the assignment. He forced his Conservative counterpart in the debate, Representative Robert Johnson of St. Paul, to concede that Sabo was correct: the bill was "betting on the come," expecting economic growth to prop up revenues and keep the state budget balanced. Nevertheless, the bill to create a 3 percent sales tax and use it for property tax relief passed the House on an 84 to 47 vote. Seven Greater Minnesota Liberals broke ranks and voted with the Conservatives to send the bill to the Senate. Despite the lopsided vote, Sabo's debate performance earned him high marks from his colleagues. He would remember that day as one that increased his visibility within the caucus.[29]

The Senate passed the sales tax bill later that same day, May 20, and sent it to LeVander—who promptly vetoed it. The referendum he required was not in the bill. Conservative legislators were ready to take the rare step of overriding the veto of a governor of their own party. But thanks to delaying tactics engineered by a future DFL governor, state Senator Wendell Anderson, the clock ran out on the regular session before the Senate's override vote was cast.

As a result, LeVander felt obliged to call a special session. The political imperative to do something about rising property taxes was evidently too intense for the new governor to dodge until 1969, when the next regular session would occur. Legislators were back in session on May 23. They sent LeVander a very similar sales tax bill on May 31. It was vetoed on the morning of June 1. Later that day, both chambers mustered more than the two-thirds majority vote required to override a governor's veto. The tallies were 93 to 41 in the House, 47 to 20 in the Senate.

It was an assertion of legislative-branch power over the executive branch on a major policy question, the likes of which had seldom been seen in Minnesota before or since. Liberals like Sabo were not pleased with the policy outcome. Nonetheless, Sabo had to be fascinated by the determination of long-serving Conservative leaders to enact tax changes they believed to be in the best interest of the state, regardless of what their party's leader said or did. They did not accept that their role was to simply echo the governor or shield him from a political storm. Rather, they took to heart their own oaths of office and duties to their constituents and stood publicly for what they believed. In so doing, they made service in the legislative branch of government seem like noble work—the sort of thing that a person of ability and principle might choose as a lifelong career.

Hubert H. Humphrey campaigning for president in 1968.

CHAPTER FOUR

MINORITY LEADER

MARTIN SABO WOULD ENDURE TWENTY-THREE GENERAL-election nights as a candidate—pacing, smoking, chatting, and impatiently waiting for ballots to be counted. It's likely that only a few of those vigils stayed etched in his memory. Election night 1968 was undoubtedly one that did.

Sabo's own election that year to a fifth term in the state House was notable only for his margin of victory. Running again for one of two at-large seats in District 42, Sabo outpolled his fellow DFL incumbent James Adams by 2,655 votes, netting his largest share of the vote to date. He and Adams defeated future Minneapolis City Council member Zollie Green and a young University of Minnesota history professor who would later become the state's first openly gay state senator and a Senate president, Allan Spear. Sabo and Spear had DFL Party endorsements, the latter securing party backing largely on the strength of his opposition to the Vietnam War. Adams had been denied the party's blessing despite seven terms of service. The DFL insiders' snub evidently didn't sit well with Martin. Despite the party's choice, Sabo and Adams ran as a team again as they had in four previous elections. Sabo was not one to abandon a colleague.[1]

Slow-arriving returns from other places likely kept Sabo awake and on edge well into the wee hours of the next day. Nationally, Minnesota's own Hubert Humphrey was losing the presidential race, albeit narrowly, to Richard Nixon. Even among his fellow Minnesotans, Vice President Humphrey's reputation had been tarnished by his association with Lyndon Johnson and the Vietnam War. But personal affection for Humphrey ran deep among DFL officeholders like Sabo, who had been an early Humphrey backer that year. It hurt to see "the happy warrior" lose.[2]

Election results in Greater Minnesota also engrossed Sabo as November 5 gave way to November 6. A few swing seats—it would be eight when the ballots were all counted—shifted from Conservative to DFL control. (The House Liberal caucus began calling itself the DFL caucus in 1967, though the Legislature remained officially nonpartisan.) That total was disappointing. It was far fewer than the twenty-six seats DFLers needed to retake the House majority.

The evening's stunner: several long-serving DFL incumbents lost their seats. Among them were minority leader Fred Cina of Aurora, assistant minority leader B. F. DuBois of Sauk Centre, and caucus secretary E. W. Quirin of Rochester. The only caucus official still standing was treasurer Joseph Prifrel, a sixty-three-year-old Teamsters Union business agent who was first elected in 1938—the year Sabo was born.

New House DFL leaders would need to be chosen promptly to prepare for the session scheduled to begin on January 7, 1969. Anyone aspiring to a leadership role would need to step forward and rally support without delay. Sabo may have been a man of few words, but he was keen-eyed about seeing opportunity and not bashful about grasping it. The DFL caucus would elect new leaders on November 23, the *Minneapolis Tribune* reported the following Sunday. Martin Sabo was named as one of several top candidates for minority leader.[3]

Sabo approached running for minority leader in much the same way he approached running for the House—one voter at a time. He set out to speak individually (most often by telephone) to each of the other forty-nine members of the caucus. His several competitors likely did much the same. But Sabo had one key advantage over his most potent rival, family physician John Salchert, who represented north Minneapolis. Though Sabo and Salchert were age contemporaries—thirty and thirty-two, respectively—Sabo had been in the House for four terms. For the most part, he was calling on people he knew well and counted as friends. By comparison, Salchert had served just one previous term, and the demands of his medical practice kept him away from some of the social occasions that allowed House members to become well acquainted. No one had filed to run against Salchert in 1968, which gave him sufficient time to serve as campaign coordinator for his caucus with the DFL Party. In that role, he became familiar with most of the year's first-time winners. But Sabo, too, had campaigned for other DFLers around the state, polishing the role he had assumed in the 1967 session as a leading DFL voice on tax policy.[4]

Both Sabo and Salchert represented Minneapolis districts. That geography mattered enough to some non-metro DFLers to become a theme in newspaper analyses of their contest. Legislators from Greater Minnesota were still smarting from the loss of clout their region had suffered as a result of court-ordered redistricting a few years earlier. It was jarring to some of them to see power shift to Minneapolis and St. Paul. For decades, legislative leaders in both parties had come from rural districts. Now, the House DFL caucus was split about fifty-fifty—half metro and/or Duluth, half Greater Minnesota—and the few potential rural candidates for minority leader weren't gaining traction. Within a few days, rural DFLers came to what for some was an uncomfortable realization: they could put their trust either in a young Minneapolis physician who had been born and raised in the city or a young Minneapolis insurance agent who grew up in Alkabo, North Dakota. Sabo's hometown had become a political asset.

Salchert told reporters he would be a more disciplined leader than Cina had been—a comment that unsettled Cina's friends. Sabo made no such promises. Salchert spoke of the need to elect a leader who represented a safe district and could therefore practice sharp-edged partisan politics without personal fear. Sabo, knowing the comment would worry legislators in swing districts, made no such argument. Salchert supporter Tom Ticen, a Bloomington attorney, told reporters he thought he should be the assistant minority leader, which would give the metro area still more control over the caucus. Sabo quietly let his backers know that he thought the assistant minority leader should be from Greater Minnesota—and that he was open to electing two assistant minority leaders for the sake of still more geographic balance on the leadership team.[5]

One by one, legislators mentioned as "possible candidates" dropped from the contest. The last to go was Fred Norton of St. Paul, a future House speaker. He announced when he exited the race that he supported Sabo. When the caucus convened for its leadership election on November 23, there were only two candidates nominated for minority leader: Sabo and Salchert. Sabo won handily on the first ballot, 34 to 16. Two assistant minority leaders from Greater Minnesota, L. J. Lee of Bagley and Earl Gustafson of Duluth, were elected without opposition in what the *Minneapolis Tribune* called "an apparent effort to satisfy DFLers outside the Twin Cities."[6]

Sabo won with both urban and rural support. All of Salchert's votes were from the metro area. That difference was not lost on Sabo. Someone with his life story needed no convincing that Minnesota is more likely to thrive if its rural and urban regions work together toward common goals. He had just seen the same formula applied to a goal of his own, with good result.

Changes at the Capitol

The customary prayers for divine guidance uttered at the Legislature's traditional opening-day interfaith prayer service might have been particularly heartfelt on January 7, 1969, at Christ Lutheran Church, across University Avenue from the Capitol. The state and nation had just come through a tough year.

The assassinations of civil rights leader Martin Luther King Jr. and Democratic presidential candidate Robert F. Kennedy rocked the nation in 1968. The presidential candidacies of two Minnesotans, Vice President Hubert Humphrey and Senator Eugene McCarthy, created an ugly split within the state's Democratic-Farmer-Labor Party. The issue at the root of their rivalry was the bloody war in Vietnam. America's military involvement in that southeast Asian nation's war between the communist north and the capitalist south was dividing Minnesotans and other Americans into increasingly hostile camps of hawks and doves. Their animosity widened other societal gaps, alienating the young from the old and rural from urban dwellers. Meanwhile, the quest for racial justice that Martin Luther King Jr. had championed was far from complete in Minnesota. A newly insistent call for equal opportunity was coming from women throughout the nation. And rising prices and still-too-high property taxes were pinching pocketbooks and political nerves throughout the state.

All of that was likely on the minds of the two legislators who joined Catholic, Protestant, and Jewish clergy in leading the interfaith prayer service that day. The two lawmakers were state Senator Joseph O'Neill, a Roman Catholic attorney from St. Paul, and Martin Sabo.[7]

A worship service in a Lutheran church was a setting in which Sabo would have felt at home. He and Sylvia and their two daughters were Sunday regulars at Trinity Lutheran, the mother congregation of Augsburg College. Once the city's largest Lutheran church, Trinity lost its sixty-four-year-old building at Twentieth Avenue and Ninth Street South to freeway construction in 1966. The congregation opted not to rebuild but instead to devote its resources to serving its Cedar-Riverside neighborhood. It rented space in a series of other churches. Eventually, Trinity made its home in Augsburg College's chapel—another place in which Martin would have felt at home.[8]

The state Capitol, on the other hand, must have felt like a different place in 1969 than it had been during Sabo's previous terms. A $2 million remodeling project in 1968 had provided every legislator with two things only committee chairs previously possessed—a desk away from the House and Senate floor and a telephone line of their own. The change was made possible when the construction of the Administration Building northeast of the Capitol allowed the offices of the state treasurer and state auditor to relocate. At the same time, the office of the secretary of state moved to the State Office Building southwest of the Capitol. Those departures gave the Legislature more committee space, including a grand round hearing room below the rotunda, and allowed for offices for House members on the ground floor and Senate offices on the second and third floors. Privacy was still in short supply, however. Members of the House majority caucus were installed in rooms of three; minority members were housed five to a room. The DFL rooms were dubbed "bull pens." Private offices were still reserved for chairs of major committees and caucus leaders. For Martin, becoming minority leader meant that for the first time in five terms he had a desk at which he could securely store supplies and a door that he could close during private conversations. Rarer still, he had his own receptionist. Other legislators shared the services of a small stenographic pool. Each caucus could hire its own stenographers—another new wrinkle in 1969. For Sabo, the improvement in his working conditions was dramatic. He began to think about how to bring a similar upgrade to every legislator.[9]

Sabo took note of two other changes, each begun modestly. In 1967 Conservative majority leader Aubrey Dirlam hired an attorney and made him available to provide research and legal assistance to individual legislators upon request. A year later a tiny library was established in the Capitol complex, geared to legislators' research needs as they prepared bills and handled constituent services. These small steps were the start of two support units that within a few years would be deemed vital to Minnesota's legislative operations—House Research and the Minnesota Legislative Reference Library.[10]

Their establishment represented, albeit subtly, a power shift that Sabo welcomed. Putting more research capability in the hands of individual legislators gently loosened the iron grip of long-serving veteran lawmakers and—perhaps more significantly—of special interests. In the first half of the twentieth century, powerful industries including railroads, mining, timber, food processing, manufacturing, and the financial services that supported them had enormous sway at state legislatures, in Minnesota and elsewhere in the nation. The redistricting reforms of the 1960s began to weaken their influence, as younger legislators arrived with a desire to make paramount the interests of constituents in their newly formed urban and suburban districts. Sabo held that all legislators, regardless of geography, had a duty to put the people's interests first—and that his job as a caucus leader included helping individual legislators fulfill that duty.

The Budget Watchdog

Sabo's new job also required him to be the voice of the loyal opposition—that is, to be among the chief critics of the Conservative majority and of Republican Governor Harold LeVander. That role may not have come naturally to someone who only a few years earlier needed nudging to contribute to debate on the House floor. No one ever accused Martin Sabo of being verbose.

But when he had something of substance to say, Sabo said it, plainly and directly. And he had plenty to say about LeVander's plans for state taxes and spending in the coming two-year state budget cycle and the years beyond. As was his wont, Sabo dug deeply into the fine print of the $1.9 billion budget proposal LeVander sent to the Legislature on January 30. He was convinced that LeVander's budget was not balanced—that its proposed expenditures exceeded projected revenue by as much as $100 million, or about 5 percent. Among the defects Sabo detected was the complete absence of funding for a proposed new teachers' retirement plan that he estimated would cost the state $7–9 million per year. He also maintained that the governor's budget underfunded the state's school aid formula by at least $6 million.[11]

Sabo had more. The 1967 tax law changes included the elimination of personal property taxes, a move that provided substantial tax relief to the state's larger businesses while doing little for average taxpayers, he said. Because the reforms also underfunded local governments, local property taxes had continued to rise in much of the state. And the new, regressive sales tax was paid largely by consumers. As a result, the total tax burden on many people of modest means had continued to grow despite the property tax relief the 1967 bill offered. Sabo saw that that situation would persist even if the Legislature adopted LeVander's proposed $37 million increase in cigarette and liquor taxes and license fees.[12]

The LeVander administration, as well as many veteran legislators, was unaccustomed to such detailed analysis and criticism from the opposition party leader. State budgeting had traditionally been the purview of a small number of legislative insiders who were tolerant of a certain amount of guesswork in projecting both future revenues and expenditures. Reliance on large national consulting firms for economic projections was still a decade away. So was the ramping up of state government's internal capacity for budget forecasting.

The administration's initial response to Sabo was to suggest that the rookie minority leader was out of his depth, inexperienced, and unfamiliar with the usual give-and-take between the governor and the legislative committee chairs who assembled budget bills. Funding for new programs is often omitted from governors' budget proposals, they claimed. They offered to "school" Sabo on the process—an offer he accepted, only to announce after a private session with state administration commissioner Rolland Hatfield that he stood by his criticism, particularly of the K–12 education budget.

Later in the session LeVander partially and tacitly conceded Sabo's point with a new proposal. He asked that state tax relief payments to local governments originally due in June be moved to July 15—that is, to the next biennium. That maneuver, known in Capitol parlance as a "shift," would become all too familiar in later decades whenever state government encountered major money trouble. It produced a one-time advantage to the state in the near biennium, while leaving state revenues and expenditures mismatched in the out years. Sabo took a dim view of the shift and said so repeatedly, calling it "camouflaged deficit spending." At best, he said, it would leave the state in a condition of "semi-solvency."[13]

Sabo's critique may have been appreciated by Minnesotans closely attuned to state government and politics. But though his message was amply covered by the state Capitol press corps, it was not the sort to capture widespread public attention or trigger demands for change. With an 85–50 majority, House Conservatives were free to ignore Sabo and enact a budget very similar to the one LeVander had proposed. The Senate's 45–22 Conservative majority followed suit on the session's final day, May 24.

The *Minneapolis Tribune*'s editorial board summed up the session's output as "uninspiring." A review by Gerry Nelson, the respected Associated Press Capitol Bureau chief, of Sabo's performance as a first-time minority leader was harsher still. House "DFLers by and large laid a political egg," Nelson wrote. They "displayed none of the zeal that had been infused into the minority in the past sessions by former Representative Fred Cina," Sabo's more voluble predecessor as caucus leader. "On the floor, young Rep. Martin Sabo, the DFL leader from Minneapolis, was the worse off for following Cina in the leadership position."[14]

Sabo evidently didn't dazzle in floor debates, and the topic he chose for his central critique of LeVander and the Conservatives lacked sex appeal. He refused to be drawn into the emerging arguments over abortion, gun control, and sports facilities. Instead, Sabo had asserted himself as a liberal budget watchdog—a breed seldom seen in latter-day American politics. He wanted honest, adequately funded state budgets so that the government services people needed—education, health care, public safety, and more—would not falter for lack of funds. He wanted to make government a reliable asset in people's lives.

Sabo may not have been a zealot in 1969. But that was the last year in the twentieth century in which Minnesota Republicans had a "trifecta"—that is, control of the governorship, the House, and the Senate. Minnesota was on the brink of political change in 1969, and Sabo helped put it there.

The Nascent Reformer

As the holiday season approached in late 1969, twenty-nine-year-old Minneapolis attorney Tom Berg found himself at a social event attended by several people attached to Augsburg College. That wasn't Berg's alma mater. A native of Willmar, Minnesota, and the son of a postal worker and a telephone operator, Berg was a University of Minnesota graduate who had started practicing law after two years in Washington, DC, in the employ of the US Navy's Office of General

Counsel. As Berg scanned the room looking for familiar faces, he recognized one—Martin Sabo. Sabo spotted him too and seemed eager to make his acquaintance.

After only a few pleasantries, Sabo got down to business. "You ought to think about running for the Legislature," he advised Berg. He made a brief argument supporting the idea, noting that Berg lived in a Minneapolis district in which the two at-large House members, Conservatives George Humphrey and Richard White, had both run unopposed in 1968. The district's political composition was shifting away from Republicans, Sabo said. Those fellows ought to have some competition.

Sabo then moved on to other guests. Berg learned later that before the party ended, Sabo made the same pitch to several other people. But on no one else would it produce the desired effect. The next morning Berg announced to his wife, Margit, that he was seriously considering running for the Legislature. One reason: he was impressed with Martin Sabo.

"He came across as someone who cares about the institution and about government," Berg recalled more than a half century later. "He definitely was trying to bring generational change to an old hidebound institution."[15]

Sabo made similar pitches to other promising possible candidates in the months before the 1970 political season. Wes Skoglund of Minneapolis was among them. Twenty-five years old and a recent University of Minnesota graduate in 1970, Skoglund had been an anti–Vietnam War activist. He was also a lifelong acquaintance of Gordon Nelson, a sociology professor at Augsburg College and Sabo's fellow parishioner at Trinity Lutheran Church. Nelson urged Skoglund to run for state House, then put Sabo in touch with Skoglund. They met for lunch.

"It wasn't a hard sell," Skoglund recalled decades later about his conversation with Sabo that day. "I'd say it was a very Norwegian sell. He made an appeal about serving the good of the state. 'You want to do something good in your life, don't you?'" Skoglund lost in 1970. He tried for the state Senate and lost in 1972. But at Sabo's urging he was back as a House candidate in 1974 and won, launching what would be a thirty-year legislative career.[16]

Candidate recruitment wasn't an uncommon role for a House caucus leader in 1970, though local political party officials then more often took the lead in finding candidates. But Berg and Skoglund understood that Sabo was seeking more than willing names with which to fill out a ballot. He was seeking able young men (the recruitment of women in large numbers was still a few years away) willing to work with him to improve state government. A new ambition was sprouting in Sabo. He could be more than a caucus leader. He could be a reformer.

Consciously or not, Sabo was emulating Republican Lyall Schwarzkopf's "Young Turks" election strategy of 1962. He was seeking to mount a loosely coordinated campaign among a handful of like-minded, relatively youthful candidates—the likes of Berg and his fellow attorneys Ray Faricy of St. Paul and Harry "Tex" Sieben Jr. of Hastings, Greater Minnesota teachers Bill Kelly of East Grand Forks and Joe Graba of Wadena, and farmer Willis Eken of Twin Valley. Sabo didn't insist on a singular campaign theme, Berg recalled, though he made sure the candidates were aware of his analysis that Conservative legislators and the LeVander administration had created a looming budget deficit. He coached them on campaign tactics, including his personal formula for success: knock on as many doors as you can. And he encouraged Berg to let voters know that Conservative incumbent Representative Richard White stood accused of a conflict of interest. He had accepted consulting fees and a Latin American trip from Twin City Lines, Inc., while sponsoring the 1967 Metropolitan Transit Commission bill that would have affected the company's future.[17]

Berg and the rest of the 1970 DFL candidates knew they had a steep hill to climb to get out of minority status. The House's 85–50 split in 1969 meant that 18 House seats would need to flip from Conservative to Liberal to put DFLers in charge. But DFL prospects in 1970 were better than they had been two years earlier. The first midterm election of a Republican president—in this case Richard

Nixon—typically favors Democrats, DFL candidates told themselves. Hubert Humphrey was back on the Minnesota ballot to reclaim his US Senate seat and, they hoped, work his old magic for other DFLers.

And the Minnesota governor's race had been transformed in January, when Republican Governor Harold LeVander announced he would not seek a second term. (Sabo said LeVander made his exit because "he wanted to get away from the fiscal mess he created.") Instead of a contest focused on LeVander and his record, the governor's race had become a spirited battle over the state's future between two young talents, DFL state Senator Wendell Anderson, thirty-seven, of St. Paul and Republican Attorney General Douglas Head, forty, of Minneapolis. Polls predicted a tight race.[18]

But polls were missing something. Minnesotans had been petitioning their state government for the redress of one aching grievance—high property taxes—for nearly a decade. Actions taken by the GOP

Governor Harold LeVander working at his desk.

governor and legislative majorities in 1967 promised relief but delivered more help to business property owners than to homeowners. That was a difference Anderson turned into a potent campaign theme. Then in early October Anderson endorsed a proposal by the Republican-dominated Citizens League for the state to assume nearly all the costs of a fundamental K–12 education. That would mean either a new state property tax or higher income and sales taxes, or both, in exchange for the elimination of local school property taxes. It was a bold proposal that Head attacked as intrusive on the prerogatives of local government. But the distinction was a nicety that did not impress tax-weary Minnesotans. Anderson's position struck voters as bold, and voters were ready to take a risk with a young governor who had a plausible plan to get their tax bills down.

Anderson was elected with 54 percent of the vote on November 3. And Sabo's House caucus gained fifteen seats. The Republican House majority in 1971 would stand at 70–65. Those numbers created a different dynamic than 85-50 had in 1969, Sabo explained to the rookies he helped elect. If the Conservative caucus split on key issues, as they were prone to do, Liberals would have a genuine chance to make a difference.

The numbers in the Senate were closer still: 34–33. A week of drama at the start of the 1971 session over the seating of Conservative Senator Richard Palmer of Duluth briefly suggested that the Senate could be tied 33–33, which would give the presiding officer, newly elected DFL Lieutenant Governor Rudy Perpich, the ability to control the chamber. The scheme—spawned in the fertile mind of St. Paul DFL leader Nicholas Coleman—alleged campaign law violations by Palmer serious enough to deny him his seat. The DFL power grab proved futile when the state Supreme Court stepped in.[19]

Coleman, the owner of a St. Paul advertising agency, was new to caucus leadership but not to the state's political limelight. As a rookie state senator, he had managed President Lyndon Johnson's presidential campaign in Minnesota in 1964. But a few years later he broke with Johnson and Humphrey, becoming one of the Legislature's most outspoken critics of the Vietnam War. That stance—as Humphrey was charting a Senate comeback—likely contributed to Coleman's loss to Wendell Anderson in the DFL gubernatorial endorsement contest in 1970. Coleman provided a quick-witted Irish American counterpoint to Sabo's stolid Scandinavian style, quickly making him a favorite with the Capitol press corps. Sabo watched Coleman's first act closely. He knew that he would need a working partnership with Coleman if they were to achieve what both wanted: DFL impact on the big decisions of 1971, followed by the election of DFL majorities in 1972.

Changing the Rules

House rules matter, Sabo preached to caucus newbies as they met before the 1971 session convened. The caucus had reelected him leader on November 21, choosing him over challenger Thomas Ticen of Bloomington, an attorney who faulted Sabo as insufficiently dynamic in floor debates. Sabo's attention had turned to the rules that would govern the House's committee organization and flow of legislation in 1971.

He was displeased in 1969 when, as a rookie leader, he approached Speaker Lloyd Duxbury to offer recommendations for minority representation on House committees. He was rebuffed. Committee appointments were the speaker's prerogative, Duxbury told him. House rules.

Sabo tried again in December 1970. The larger size of the DFL caucus warranted him some say over the composition of committees, he told incoming Speaker Aubrey Dirlam. (Duxbury had stepped down to take a railroad industry lobbying job.) Sabo went to the effort of preparing lists of proposed committee appointees. No, Dirlam replied. House rules.

Then it's time to change the rules, Sabo resolved. He was ready to advocate for what he considered the rightful role of all duly elected legislators—majority or minority—to bring their voices to bear on decisions at the state Capitol. He believed that the Minnesota House had operated as an oligarchy long enough.

Sabo had his sights on all the House's standing committees. But one committee—the powerful Rules committee, which controls whether and when bills arrive on the House floor—was his focus. That committee was comprised entirely of members of the majority caucus. It operated in such secrecy that no House members other than the committee itself were allowed to witness its meetings. The proceedings of that committee were not recorded, nor were any votes made public.

One more thing: vote totals on amendments offered on the House floor were not recorded in the House Journal, the daily record of proceedings. The official record created the impression that the minority docilely went along with majority proposals, offering no alternatives. "We never thought that was really fair," Sabo, ever understated, said of the situation years later.[20]

Sabo got busy, schooling his caucus mates in the importance of House rules in the lawmaking enterprise and the value of sticking together on rules change proposals. Sabo prided himself on never imposing a "caucus issue," requiring his fellow DFLers to either vote as a bloc or face internal sanction. But he impressed upon his colleagues, then and in the months that followed, that they were a group preparing to retake control of the House in the coming election. They should seize every opportunity to show Minnesotans how they would operate the House if given the chance. Thus, he asked DFLers to focus their proposed rules changes in a way most likely to attract media attention and public support. Further, he counseled, they should offer no amendment to the Conservatives' proposed rules that the DFL caucus was not prepared to adopt when voters give them the majority. Frivolous or "gotcha" amendments ought not go forward, Sabo stressed. The rules debate was the chance to describe a new, more democratic course for the Minnesota House.

With his full caucus behind him, Sabo went public on December 11 with his request to appear before the Rules committee to propose changes—a request he fully expected to be denied. That day and in subsequent days, he laid out the DFL proposal for rules changes: all committees, including the Rules committee, should have minority-caucus representation proportionate to their strength in the full House, with the minority leader empowered to choose which members would represent his caucus; all proceedings and votes on the House floor should be recorded, including those cast when the House operates as a committee of the whole to give bills preliminary approval; lobbyists should be required to regularly disclose the sources of their compensation; and House members should adhere to a code of ethics, including disclosure in broad categories of their own financial interests.[21]

Dirlam and the new Conservative majority leader, Ernest Lindstrom of Richfield, came up with their own versions of the lobbyist disclosure and legislator code-of-ethics requirements. Those measures were adopted on January 7, 1971. But the DFL amendments seeking more openness and opportunity for minority voices to be heard were voted down—as Sabo expected. Dirlam went so far as to fault the proposal to record House floor sessions as a DFL stunt, "so you can have your speeches ready for the next campaign."[22]

On the contrary, Sabo's interest in opening the House to more public scrutiny was no stunt. But in detecting potential DFL campaign fodder in the 1971 House rules fight, Dirlam wasn't wrong.

CHAPTER FIVE

IT'S A MIRACLE!

HE OWED IT TO PLAYING DOMINOES, MARTIN SABO ALWAYS said with a smile when someone at the state Capitol complimented him on his agility with numbers. He may have been acknowledging a more profound lesson than even he realized. To be sure, playing numbers-based games like dominoes with his parents and older sister to while away long winter nights in Alkabo honed his ability to add, subtract, multiply, and divide. But those games also taught him that mathematics isn't kid stuff. He saw that skill with numbers could put him on an equal plane with adults. He learned that numbers are worthy of respect. They tell the tale between winning and losing, gain and loss, acclaim and reproach. The boy who became a lawmaker learned that success requires paying close attention to numbers—such as the ones that reveal how much government costs, and who pays for it.

When Sabo said in 1970 that outgoing Republican Governor Harold LeVander was leaving a "fiscal mess" to his successor, he wasn't making a flimsy partisan accusation. He had numbers to back it up—and Capitol observers knew it. They had already seen that Sabo could be trusted to offer a data-based assessment of the state's fiscal condition. Sabo was accurately describing what Governor Wendell Anderson and his new DFL regime faced in January 1971.

Their task was to craft a budget proposal for the state's 1972–73 biennium that would both durably balance the forecasted $3 billion

Governor Wendell R. Anderson at his desk in 1971.

state budget—which was some $500 million short of the revenue needed for existing commitments—and honor Anderson's campaign promise to deliver both homeowner property tax relief and more state support for public schools. With a budget proposal due to be sent to the Legislature by the end of January, Anderson's crew set to work weeks before his January 4 inauguration.

Sabo was not part of the governor's original drafting team. It was headed by forty-one-year-old Gerald W. Christenson, a Litchfield native and PhD educator whose doctoral dissertation—still a work in progress in 1971—analyzed disparities among districts in public school funding. The topic was on point for the exercise at hand. Christenson, a former aide to US Representative Joe Karth of St. Paul, was Anderson's choice to head the state planning agency, a small bureau that had been created by LeVander and the Legislature only four years earlier. It worked closely with the governor's office. Assisting Christenson was Eileen Baumgartner, twenty-eight, a College of St. Catherine chemistry major, Peace Corps alumna, and University of Minnesota public administration graduate who was also new to the planning agency. The team also included John Earl Haynes, twenty-six, the gubernatorial campaign's research aide and former state Senate tax analyst who had been slotted into the governor's office as its chief fiscal advisor.[1]

Sabo was invited to join the team soon after it developed preliminary ideas, Haynes said. Why Sabo—and no other legislator—was chosen for consultation at that early stage isn't clear, though his affinity for numbers surely helped. "Sabo was more sensitive to math issues than I was," Haynes said years later. It undoubtedly helped too that Anderson and Sabo knew each other well. They had been together as the Minnesota House's "kids" in 1961. Anderson was five years older and had arrived at the Capitol two years earlier than Sabo.[2]

Baumgartner, the team's mathematics whiz, welcomed the House DFL leader. "I had seen him operate before," she recalled years later. "I had seen his intelligence. He's a very mathematical guy. We're both data hogs." Sabo was soon present at every meeting. "They trusted him," Baumgartner said of the politicians in the room. "They didn't understand all the technicalities, but they knew he did."[3]

Sabo joined the team as they were exploring what would have been a jaw-dropping change—the complete abolition of the local property tax. A state property tax would take its place, to be distributed to schools, counties, and municipalities according to formulas set in St. Paul. The idea had the virtues of simplicity and efficiency. But Sabo convinced the team to think again. A proposal to remove taxing authority from the hands of local school boards, county commissioners, and city councils would set off a political firestorm, he argued. And a state takeover was not necessary to achieve the governor's goals. Rather, by imposing yearly maximum increases—"levy limits"—local appetites for higher taxes could be constrained within the existing system. "Legislators would be far more comfortable with that approach because it's more familiar," Haynes said, recapping Sabo's argument. "Sabo was interested in finding the most practical way to get the job done." His idea prevailed.[4]

When Anderson appeared before a joint House and Senate session on January 27 to propose the largest income tax increase and state/local tax swap in Minnesota history, Sabo was ready to help sell it. Anderson asked for a whopping 37 percent increase in state taxes—$762 million. Nearly $500 million of that total would come from the elimination of a state tax deduction for paid federal income taxes—an approach that would result in progressively higher taxes for higher-income Minnesotans. The rest of Anderson's new tax load was also chosen to fall harder on upper-income Minnesotans than lower-income ones, though he also included new taxes on tobacco and alcohol. He avoided calling for an increase in the sales tax, then barely four years old and still resisted by many DFLers because of its disproportionate impact on lower-income consumers.

Anderson planned to use the lion's share of his proposed new tax revenue to reduce school property taxes. Further, he advised that school boards no longer be allowed to increase spending—and hence their local tax bite—beyond an annually adjusted state-derived threshold, unless they sought voters' permission to do so with an "excess levy referendum." That was Sabo's "levy limit."[5]

Sabo told reporters he considered Anderson's budget "courageous." That it was. But it risked being so far beyond the political tolerance levels of the Conservatives in charge of the House and Senate that it would be declared dead on arrival. Sabo advised Anderson's team to break the proposal into component parts and, at least initially, see which of them might find bipartisan support. He agreed to personally sponsor the changes in the income tax rates and federal tax deductibility that, taken together, would give Minnesota one of the most progressive state income taxes in the nation. The state's existing tax system—the combination of income, sales, and property taxes—imposed an "inequitable burden on those least able to pay," Sabo told interest groups that visited the Capitol. For him, one of the most attractive features of Anderson's proposal was the opportunity it presented to shift more of the state/local tax burden onto the shoulders of those with larger means to bear it.[6]

As Sabo defended that feature of Anderson's plan, he continued to keep his eye on the bottom line. His first measure of any proposal, whether of Liberal or Conservative origin, was whether it would keep the state budget balanced through the coming biennium and preferably beyond. He was one of perhaps a half dozen legislators for whom maintaining a balanced budget had become a fixation. To him, stewardship of the budget was an obligation that went with caucus leadership.[7]

Minnesota's balanced biennial budget requirement is set by the state constitution, albeit indirectly. It derives from a prohibition on borrowing at the end of a biennium for the purpose of balancing a budget. If a budget is out of balance, a governor is obliged to make unilateral spending cuts—a process known as "unallotment"—to stay in the black. Unallotment inevitably falls on programs that benefit lower-income Minnesotans, Sabo knew, since those programs lack political constituencies potent enough to shield them. Unallotment was something Sabo was keen to avoid.[8]

Sabo wasn't happy with the bill the House majority crafted in May in response to Anderson's proposal. He pointed out that it overestimated the tax revenue it would generate by $13–14 million—a small amount, but one that had not escaped Sabo's notice. But the larger disagreement between DFLers and House Conservatives was on the size of the House plan—it was about a third smaller than the governor's—and its distribution of new state taxes. House Conservatives wanted to rely much less on income tax increases and opted instead for a one-cent increase in the state sales tax. DFLers charged that the Conservatives' proposal would keep property taxes unacceptably high and hit lower- and middle-income Minnesotans disproportionately hard.[9]

Those DFL messages were well covered by Capitol reporters, with whose working ways Sabo had become familiar. He knew that if he wanted attention drawn to the Liberal minority's positions, those positions should be uncomplicated and few. It was never Sabo's practice to demand that his caucus mates vote in unison or strictly follow his lead during floor debates. But his requests were respected and generally heeded, remembers Joe Graba, in 1971 a Liberal freshman representative from Wadena and a future executive director of the state's technical college system.

"He told us in a caucus meeting, 'I want us to agree on four amendments, and I hope we won't offer any more than four. If you offer too many, the newspaper tomorrow will write articles about how many amendments we offered. If we do just four, the articles will be about what we disagreed with, not how many disagreements we have.'" Sabo had acquired good PR sense.[10]

Keeping Count

Sabo had also honed the ability to calmly count votes under stressful circumstances. That knack was on rich display on May 13 when the House and Senate met jointly to fulfill their constitutional duty to elect members of the Board of Regents of the University of Minnesota. When the two legislative bodies combined, Conservatives had a clear majority, 104 to 98. Yet Sabo was able to take advantage of a convoluted voice voting procedure and disarray among Conservatives to elect a DFL-preferred candidate, educator and Minneapolis civil rights leader Josie Johnson, to one of three seats being filled in that exercise.

Sabo was the floor engineer, directing "a series of moves so intricate as to almost defy description," reported Gerry Nelson of the Associated Press. Legislators voted by naming aloud their votes for a three-candidate slate. Most Conservatives voted for incumbent Albert Hartl of Fergus Falls, farmer-businessman George Rauenhorst of Olivia, and LoAnne Thrane, a Republican activist from Chanhassen. But some Conservatives preferred Hal Greenwood, president of Twin Cities–based Midwest Federal Savings & Loan, over Hartl. They promised DFLers they would support Johnson if enough Liberals supported Greenwood.[11]

Sabo kept a painstaking tally as the voice votes were cast and saw that the promised Conservative votes for Johnson were not forthcoming. He signaled to the Liberals who had voted for Greenwood that they in turn should rise to change their votes. The result was a parade of vote-changing that lasted several hours and involved both caucuses before all the votes were cast. The final tally: Rauenhorst 112, Thrane 108, Johnson 100, Greenwood 91. The top three vote-getters were elected—and Josie Johnson, who would go on to be an icon in Minnesota civil rights annals, became the first African American to take a seat on the twelve-member Board of Regents.

"Martin was so quick at making the counts. He had us set up and was sending signals to us constantly," Graba recalled. Other people who had not been previously nominated—twenty-eight in all—were receiving votes in an elaborate dance before the voting ceased. "Martin juggled that vote until the Conservatives were so confused that they couldn't see that Josie had the majority. But Martin did. When he finally said, 'Mr. Speaker, move that voting cease,' they allowed a voice vote on the motion," Graba said. Conservative leaders evidently were unaware at that moment that Johnson was among the winning three candidates.[12]

When Sabo was interviewed late in life about memorable accomplishments during his legislative career, the first episode he mentioned was Josie Johnson's election to the Board of Regents. It was "the one that was the most fun," he said.[13]

The Hard Work of Miracles

As the 1971 regular session wound down to a few days, Sabo recommended a veto of the House's tax bill should it reach the governor's desk, and Anderson seemed ready to comply. John Haynes told a reporter that he did not believe there was a "smidgen of difference" between Sabo and Anderson on tax policy. The Norwegian American from Alkabo and the Swedish American from east St. Paul had become solid lawmaking partners. "They had similar attitudes about a great many matters," Haynes said about Sabo and Anderson years later.[14]

Their personalities meshed well too—in part because Sabo was content to yield the spotlight to Anderson. It likely mattered to Anderson that Sabo evinced no desire to run for statewide office. In Anderson's eyes, that put him in a different light than Sabo's Senate counterpart, DFL minority leader Nicholas Coleman, who had been one of Anderson's rivals for the DFL endorsement for governor in 1970.

But no tax bill was forthcoming from the Senate. Its Conservatives had splintered over the tax/school funding issue. Senate majority leader Stanley Holmquist, a former Grove City school superintendent who was serving his last session in a twenty-five-year legislative career, decided in early May to back Anderson's plan. He saw it as a way to ease the financial distress that had long plagued rural school districts like his. Other Conservative senators either fell in line with Holmquist or opted for one of several smaller versions less dependent on a progressive income tax increase. The result: no tax bill was sent to the governor at the end of the regular session. Everyone at the Capitol acknowledged that the work wasn't done. Anderson called a special session on May 25, the day after the regular session was constitutionally compelled to adjourn.[15]

The Legislature's Conservatives then did something commendable that provided stability for Minnesota, even as it undercut their negotiating leverage with Anderson. They passed a bill extending the life of the current biennium's state taxing and spending authority into the new budget period, which was set to begin on July 1. Doing so meant that sufficient revenue was assured to pay for several spending bills that had been enacted during the regular session—bills Anderson said he might be compelled to veto unless taxing authority to pay for them had been provided. Had he vetoed the bills—and had the tax/school funding stalemate dragged on, which appeared likely—the state would have lurched toward a highly disruptive government shutdown beginning July 1. A shutdown would have put much more pressure on Anderson to cave to Conservative calls for smaller tax increases and less school property tax relief. Anderson signed the spending bills on June 7. Among the legislators applauding the move were two lawmakers who had become allies, likely to the surprise of both—Stanley Holmquist and Martin Sabo.[16]

The lifting of a July 1 government shutdown threat removed something legislative bodies generally require to compel compromise—a deadline. The special session shifted into slow motion as summer arrived. The leading legislators on the tax and school finance conference committees—five House and five Senate members on each, for a total of twenty—continued to work behind closed doors. The Senate panels included several members of the Liberal minority; the House committees were all Conservatives. That left Sabo and 181 other legislators out in the cold—or rather, as summer progressed, the heat. The state constitution required that the House and Senate convene every three business days to remain in session. That meant a series of increasingly annoying and costly trips to the state Capitol for people elected to what was purportedly a part-time gig that paid $4,800 a year. Most legislators had other jobs that provided the bulk of their incomes—Sabo, for example, sold life insurance. Those jobs required time and effort during summer months that in 1971 were increasingly being consumed by fruitless trips to St. Paul. Senator Florian Chmielewski, a polka band leader from Sturgeon Lake, voiced the sentiments of many when he strapped on his accordion outside the Senate chamber on June 8 and crooned a specially adapted version of the country song "Please Release Me, Let Me Go." He found several other DFLers willing to join his impromptu chorus. But they were unable to accelerate the pace of negotiations.[17]

Reporters watching the comings and goings of negotiators in closed-door talks in mid-June detected that most Senate Conservatives, led by Holmquist, and DFLers in the governor's office were nearing a compromise. But House Conservatives weren't budging from their desire for a tax increase at least $200 million smaller than Anderson and Sabo originally sought, with consequently less property tax relief as well. And as long as the House wasn't moving, a few Senate Conservatives were holding out too. The House's majority caucus had embraced a smaller-is-better philosophy of government that would become Republican dogma with the rise of President Ronald Reagan a decade later. House Conservative majority leader Ernie Lindstrom's oft-repeated line was: "The best tax relief you will ever get is the tax dollar that wasn't taken away from you in the first place."[18]

Sabo's rejoinder to Lindstrom was picked up by the Associated Press and published around the state. He stressed that the fight at the state Capitol was less about the size of government than about who should bear the responsibility for paying for it. "The real issue is whether we have the foresight and courage to reform an unjust tax system," Sabo said. "The issue is whether we are willing to raise enough money at the state level to lower local property taxes, which are regressive and unfair."[19]

After weeks of futility, House and Senate Conservatives finally came up with a tax bill in late July that would unite their caucuses. On near-party line votes—with only one Liberal legislator in each chamber voting with Conservatives—the Legislature approved a $600 million bill on July 30 that included a one-cent sales tax increase, income tax rate changes that functioned as a 23 percent across-the-board surtax, a five-cent per pack cigarette tax, and considerable business tax relief. It increased state school spending sufficiently to cover 61 percent of basic educational costs, up from the existing 43 percent.[20]

At Sabo's urging, Anderson vetoed the bill on August 3. His veto message picked up on points Sabo had been making all year. He blasted a bill that did little to relieve the total state-plus-local tax burden on lower-income Minnesotans while easing taxes on businesses. What's more, it had been crafted by closed-door conference committees, with undisclosed input from corporate lobbyists. "It's not only a tax bill that I am vetoing today," Anderson wrote. "It is an approach to the problems of our people. . . . I am vetoing the idea that the special interests are entitled to write the people's laws. I am vetoing the idea that the people don't have to be consulted. I am vetoing the idea that those with the most power and wealth should get the most tax relief."[21]

After sending Anderson the ill-fated bill, the Legislature had recessed until a date certain—October 12. That ended the irritation of check-ins at the Capitol every three days while keeping the session alive. A two-month window had been created for more negotiation.

Anderson proposed a new approach to resolving the tax/school funding question: A new conference committee of ten legislators should take up the task of preparing a bill—in public. No more closed meetings, he urged. (That was a plea he could not make stick.) Further, Anderson said, the committee should contain at least four DFLers. The Senate's prior conferees included two DFLers, but the House had frozen out Sabo and his caucus mates. In effect, Anderson was insisting that Sabo be allowed to join them. "Martin was one of the guys who really knew the tax and school issues—knew them better than anybody," Haynes said. "He needed to be part of any all-party negotiations." Anderson went so far as to turn over the dining room in the governor's official residence for the new committee's use. Republicans in the House must have understood that they were running out of options. Reluctantly, they agreed to Anderson's plan for negotiations.[22]

Press reports in subsequent weeks contained hints about new possibilities and potential compromises. Sabo recalled years later that when he joined the talks, he immersed himself in two complex aspects of the work—the formula by which school aid is distributed, and the way the state supplies aid to cities and counties. Both of those distribution schemes were critical to achieving Sabo's aim of equalizing the quality of schools and public safety around the state. Sabo believed that the quality of government services—particularly education—should not be solely dependent on a community's wealth. He proposed a major change in the state's aid distribution to cities and counties. Rather than basing aid amounts on how much sales tax a community collected or how much revenue it lost in 1967 when the state's personal property tax was repealed, as had been the case for several years, Sabo urged adoption of a simple new formula based on population.[23]

His idea was not fully adopted in 1971. But it was the first step in a major shift toward awarding state aid to cities based on measures of need and means rather than on prior tax collections. That change is at the heart of Local Government Aid (LGA), the program that for more than a half century has used state government's fundraising muscle to help pay for police, fire, infrastructure, and other municipal services throughout most of Minnesota. The LGA program has continued to reach the lion's share of Minnesota's 854 cities. In 2023 about 90 percent of the state's cities qualified for the aid. The distribution scheme has changed several times through the years. But it has always been based on both assessments of a city's needs and its ability to pay via locally raised revenue. The idea behind the program is still Sabo's: in Minnesota, whether your community has decent police, fire, sewer, and water services should not depend solely on its property wealth.[24]

Sabo and his Senate counterpart Coleman insisted on one other feature of the new city aid program: it needed to serve Minneapolis and St. Paul as well as the rest of the state. The phrase "municipal overburden" was used to describe places like Minneapolis, St. Paul, and regional commercial centers where demand for public safety and other city services is enlarged by a daily influx of workers and a shared responsibility for surrounding communities. Their success in securing LGA for the "cities of the first class"—Minneapolis, St. Paul, and Duluth—also secured the votes of legislators from those cities for a final bill.

That was just one item among several moving pieces that needed to be set in place for another bill to pass and reach the governor's desk. The October 12 reconvening date provided a deadline of sorts for the work. But a more potent one emerged in September, when State Auditor Rolland Hatfield, a Republican, announced that without a new tax bill, the state would be unable to pay its bills after November 15. More impetus for action appeared at about the same time in the form of a pair of lawsuits, one by the Minnesota Federation of Teachers and another by the Minnesota Real Estate Taxpayers Association. They challenged Minnesota's school finance system for overreliance on the taxation of property wealth. A similar suit had recently succeeded before the California Supreme Court.[25]

With Holmquist, the twenty-four-year veteran, holding the gavel in the governor's dining room and Sabo in deal-making mode, agreements slid into place—sometimes in ways that observers did not grasp. Holmquist was not a fan of public meetings. When reporters were present, he used his position to end public discussions of finer policy points when he sensed that agreement was near. He feared that more talk risked bogging things down or generating news coverage he didn't want. "I sense that we're close. We'll let the staff take it from there," he would say, then move to another topic.[26]

It was an adroit performance. But when the Legislature returned on October 12, the tax/school bill was still not ready. Two more weeks of talks—most of them behind closed doors, as Holmquist preferred—were required before a bill emerged with the support of the bipartisan negotiating team. The size of the total tax increase—$580 million—more nearly aligned with Conservative preferences. But the income tax increase it included was structured in progressive fashion to spare lower-income Minnesotans. A one-cent sales tax increase was included; so was an increase in corporate income taxes. Gone were the business tax breaks House Conservatives had sought. A boost for both cigarette and liquor taxes was added. And substantial increases in aid to schools, cities, and counties—combined with levy limits to constrain new local taxes—promised property tax reductions of at least 20 percent throughout the state. The state's share of public school costs, in aggregate, would go from 43 percent to 65 percent.[27]

It was a package that cleaved both the Conservative and Liberal caucuses, disappointing some on both the left and the right. In both the House and Senate on October 27, it received more support from the DFL minority than the Conservative majority. Sabo made his own support clear, but he did not pressure his fellow House DFLers to join him. Yet 46 of the 64 others did. Sabo remembered years later how proud he was of that vote—not because his caucus mates had followed his lead, but because they decided for themselves that they had a duty to compromise for the good of the state. "Here was a big substantive piece of legislation that was controversial, and might or might not be good politics, but our folks were voting for it and making it law," Sabo said in 2015. "That was when I thought that we knew how to be a majority in the future."[28]

Going National

An obscure organization with a mouthful of a name—the US Advisory Commission on Intergovernmental Relations—gave the 1971 Minnesota tax/school funding legislation the name that would stick: the Minnesota Miracle. That was the headline in a February 1972 report in which the commission hailed a "cluster of highly innovative actions" by Minnesota's governor and legislators. They "may well claim the outstanding fiscal performance award of 1971. . . . By assuming a dominant role in state-local fiscal policymaking, they intended to reduce the fiscal disparities among school districts, strengthen the general fiscal position of cities and counties and ease the burden of property taxes on homeowners and business firms. In the process, they made Minnesota a model for other states to follow."[29]

It was sweet music to Minnesota policymakers' ears. Among the enduring characteristics of Minnesotans' shared psyche is ambition for their state to be seen as a shining North Star ("E'toile du Nord" is the state's motto) in comparison with other states. Politicians in both parties were prone to believing that their state provided its citizens with a higher quality of life than offered elsewhere. Hubris lies not far beneath Minnesotans' veneer of modest reserve.

Modesty and reserve ran deeper in Martin Sabo than in many Minnesota politicians. But he evidently believed that Minnesota in 1971 had accomplished something noteworthy that could be a model for other states. He also saw that Minnesota could hold its own in comparison with other states, and that he could learn from others as well.

"At that point, I got started in national legislative activities," Sabo said with characteristic understatement about his work in the months that followed the longest special session in Minnesota history. In fact, he plunged in. He joined both the National Legislative Conference and the National Conference of State Legislative Leaders. When he was invited to join the Eagleton Institute for Young Legislators, he said yes to that group too.

He was undoubtedly encouraged to get involved in national organizations by the House's top staff administrator, chief clerk Edward Burdick, who in 1971 was president of the American Society of Legislative Clerks and Secretaries. Already then Burdick was a thirty-year veteran of legislative service and one of the most respected people in the Capitol. A native of Vernon Center in southeastern Minnesota, Burdick began service to the House as a page in 1941, at age nineteen. He became chief clerk in 1967; he would preside over floor sessions and manage House operations for the next thirty-eight years. With a distinctive stentorian voice and a firm grasp of parliamentary procedure, Burdick kept House floor sessions orderly and debates moving. He was revered by legislative leaders of both parties.

Sabo's interest in joining national legislative organizations would have been heartily endorsed by Burdick—and Sabo would have listened. They had become friends as well as mutual admirers, Burdick's adopted son Patrick Mendis said years later. Each saw in the other a deep commitment to the legislature as an institution. Each felt an obligation to make that institution function in an optimal way. "Martin was a stability guy who liked to make order out of chaos," Mendis said. "Ed liked stability, consistency, and following the rules." Burdick probably expressed a preference for the National Legislative Conference, a 2,000-member group that included both elected officials and staffers as members.[30]

In 1974, only three years after Sabo started participating in national organizations, he was elected president of the National Legislative Conference. That same year, Burdick took a seat on that organization's twenty-member governing board. That put them in the thick of major change. In January 1975 their organization would merge with the smaller National Society of State Legislatures and the National Conference of State Legislative Leaders, forming the National Conference of State Legislatures (NCSL), today's much-respected source for best practices information for state governments. Burdick's American Society of Legislative Clerks and Secretaries became an NCSL affiliate. The combination would provide the nation's legislatures with "one forum for the discussion of state and national issues," news coverage explained. The first NCSL presidencies would go one by one to the presidents of the three predecessor organizations. Martin's turn would come in 1976–77.[31]

"Martin had a lot of influence because he was interested in legislative staff and supported the national staff organization," attested Bill Pound, who served as NCSL's executive director for thirty-two years. "Not all legislators were strong on that. But Martin understood that clerks were the main spokespeople for legislatures and did a great deal to control their operations and set their tones." Burdick had schooled him well.[32]

Redistricting Again

The wind of change in many state legislatures in the early 1970s was the same one that had blown hard in the mid-1960s—the federal courts' insistence that legislative districts be drawn in accordance with the "one person, one vote" rule. No longer could legislatures regard the drawing of new maps as optional after a census, as Minnesota legislators had done for nearly half a century. Every new decennial census now would trigger an imperative to equalize district populations via the realignment of district boundaries. If legislators did not act, the courts would.

Even throughout the battle over tax burdens and school funding, the obligation to respond to the 1970 census by drawing new maps hung over Minnesota legislators during the 1971 session. It's why the Conservative majorities in the House and Senate sent legislation containing new legislative district maps to Anderson before the special session ended on October 30. Two days earlier, the *Minneapolis Star*'s Deborah Howell had advised readers that the Legislature's majorities were not likely to get their way. "Sabo's View May Decide Redistricting Plan's Fate," the October 28 *Star* headline reported. While some of the Senate's DFLers evidently found the Conservative plan acceptable, Sabo did not, Howell reported, and his views mattered most in the governor's office. "If Sabo decides he does not like the plan, his

House DFL caucus is likely to agree with him. This means that DFL Gov. Wendell Anderson most likely would veto it, even if it passes both houses."[33]

Howell's forecast was spot-on. Anderson vetoed the GOP plan on November 1 after receiving requests to do so from both Sabo and DFL state chairman Richard Moe. Anderson's move signaled his willingness—and Sabo's—to let the federal courts decide the shape of Minnesota's legislative map. More specifically, they would let a three-judge panel of the US Eighth Circuit Court of Appeals take over, knowing precisely into whose hands they were placing the matter. The panel that had been assigned in October was led by former Minnesota Democratic National Committee member Gerald Heaney of Duluth and included Judge Earl Larson of Minneapolis, a former law partner of DFL Governor Orville Freeman, and Judge Edward Devitt, a former Republican congressman from St. Paul. Republican state Representative Lyall Schwarzkopf drew the obvious conclusion from the panel's composition: "I think that some sort of partisan DFL plan will come out of that court."[34]

Sabo understood that with judges in charge incumbent protection would not be a major consideration in the mapmaking. The new maps were bound to put a sizeable number of incumbents in the same districts, ending careers, while creating some new districts without a resident incumbent. That "applecart-upset" prospect evidently appealed to him. It presented a rare opportunity to infuse a large amount of new blood into a seniority-loving, sclerotic institution. It might even produce new majorities.

But in the near term, the federal panel delivered more confusion and anxiety than Sabo likely bargained for. On December 3, 1971, it ordered that the size of the Minnesota Legislature be reduced from 202 to 140 members—the Senate shrinking from 67 to 35, the House from 135 to 105. The court's move was triggered by its objection to the state's long-standing arrangement of allowing one Senate district to include three House members while the other sixty-six districts had two. The desire for an odd number of members in both chambers while minimizing population deviation among the districts could be better met with a Senate one-third the size of the House—thus three House members in every Senate district, the court argued.[35]

The proposal was a shockwave hitting the state's political establishment, especially in the state Senate. Minnesota had the nation's fifth largest legislature and its largest senate. It was a design traceable to the state's New England origins. Many of Minnesota's founders were from New Hampshire, Maine, Vermont, and Massachusetts, where they were schooled in the broadly participatory democracy of town-meeting governance and the expectation that many citizens would take a turn at public office. It's no coincidence that the nation's largest legislature is in New Hampshire. A large legislature meant districts could be geographically small enough to allow for in-person, door-to-door campaigning—Sabo style.[36]

The three-judge panel gave interested parties less than a month to submit possible maps for a legislature of 140 members. It also allowed that there was still time for the Legislature and governor to enact an alternative plan of their own, in a special session. Conservative Senate leader Holmquist came up with one that called for a 135-member House and 45-member Senate and convinced several leading legislators, including Sabo, to sign on to the idea. But interest in a special session was not high in the governor's office, where it counted. (In Minnesota, only a governor can call a special session of the Legislature.)[37]

Simultaneously, senators were employing another tactic to avert the shrinkage of their chamber. They sent an appeal to the US Supreme Court asking that the three-judge panel's order reducing the Legislature's size be overturned. But Judges Heaney, Devitt, and Larson would not be deterred. They issued maps with 35 Senate and 105 House districts on January 25, 1972. Precinct caucuses, the first step in the political party endorsement process, went forward on February 22 with many legislative campaigns in limbo.

Finally on April 29, in a rare Saturday order, the US Supreme Court spoke. The three-judge panel had gone too far, the justices said in an 8-1 opinion. "So drastically changing the number of districts and the size of the houses of the state legislature is not required by the federal constitution, and is not justified as an exercise of federal power." They called the panel's approach "radical surgery." Heaney, Devitt, and Larson were ordered back to the drawing board.[38]

The chastened panel set to work and on June 2 released the map that would govern Minnesota's legislative geography for the next ten years. Every Senate district would henceforward contain two distinct House districts—no more running at-large, as Sabo had done since 1960 in Minneapolis. The plan reduced by one the number of House members, from 135 to 134. The court was evidently willing to take the chance that Minnesota voters would not elect a House divided at 67 to 67. (It was a risk they likely regretted only a few years later.) The new map created 10 Senate districts and 29 House districts without a resident incumbent. (The Minnesota Constitution requires legislators to reside in the district they represent.) It also paired incumbents in 10 Senate and 26 House districts. Analysts said the maps were not particularly favorable to either party, rating as "toss-ups" more than a dozen Senate contests and 16 to 23 House races. But DFL state chairman Richard Moe, noting that 31 legislators had already announced that they would not run again, had a different read of the new maps: "It's our best opportunity in years to win control of the Legislature."[39]

CHAPTER SIX

THE KEY TURNS

RICHARD MOE, AN EARNEST, NO-NONSENSE ATTORNEY, WAS heading into his second election at the helm of the state DFL Party in the spring of 1972. Like Sabo, he sprang from Norwegian roots—and like Sabo, he believed that politics should be a tool for improving people's lives. The two men were contemporaries, with Moe just fifteen months older than Sabo, and kindred in their serious-minded approach to politics. Moe was a native of Duluth who landed in Minneapolis after graduating in 1959 from Williams College in Massachusetts; he would get his law degree from the University of Minnesota in 1966. Moe first noticed Sabo at the city's DFL convention in 1960 when Sabo was a greenhorn candidate for the Legislature. Moe was elected a state convention delegate that day, launching his career in politics. That same day, he decided to support Sabo's state House bid. It was the start of a lasting relationship. Twelve years later, they were partners with a shared goal: to win a majority for the DFL in the 1973 Legislature.[1]

The 1970 election had produced DFL gains but not majorities. It also provided several lessons for Moe. He had succeeded Warren Spannaus as DFL chairman. Spannaus resigned in December 1969, first to run for governor, then in February 1970 switching his target to attorney general—a post Spannaus would win and hold for the next twelve years. (Moe's unsuccessful rival at the December 6, 1969, DFL state central committee meeting that elected Spannaus's replacement was Sabo's Augsburg College chum Jim Pederson.)[2]

Though the 1970 election was still eleven months away, Moe arrived at DFL headquarters with the nagging feeling that he was already behind schedule. As chairman, he bore considerable responsibility for legislative candidate recruitment. (A half century later, leaders of legislative caucuses play a much larger role in helping local parties identify and attract candidates.) He regretted that in fifteen state House districts and five Senate districts that fall, Conservative candidates ran unopposed. When Liberals fell only three votes short of a majority in the state House and one vote short in the Senate, his regret turned to resolve. During his regular planning meetings in 1971 and early 1972 with minority leaders Nicholas Coleman and Martin Sabo, Moe told them he intended to find and field a candidate who would caucus with the Liberals in each of the 134 House and 67 Senate districts.[3]

"Our strategy was to get a candidate in every district and run hard," Moe recalled years later. "My sense was that there was a lot of complacency then on the part of Conservatives. They thought they were impregnable. We caught a lot of those guys sleeping." That attitude was understandable. The House had not had a Liberal majority since 1961; the Senate had been in Republican/Conservative hands since Minnesota became a state in 1858.[4]

Moe came close to meeting his recruitment goal. Conservatives ran unopposed in just three House districts in 1972. No Conservative Senate candidates went unchallenged. Though the DFL Party was nearly thirty years old in 1972, it could be said that it was functioning as a statewide party for the first time.

Moe believed in face-to-face candidate recruitment. That meant hitting the road. "We scoured the counties in Greater Minnesota for candidates who were well known locally," he said. "We'd even get guys off their tractors to talk to us." "We" generally meant Moe and his younger aide Robert Hurner. Sabo made a few early trips. But he and Coleman were more often part of a follow-up calling crew that also included Governor Wendell Anderson and the state's two US senators, Hubert Humphrey and Walter Mondale. Humphrey, again in good graces with most of his party as the bruises of 1968 healed, was said to be particularly effective at sealing the deal with would-be candidates. The former vice president's largesse also helped pay for Moe's travels. After Humphrey secured his return to the Senate in 1970, he donated half of his remaining campaign funds to state DFL operations.[5]

Moe planned to spend the state party's money on more than gasoline. He disclosed to the *Minneapolis Star*'s Peter Ackerberg in late 1971 that he was taken with the ideas of a political scientist from Illinois, Robert Agranoff, who a few years earlier had served a stint as DFL legislative coordinator in the employ of the state party. Agranoff advised that the modern media landscape required a change in the role state political parties played in legislative races. No longer should they operate district by district with a series of distinct, highly variable campaigns, he said. Instead, state parties should serve as coordinators for larger regions, those defined by zip codes and available address lists for mass mailings, and television, radio, and newspaper markets for advertising. The state office should provide messaging advice, research, fundraising, and advertising help, Agranoff counseled.[6]

When Moe brought that counsel to Sabo's attention, the House leader knew exactly what messaging advice he wanted to dispense. Openness in government—the same theme he convinced Wendell Anderson to sound during the long special-session summer of 1971—could be a winner for DFL legislative candidates, Sabo believed.

Sabo was not making a conventional strategic choice. It's unlikely that many legislative leaders would have argued then—and fewer would say now—that the transparency of government work would concern enough voters to sway their votes. Sabo's choice may have sprung in part from his irritation at being excluded from tax-and-school-finance negotiations in the summer of 1971. But it's more likely that Sabo's focus on the visibility of legislative proceedings had deeper roots, even tracing back to the role lay people and local congregations played in governing the anti-hierarchical Lutheran Free Church of his youth. Sabo also remembered well his days as a freshman legislator, learning by sitting in on committee hearings—and then being told to leave those rooms when the big decisions were at hand. He sensed that the Legislature's 1971 closed-door marathon had convinced more than a few voters that more public scrutiny was in order at the Capitol.

The result was a brochure prepared by the state DFL party and made available to candidates who intended to caucus with the Liberals if elected. Candidates were counseled to distribute the brochure as they knocked on doors and passed out their own literature. "Your Key to Open Government" read the brochure's headline, the words splayed over an ornate, arched white door that had been padlocked shut. Open the brochure, and there was portrayed a large key over a drawing of the state Capitol with the words, "Your vote will turn the key! Open State Government to the people. Elect a DFL Legislature in 1972."[7]

The brochure's text focused on 1971 decisions in the state House—revealing Sabo's handiwork without citing him by name:

> In the 1971 session every House Republican voted against a requirement that all legislative committee meetings be open to the public. Every Republican in the House voted against a requirement that lawmakers disclose their financial interests. . . . Every Republican member of the House of Representatives voted against making a tape recording of all floor sessions. . . .
>
> With only one exception, every DFL member of the House voted for recording of all floor sessions, for recorded votes in the committee of the whole for open committee meetings, for disclosure of legislators' financial interests. . . . The DFL is pledged to end the long reign of secrecy in the Minnesota Legislature. It's your Legislature and you have a right to know what's going on there.

A New Map Needs a New Strategy

First-time candidate Robert Vanasek made ample use of the DFL's openness-in-government brochure, distributing it along with a flyer bearing his own name, face, and credentials as he knocked on doors in mostly rural District 24A. If the two pieces had not arrived together, voters would not have known Vanasek's party affiliation. His brochure made no mention of the fact that he had won DFL endorsement for the open seat at the party's district convention at New Prague High School that spring. (At that convention, Vanasek endured a grilling about welfare policy from a young Carleton College professor named Paul Wellstone.)[8]

The 1972 ballots provided voters no clue about legislative candidates' party loyalties, not in Vanasek's district nor any other around the state. As had been the case since the 1914 election, the 1972 legislative election was a nonpartisan affair. Officially, the DFL Party wanted that changed. Keeping voters in the dark about a candidate's party loyalty denied them information that was crucial to informed decision-making, party leaders and the DFL platform argued. A change to partisan elections could be done by statute, they noted, making it much easier to accomplish than changes requiring a constitutional amendment.

But in various places around the state in 1972, Moe, Sabo, and other party leaders quietly delivered a different message to candidates who intended to caucus with the Liberals: if you deem the DFL Party's endorsement a liability, either skip it or don't advertise it; we won't hold it against you and, in fact, we'll still offer you fundraising and messaging help.

That advice was delivered to Vanasek, a twenty-three-year-old political science graduate of the University of Minnesota, via state Representative Dick Menke, the DFLer in whose district Vanasek had previously lived. Redistricting had shifted Menke's district away from Vanasek's hometown, New Prague, a rural town of about 2,600 people thirty-five miles southwest of Minneapolis. As its name implies, New Prague bore a strong German and Bohemian immigrant imprint, and it had a conservative bent. The new map put New Prague in an open seat, one Vanasek was willing to try to fill. It was precisely the kind of swing district the DFL would need to carry if the party were to recapture control of the House.

Vanasek had spent a portion of the 1971 session at the Capitol conducting research for his senior thesis, which examined the influence of lobbyists at the Legislature. While there, he had become acquainted with several young liberal legislators—Menke, Harry "Tex" Sieben of Hastings, William "Bill" Kelly of East Grand Forks, Tom Berg of Minneapolis, Ray Faricy of St. Paul, and Joe Graba of Wadena. They were a change-minded cohort within their caucus, contemporaries in age, ambition, and political thinking. They were also united in their admiration for Martin Sabo.

"I got my appetite whetted," recalled Vanasek. Though at least a decade younger than most of them, he could imagine himself joining their club in 1973. (He would serve as House speaker from 1987 to 1992.)[9]

The Platform of 1972

Vanasek's decision to downplay his DFL ties was likely reinforced as the 1972 political year unfolded. Though not as bruising as the 1968 contest had been, the 1972 Democratic competition for president pitted moderates against liberals, hawks against doves, and Minnesota's Hubert Humphrey against South Dakota Senator George McGovern—both of whom, ironically, were sons of the South Dakota prairie, both shaped by the privations of the Great Depression, and both swayed by the social gospel movement of the Methodist Church. They had been allies and friends in the US Senate in the early 1960s. But the Vietnam War drove a wedge between them while Humphrey served as Lyndon Johnson's vice president. McGovern's record as one of the Senate's most outspoken critics of US involvement in Vietnam propelled him to the Democratic nomination in 1972, quashing Humphrey's presidential quest and leaving Humphrey's still-numerous Minnesota loyalists dispirited.

McGovern's bid to unseat Republican President Richard Nixon faltered soon after the Democratic National Convention in mid-July. His vice presidential running mate, Missouri Senator Thomas Eagleton, withdrew from the ticket on August 1 after revelations about his history of mental illness and his failure to disclose his condition to

George McGovern (second from right) with (from left) Wendell Anderson, Hubert Humphrey, and Walter Mondale in 1972.

McGovern before the convention. That embarrassing episode only added to the antipathy a significant cadre of party leaders (most of them Humphrey allies) felt toward the more liberal McGovern.

In Minnesota, US Senator Walter Mondale—who considered Humphrey his political mentor—was on the ballot that year and plainly less than eager to embrace McGovern. Richard Moe remembers a McGovern campaign stop in the Twin Cities in mid-October during which it was difficult to get prominent DFLers to appear publicly with the party's presidential nominee. Moe himself picked up McGovern from the airport; Wendell Anderson, who was not on the ballot in 1972, squired the presidential candidate to several media stops. The headline in the next day's *Minneapolis Star* summarized the party's gloom about McGovern's candidacy. "Anderson says McGovern has made state gains, needs more," the story said.[10]

More worrisome to DFL legislative candidates in swing districts than McGovern's standing was the aftertaste of the 1972 DFL state convention. The confab in Rochester June 10–11 produced a platform that was well ahead of its political time—supporting legalization of marijuana, unconditional amnesty for war resisters, and a guarantee of full civil rights for homosexuals. "DFL Endorses Homosexuals' Right to Marry," the *Minneapolis Tribune* headline reported on June 12, though the article went on to say that allies of Governor Anderson succeeded in mounting a procedural challenge to the marriage question just before the convention adjourned. Each of those planks in the party's platform would become state or national law years or decades later. But in 1972, the convention's policy choices were derided by state AFL-CIO president David Roe as the "platform of grass, ass, and amnesty." Moe and DFL associate chair Ruth Cain issued a statement after the convention that called its platform "a misordering of priorities." Within a week Governor Anderson disavowed several platform planks, adding, "I don't know of a single candidate for the Legislature who supports them."[11]

The public rebuke DFL convention delegates received from party leaders might have been of concern to a few legislative candidates who looked to state convention delegates as campaign workers and donors. But more DFL candidates likely breathed easier as Anderson, Moe, and Roe painted a picture of party activists as out-of-touch extremists and the state party's platform as an aberration that could be safely ignored. That was an expedient message for 1972. But it was the beginning of a lasting change in the way Minnesota legislative campaigns were run. Control of legislative campaigns would shift in coming years away from state parties, moving into the hands of legislative caucuses, their allied special interest groups, and purportedly independent political action committees. Political party activists and their grassroots organizing would come to play a lesser role in legislative races, with the 1972 DFL convention often cited as an impetus for that shift.

Clean Campaigning

In the years to come, legislative caucus leaders, sometimes with the aid of one or more designated caucus veterans, would function as campaign generals, recruiting candidates, plotting strategy, and raising and dispensing campaign funds. Sabo did some of each of those things in 1972. But local and state party organizations were in the driver's seat, and campaigns relied more on shoe leather and gasoline than on expensive direct mail and advertising. A typical candidate's total budget was generally between $3,000 and $6,000. With the consultation of a caucus steering committee, Sabo was empowered to dispense small contributions to strategically chosen candidates, generally in increments of only a few hundred dollars.[12]

But candidates in districts deemed strategically important got something they may have prized more than funds—Sabo's attention and advice. Joe Graba, a science teacher in north-central Wadena who was seeking his second term in 1972, had been handed a raw deal by redistricting. All but three townships in his original district were lost to another. Graba would need to introduce himself to new voters while defending his votes for tax increases as large as $700 million. He wasn't sure he should run again—but he couldn't bring himself to confess his misgivings to Martin Sabo.

"Martin would call and ask what I needed," Graba recalled years later. "He didn't try to tell me how to campaign." But Sabo wasn't without advice. When Graba ran in 1970, Sabo had encouraged him to try door-knocking. "That was kind of new then," Graba said. He had opted not to seek DFL endorsement in 1970 and had spurned offers of help from US Senators Mondale and Humphrey, sure that their visibility would not serve him well in his rural swing district. But he paid heed to Sabo.[13]

One other Saboism guided him, Graba said. "I remember him saying, 'I never talk negatively about the Republican opponent, especially when I'm in their district.'" Graba took that message to heart and refrained from attacking his opponents—even when one opponent's conduct had generated considerable local gossip.

Fifty years later, refusal to criticize one's opponent in a political campaign is such an anachronism that it seems implausible. But it was a firm Sabo rule, Richard Moe confirmed. In the 1972 campaign's final weeks, Moe and Sabo traveled together to key districts, appearing at bean feeds, potluck dinners, and other campaign events to raise money and bolster volunteer spirits.

"Martin tried not to personally attack anyone. He thought politics shouldn't be personal," Moe said. "He kept his eye on the ball—which for him was always policy. He liked politics because he saw it had a purpose." Sabo talked about DFL efforts to make state taxes fairer, keep property taxes low, and make sure schools throughout the state were as good as those in wealthy suburbs. "He could sell his politics anywhere, rural, suburban, or urban, but he was particularly good in rural areas. He had such a pleasant way about him, unthreatening and charming, that he commanded respect."[14]

Sabo was the featured speaker at the New Prague Country Club on October 14 at a fundraising dinner for Bob Vanasek that was so unthreatening that the *New Prague Times* congratulated its organizers for the event's pleasant "Gemuetlichkeit" spirit. Moe and Sabo were encouraged by what they were hearing about Vanasek's campaign. "Sabo was pretty impressed with the size of the crowd," Vanasek recalled—noting that a ticket to the fundraising dinner cost just $7.50 per person. Even in 1972, that was a bargain price—one Vanasek chose for strategic reasons. "I wanted to get as many people as possible to feel invested in my campaign. That way, they would defend me in conversations with their family and friends. That was worth more to me than an extra fifteen or twenty dollars."[15]

The same spirit of inclusivity inspired Vanasek to ask Sabo to avoid delivering a strongly partisan message at the event. "Please don't go after the Republicans. At least a third of the people in the room will be Republicans," he told the caucus leader. "Sabo got that immediately" and complied nicely, Vanasek recalled—so much so that readers of the *New Prague Times*, which covered the event, were left to discern the party affiliation of Sabo and Vanasek by a single mention of the presence of the local DFL chairman.[16]

A Breakthrough Year

Sabo was keenly focused on legislative races in 1972—but not all of them, and not on a full-time basis. His $4,800 annual legislative salary included a $16 per diem on days that included official meetings—which were few between sessions. Extra compensation for legislative caucus leaders was still seven years away. That low salary plus the needs of his growing family—which included daughters Karin, age eight in 1972, and Julie, age six—meant that Sabo could not afford to stop selling insurance for the Aetna Company during campaign seasons. He had to allocate his time carefully, heeding advice from Moe and the DFL's small staff of field-workers—some of them college interns who had first worked for Humphrey's short-lived 1972 presidential campaign—about which districts presented DFLers with the best chance to gain seats.[17]

It may have been the state party's assessment that kept District 40A in Minnetonka, an affluent, Republican-leaning suburb west of Minneapolis, off of Sabo's radar. For that or some other reason, Sabo did not personally call Joan Anderson Growe before election day to inquire about her campaign or offer support. If he had, he might have become engaged in something important that was stirring that year among women in politics.

Since 1961 Sabo had served in a nearly all-male legislative body. He developed an admiring friendship during his freshman session with state Representative Sally Luther, a Minneapolis liberal and Vassar-educated former journalist who had been in office since 1951. For several terms, she had been the House's only female member. Luther served her last term in 1961–62 and chaired the Civil Administration committee, wielding her gavel with a competent efficiency that Sabo admired. She was "just incredibly knowledgeable," he would say years later. But she was exceedingly rare. The number of women in the state House dwindled from three in 1963 to one in 1971.[18]

As what would later be called the "second wave" of American feminism began rolling in the late 1960s, women in Minnesota and around the country expanded their thinking about their rightful roles

Martin Sabo (left) presenting Helen McMillan with a plaque at a recognition banquet in Austin, Minnesota, in 1975.

in the nation's democracy. Fifty years after the feminist "first wave" brought women the vote, women were no longer satisfied to participate in government merely by being voters, campaign volunteers, and secretaries to powerful men. In larger numbers, women began seeking elective office. In Minnesota many of those candidacies, including Growe's, came at the instigation of local chapters of the League of Women Voters, not political parties. The only woman elected to the Legislature in 1970 was former state League of Women Voters president Helen McMillan of Austin. In 1972 forty-one women filed for legislative seats; twenty-nine of them survived the primary election. One of them, Georgia M. Smith, was Sabo's own long-shot opponent in District 57B.

Sabo and the state DFL office would have done well to take notice of their party's rising female tide and offer their support. Instead, Growe recalls, she and her energetic, all-female volunteer team had no communication from Sabo. The caucus leader likely doubted that she could win, Growe said years later. In a Minneapolis district abutting Sabo's own, Phyllis Kahn, running against another DFLer, Matthew Stark, recalled years later that she was similarly ignored, likely for a different reason. While Growe was seen as unlikely to produce a win for the Liberal caucus, the Kahn–Stark contest was sure to do so. Neither district was seen as "in play."[19]

In Minnetonka the only offer of help from the state DFL office came about a week before the election when the party's executive director, Hank Fischer (who lived in Growe's district), dispatched a young aide named Mark Winkler to Growe's house. "Great! You can babysit while I go door-knocking!" Growe told Winkler, informing him that she was the mother of three teenagers and a five-year-old. Winkler took the assignment for one day, then vanished—only to turn up a few years later on the staff of Minnesota Secretary of State Joan Growe.[20]

When Growe was one of six women elected to the House on November 7, 1972, her victory evidently came as a surprise to Sabo. "Joan Growe won? Who's Joan Growe?" he reportedly said at an election-night victory party, according to word that quickly got back

Joan Growe as Minnesota Secretary of State in 1977.

to the Growe campaign party in Minnetonka. Not only had Growe defeated her Republican opponent, Richard Stranik, she had carried every precinct in the district.

Three other DFL women won that day: McMillan, Kahn, and Linda Berglin, who like Kahn represented Minneapolis and, like Kahn, would go on to long and distinguished legislative service. Two Republican women, Mary Forsythe of Edina and Ernee McArthur of Brooklyn Center, joined them in a breakthrough year for women in the Minnesota Legislature. Starting in 1972 and through the next several decades, the Legislature's female ranks would grow with each election. In 2024 their numbers stood at 76 of 201.

Trifecta

Moe and Sabo fretted about turnout all day on November 7, election day. It was clear that George McGovern's presidential candidacy had not caught fire in Minnesota. A small but sometimes decisive share of Democratic voters were notorious for turning out only for presidential elections. Would they come to the polls with McGovern at the top of the Democratic ticket and all the polls showing Nixon cruising to a second term?

Their concern was not unfounded. Official turnout in Minnesota in the 1972 general election was 70.3 percent, lower than in any presidential election since records started being kept in 1950. But another factor was at work affecting the partisan bent of the 1972 electorate. Minnesota Secretary of State Arlen Erdahl reported that the state had 225,000 more eligible voters in 1972 than it had in previous presidential elections, thanks to a reduction in the nation's voter-eligibility age from twenty-one to eighteen. That change was made via constitutional amendment in 1971 in response to pressure from young adults who resented being eligible for military service at age eighteen but unable to vote until age twenty-one. Younger voters tended to favor the Democratic Party. While their support for McGovern was not sufficient to push him ahead in Minnesota—which Nixon carried with 51.6 percent of the vote—they helped make Minnesota's presidential vote the closest in the nation that day. They pushed Senator Walter Mondale's winning share of the vote to 57 percent. And they helped downballot DFLers—the ones on Sabo's mind.[21]

That night's election returns were probably no slower than in any other year. But for Sabo, the wait for state House results had to have been among the most agonizing. Senate results were known earlier and gave the DFL election-night party much reason to cheer. In the wee hours of November 8, it was clear that DFLers had won 36 of 67 Senate seats. For the first time in state history, the Senate would be in DFL hands. House results were encouraging, with surprisingly easy wins by the likes of Robert Vanasek in New Prague and Joe Graba in Wadena boosting Sabo's optimism. When the *Minneapolis Star* went to press at midmorning November 8, House Liberals were "assured of 60 seats and leading in 12" of 134 total seats, it reported. By that evening, at deadline time for the November 9 edition of the *Minneapolis Tribune*, the House's flip to DFL control was clear. The newspaper reported that the 1973 session would have a House composed of 78 Liberals and 56 Conservatives. After recounts were complete a few weeks later, the final House count was 77 to 57—and DFLers were still smiling over a Jerry Fearing cartoon published in the *St. Paul Pioneer Press* on November 9. It showed Governor Wendell Anderson at the door of the Legislature, receiving a birthing basket containing two donkey colts labeled "House" and "Senate." The caption: "Just what I always wanted—twins!"[22]

CHAPTER SEVEN

IN CHARGE

SABO HAD TO BE EUPHORIC IN THE HOURS AFTER IT WAS CERtain that the 1973 Minnesota House would have a Liberal majority, the first since 1961. He undoubtedly was also pleased with the composition of the new House. More than a third of the members of the 1973 House would be serving their first term. Together, the newbies significantly reduced the average age of House members. The number of women in the House would jump from one in 1971 to six in 1973. And for the first time in the twentieth century, the House would have an African American member, Conservative Ray Pleasant of Bloomington.[1]

But satisfaction was not the only sentiment Sabo experienced the day after the 1972 election. Sabo confessed years later that he was also struggling with indecision about his own position in the coming session. As minority leader for the past four years and one of the architects of the campaign that produced the new DFL majority, Sabo was clearly in line to be the next House speaker. But was that the role he ought to play? Should he run for speaker?

Sabo's hesitation did not spring from shyness. He was now thirty-four years old and beginning his seventh term. He had long since overcome his initial reluctance to occupy legislative limelight. "I'd gone from the person who didn't say much to sort of enjoying the give and take of the floor," he said on reflection years later.[2]

He had also become good at it. "I loved to watch him on the floor," said state Representative Joe Graba about Sabo as the floor leader in the 1971 session. "He knew the process. He knew the issues. He had excellent command of details. He was always well prepared. You could tell that he had spent the night before a debate doing his homework. It was fun and so educational to watch him in action."[3]

Rather, Sabo wondered whether he was better suited to verbal jousting on the House floor than juggling the often-competing obligations a speaker holds. "The speaker is in a unique spot," Sabo said. He or she is "both the head of the party and the institution," with a duty of stewardship for both that he took seriously. As he understood the speaker's role, he would face limits in the extent to which he could strive for partisan advantage. As speaker, he could control which bills came to the floor and influence the flow of debate by choosing which lawmakers to recognize for comments. But he would be obliged to leave the actual debating to others. Others would make the case for legislation as they saw fit. For someone who cared deeply about passing bills for the right reasons, that was a lot of control to surrender.

He decided to confide in someone who he believed would appreciate his dilemma, someone who knew well the singular role of the speaker in the Minnesota House. He called Lloyd Duxbury.

That call bears notice, for what it says both about Sabo and about Minnesota politics in the mid-twentieth century. Sabo had known Duxbury only as the leader of the Conservative caucus. He had been first minority leader, then speaker, from 1959 until 1970. That meant Duxbury was in what latter-day DFL partisans would consider the "enemy camp" and hence not to be trusted, let alone befriended and consulted. Duxbury's last session as speaker was Sabo's first as minority leader. The two would not have sparred directly during floor debates—that was the majority leader's role—but they were rivals in setting legislative strategy and describing the merits of bills to ever-watchful Capitol reporters.

Yet Sabo regarded Duxbury with enough respect, trust, and friendship to reach out to him as he pondered a move that would be significant both for him and for the Legislature. Duxbury was sixteen years Sabo's senior and, like Sabo, had a rural background. But they came of age in very different circumstances. Duxbury's father was an attorney and state senator from Caledonia, a small town in southeastern Minnesota, who sent his son to the prestigious Philips Exeter Academy in New Hampshire for high school. After military service in World War II, Lloyd Duxbury earned both his undergraduate and law degrees from Harvard University. When he stepped down from the Legislature, Duxbury became a vice president at Burlington Northern, one of the nation's largest railroad companies.[4]

Those are credentials Sabo would have admired, perhaps with a tinge of jealousy, regardless of the political affiliation of their bearer. He obviously also believed Duxbury's counsel would be grounded in the elder man's sincere judgment about the best interests of both Sabo and the House—and that their call would remain confidential, as it did until Sabo himself disclosed it late in life. It was possible in those years for Minnesota politicians of differing parties to build and sustain relationships of that caliber. Each understood the other to possess primary loyalty to the state and its governance, with party loyalty secondary.

"In very colorful language," Duxbury "described what I was if I didn't make that decision to run for speaker," Sabo said in 2015, summarizing their conversation. "So I decided I'd better do that." Former state Representative Tom Berg reported a more unvarnished Sabo account of Duxbury's words in his 2012 book, *Minnesota's Miracle*: "You dumb son of a bitch, of course you should be speaker."[5]

Sabo announced his bid for the speaker's chair on November 10. News stories immediately began referring to him as the likely next speaker, making no mention of any challenger within DFL ranks. In fact, the phones of some of the caucus's more liberal members buzzed for a few days over the possibility that someone who had been a more outspoken opponent of the Vietnam War might be found to challenge Sabo. But that idea came to naught. Sabo was the unanimous choice of his caucus as their candidate for speaker when they met on November 25. The full House made it official when it convened on January 2, 1973.[6]

New Leadership

The rest of the 1973 House leadership team was in place as well. Leading the Conservatives in the minority was Aubrey Dirlam of Redwood Falls, who had been their speaker during their last term in the majority. His elevation to that position was not a sure thing. After an election setback like the one the House Conservatives were dealt in 1972, legislative caucuses often opt for new leadership. The 1971 majority leader, Ernie Lindstrom of Richfield, declined to run for minority leader. But he was openly critical of Dirlam, faulting him and other longtime Conservatives for allowing special interests too much sway over both legislation and campaigns. Lindstrom backed Representative Arlan Stangland—a future congressman—for minority leader. When that effort came up short, Lindstrom secured Dirlam's support for the creation of a nine-member caucus steering committee that would approve the hiring of caucus staff, help formulate caucus positions on key legislation, and—if given the opportunity—advise Dirlam on appointments to House committees. Dirlam explained his acquiescence to that move with an admission that he was "running scared" during the leadership election. He had agreed to a major break from the one-man rule that had long been House tradition.[7]

With Sabo in the speaker's chair, DFLers needed a new majority leader to manage floor debates—and the tradition of geographic balance dictated that the choice should come from greater Minnesota, since Sabo represented a Minneapolis district. Irvin Anderson, forty-nine, a feisty quality inspector at Boise Cascade Corporation in International Falls, got that nod from the DFL caucus. A World War II naval aviator who had first been elected in 1964, Anderson was a conservative Democrat and an ally of organized labor who relished controlling the levers of power. In many ways, he was Sabo's alter ego—bombastic rather than temperate, abrupt rather than careful, provocative rather than reassuring. The caucus vote to elevate Anderson to majority leader was unanimous. He evidently had at least the tacit backing of the speaker designate. Any reservations Sabo may have had about the choice were kept private.[8]

It's possible that Sabo may have seen Anderson's pugnacious style as an asset. "Martin understood that as speaker, he was the leader of the whole institution," Joe Graba said years later. "He understood that he had to lead both caucuses. He did not want the speaker to be seen as excessively partisan, or his decisions from the chair to be seen as tainted." With Anderson dependably occupying the DFL's partisan corner, Sabo could stay above the fray.[9]

Anderson's position meant that when the DFL caucus met during the 1973 session, he would function as its presiding officer. Sabo likely could have taken that up-front role himself. Instead, during caucus meetings Martin preferred to sit quietly to one side and observe, Bob Vanasek said. Nevertheless, Vanasek added, "everybody knew who the boss was."[10]

A New Era of Openness

None of the speaker's traditional "bossy" powers was greater than the control he had over the number and composition of House committees. Sabo was the rare boss who sought to yield some of that control to others. He had been in earnest two years earlier when he sought to bring a greater measure of democracy to House operations. He had chafed then at the minority's inability to choose its own appointees to House committees and at the majority's refusal to seat any minority members on the powerful Rules committee. He hated that Rules committee meetings were closed to the public and even to other House members. "I always said to our folks, we should not be proposing anything in the minority that we weren't willing to do in the majority," Sabo said years later. "I think we pretty much followed through with that."[11]

Following through meant advising Dirlam in December about the change Sabo was making in the committee structure—reducing the number of committees from twenty-four to nineteen—and inviting the minority leader to recommend committee assignments for members of his caucus. Sabo accepted all of Dirlam's recommendations.

Following through meant assuring the minority of proportional representation on all committees save for one—the Rules committee. On that powerful committee, Sabo wanted members of the minority included and meetings opened to the public—a first in both instances. But he opted for an eighteen to seven split on the committee between majority DFLers and minority Republicans—and hence provoked howls of Republican protest that they were being treated unfairly.[12]

Minneapolis DFL Representative James Rice, a former gubernatorial chief of staff known for his wit, couldn't resist calling attention to the Conservatives' reversal as they argued for minority-caucus representation on the Rules committee—something they had fiercely opposed just two years earlier. "We are witnessing the most amazing conversion since Saint Paul on the road to Damascus," Rice quipped during the January 3 floor debate.[13]

Dirlam went so far as to refuse to name seven Republicans to the Rules committee. He would leave that task to Sabo. "I think they didn't appoint them because they had a fight going on internally," Sabo said. "So I appointed their members and I never had any complaints about who was appointed."[14]

Following through also meant bringing to the full House a package of rules changes that Capitol reporters described as "sweeping" and "liberalizing." In addition to the Rules committee changes, Sabo and his DFL caucus proposed opening all committee meetings to the public and tape-recording their proceedings for future public access. They sought to require the recording of roll call votes when a bill was on the House floor for preliminary consideration (provided at least fifteen members indicated that desire with a show of hands). They asked for minority-caucus control of the selection of minority members of committees, codifying in House rules what Sabo had done voluntarily in December. And they proposed to require each House member to disclose his or her personal financial assets and liabilities, not including home mortgages, cars, household items, and personal savings.

On January 3, moments after listening to Governor Wendell Anderson's State of the State address, the House took up the DFL rules package. During seven hours of debate and through votes on multiple amendments, Conservatives chided DFLers for not going further. For example, former minority leader Lindstrom proposed allowing a committee's members by majority vote to put a bill on a committee's agenda—a prerogative that belonged to the committee's chair. That and other GOP amendments were defeated as the new majority got its first exercise in sticking together during important votes. At the end of a long day and evening, Republicans did not want to vote against the open-government measures DFLers were proposing. Sabo's rules package passed 131 to 1.[15]

The House had witnessed something rare in American legislative annals—the voluntary surrender of power by a legislative leader. Sabo felt good about his decision. He was particularly proud of assuring minority caucus members their rightful representation on committees. "I always thought that we should maximize their input in the process to the degree that we did," he said in 2015. "We had a better product because of Republican suggestions. That was a plus for them as well as for us."[16]

The irony in Sabo's session-starting rules changes is that while giving up authority over some aspects of House operations, he gained "soft power"—that is, the respect he enjoyed in the eyes of his colleagues and others at the Capitol. He had made good on promises about bringing more openness to the state's lawmaking enterprise. And he had done so in a timely and orderly way, with a minimum of partisan hostility. The power of the speaker may have shrunk, but Sabo grew in stature.

Investing in Talent

Republicans would now decide who would fill minority seats on House committees. But it was up to Martin Sabo to assign DFLers to the body's nineteen committees and to select their chairs. That task presented Sabo with what must have been a tantalizing opportunity. He could adhere to the time-honored practice of allowing seniority to strictly dictate who would wield gavels. Or he could break with tradition and install chairs based on his assessment of members' abilities, thereby signaling a crumbling of the old order and striking a blow for institutional betterment. A different speaker also may have considered matters such as personal loyalty or the payback of a political favor.

Sabo was not the latter sort. But he spent the better part of the month after the 1972 election pondering the House's committee rosters, balancing his genuine respect for members' durability and for institutional norms with a desire to optimize committee performance. He decided to hew closely to "seniority rules" as he named chairs. With thirty new members in his seventy-seven-member caucus, experience was not in abundant supply and deserved to be acknowledged, he decided. But he would pay less attention to seniority and more to talent and vigor as he designated vice chairs, positions whose status he intended to elevate on key committees.

"His emphasis to me was that legislating is a team sport, and vice chairs are important players. We were told we were there to help," said Bill Kelly, the quick-witted teacher from East Grand Forks who was starting his second term in 1973. He was three years younger than Sabo and born in North Dakota; their shared North Dakota roots helped solidify their friendship. Sabo made Kelly vice chair of the powerful Rules committee, second to majority leader Irv Anderson. Sabo knew Anderson possessed an independent streak. Kelly provided Sabo with a watchful ally on the committee.[17]

The pattern played out on other key committees as well. For example, as chair of the busy General Legislation and Veterans Affairs committee, Sabo installed Stan Fudro, a home builder and decorated World War II veteran from northeast Minneapolis who was first elected to the House in 1956. As the committee's vice chair, he chose second-term legislator Joe Graba of Wadena, who was Sabo's contemporary in age and like-minded in political outlook. Chairing the Agriculture committee was George Mann, a soft-spoken farmer from Windom who had been in the House since 1959. As vice chair, Sabo tapped Willis Eken, a second-term farmer from Twin Valley near the North Dakota border who would go on to be House majority leader and president of the Minnesota Farmers Union in the 1980s. The Transportation committee gavel went to Bernie Carlson of Cloquet, a sixty-year-old paper mill employee first elected in 1960; his vice chair was Dick Lemke, a Lake City farmer seventeen years Carlson's junior who arrived in the House via special election in May 1971. Sabo scored headlines by making five-term Representative Helen McMillan of Austin the chair of the Crime Prevention and Corrections committee. It was only the second time in state House history that a woman had chaired a major committee. McMillan's vice chair was Don Moe of St. Paul, an energetic second-term member who would serve twenty years in the Legislature and become the body's authority on public pensions.[18]

Sabo was seeding key committees with allies. But he was also making smart bets on the "comers"—the junior legislators whom he deemed likely to become leaders a few sessions hence. He made strong picks. By adding freshman Representative Linda Berglin of Minneapolis to the Health and Welfare committee, he was launching the career of one who, as a state senator from 1983 until 2011, would become perhaps the nation's leading state legislative voice on health care policy. By tapping twenty-nine-year-old Doug Johnson as vice chair of the Taxes committee, Sabo was encouraging the high school guidance counselor from Cook, in remote northeastern Minnesota, to become an expert on tax policy. Johnson took that expertise to the state Senate beginning in 1977; within a few years he became the Legislature's top "tax man." By making Harry "Tex" Sieben, a two-term lawyer from Hastings, the vice chair of the Government Operations committee, Sabo was displaying confidence in Sieben's ability to master the complexities of state agencies and Minnesota's state/local government relationships. That knowledge was good preparation for a future House speaker. Likewise, serving as vice chair of the Judiciary committee was good training for future US Representative Bruce Vento of St. Paul, then a second-term member of the House.

Sabo largely kept his own counsel as he made committee assignments. He drew on the observations about his colleagues' abilities that he had made through years of quiet attention to House committee work. With the Legislature not in session in late 1972, most of Sabo's conversations about committee assignments occurred by telephone. Years later Sabo described his decision-making process: "When you make committee assignments, you're trying to have workable committees that somewhat reflect the caucus," he said. In addition, "On some crucial committees . . . you want to make sure you can do what's needed to govern. Some things are optional; some are necessary. You need to have that in mind." Making sure the institution could function well was his top priority.[19]

Even if legislators had been in St. Paul when Sabo sorted the committee rosters, it's not likely that he would have shared his thinking with many confidants, if any. He was not much inclined to single out friends for bull sessions or socializing, and he avoided glad-handing for popularity's sake. He relished time for quiet reflection. What's more, as a family man with small children at home and a wife who had resumed her nursing career with part-time evening shifts at a local nursing home, Sabo had heavy demands on his time. His elder daughter, Karin, remembers evenings with Dad, eating frozen pizza dinners. As soon as his daughters were old enough, Martin taught them to play card games such as rook, whist, and hearts. Sometimes father and daughters would venture to an Augsburg College basketball game on the campus near their home. Martin would cheer for the Auggies while Karin and Julie played under the bleachers.[20]

Sabo was aware that other legislators were similarly stretched. "We did not do a lot of socializing," Kelly said about his friend Sabo. "Martin liked a glass of beer, but we did not grab one very often. He understood that people had a lot on their plates. They had to engage with constituents and meet with lobbyists. He was respectful of their time."[21]

Kelly recalled that as Sabo contacted members to advise them about their committee assignments, he conveyed a sense that every assignment was important to the enterprise of governing and deserved their best efforts. "He expected every member of the House, in both parties, to do their very best. He respected them for where they came from and what job they had to do, and he wanted them to respect themselves and each other," Kelly said. It was a miniature Lutheran Free Church sermon, adapted for a new congregation.

Expanding the Calendar

It was said by latter-day Capitol wags that the Minnesota Legislature had switched from annual to biennial sessions in the late 1870s because "the railroads got tired of having to buy the Legislature every year." Like many wisecracks, that one likely contained a germ of truth. But it took a vote of the people in 1877 on a constitutional amendment to put legislative elections and sessions on a two-year cycle, with no regularly scheduled sessions in even-numbered years.

The people voted on the Legislature's calendar again in 1972. An amendment to "alter the manner of determining the length of legislative sessions, permitting variations in the times for meetings of the legislature" won the approval of 55 percent of those voting. The change was sold as a way to minimize special sessions, which had become commonplace beginning in the 1950s. The five-month special session ordeal in 1971 had been fruitful, but its duration had outlasted public tolerance. The oddly worded amendment did not make a direct promise about the length of sessions, which would still be limited to 120 "legislative days." News organizations were left to advise voters that the change on offer was permission for the Legislature to meet every year.[22]

More explanation was in order when the first bill of the 1973 session was sent to the governor's desk on January 3. That bill redefined the legal meaning of "legislative day." Previously, a legislative day was any calendar day except Sunday after the Legislature convenes. The bill Anderson signed on January 4 defined a legislative day as any day when the full House and/or the full Senate meets. Days when lawmakers meet only in committees would no longer count toward the 120-day limit. Two floor sessions per week would still be required, under a constitutional provision that does not allow either chamber to adjourn for more than three calendar days (except Sunday) without the consent of the other chamber. And the Constitution's rule governing the adjournment date also stayed in place. It stipulated that the Legislature could not meet in regular session after the first Monday following the third Saturday in May in any year. The upshot: the

Legislature would be permitted to meet in any year from January to mid-May, with starting dates of its own choosing.[23]

A big change in the Legislature's workflow was in the offing. Before the 1973 session began, House and Senate leaders opted to assemble a twelve-member, bipartisan, bicameral committee to make decisions about when bills should clear committees, clear the floors, and head to conference committees under the new calendar. Chosen to head that committee: Martin Sabo.[24]

As Sabo knew well from his involvement with the National Legislative Conference, Minnesota's move to annual sessions was part of a national trend. In the early 1960s only nineteen of the fifty states' legislatures met annually. By the mid-1970s that number had grown to forty-one. Minnesota was one of four states—North Carolina, Tennessee, and Vermont the others—that used the flexible scheduling approach, allowing a fixed number of legislative days to be spread over two years. By 2023 only four states—Montana, Nevada, North Dakota, and Texas—still conducted sessions every other year.[25]

When Sabo was asked in 2015 about the many institutional changes he engineered in 1973, the first one on his lips—"a big change," he said—was the move to annual sessions. "People were around more," he said. That meant that legislators' knowledge of their topical specialties could deepen. Their relationships with each other, plus staffers, lobbyists, and journalists, could deepen. Their commitment to stewardship of their lawmaking institution and of the state itself could deepen. Annual sessions were part of a movement to elevate the competence and capacities of state governments, lifting them from the sleepy backwater status they had acquired in many states.[26]

But annual sessions had a downside. Some gifted, civic-minded people who might have sought election to a legislature that met every other year would not consider a candidacy when the requisite time commitment was five months every year in St. Paul, plus campaigning. A 2015 comparison between that year's Minnesota Legislature and the one that met in 1971 found a big decline in the number of legislators in their forties and an increase in those past age sixty. Sabo had arrived at age twenty-two in a legislature dominated by old men and had done much by 1973 to bring down legislators' average age. He may have been surprised and disappointed in subsequent decades to see that trend gradually reversed.[27]

Removing the Blindfolds

"I favor party designation for the state Legislature," Sabo told the *Minneapolis Tribune*—in 1964. "The idea that the election of legislators is nonpartisan is fiction. The people have the right to know of which party a candidate considers himself a member."[28]

He was far from alone in making that argument. But putting party labels next to the names of legislative candidates on state ballots was not a simple rules-change matter. It required statutory revision—the undoing of a 1913 law that made the Legislature officially a nonpartisan body. During the heyday of the early twentieth century's political reform movement, legislators were trying to lessen the partisan divide in state lawmaking. But their move had allowed Democrats and Farmer-Laborites to take the name Liberals and Republicans Conservatives and then continue to function as partisans in nearly every respect. The nonpartisan idea did not catch on elsewhere. Only one other state—Nebraska, which also has the nation's only unicameral legislature—followed Minnesota's lead.[29]

House DFLers had been asking for many years for a return to party labels in legislative elections, arguing that honesty and transparency demanded it. But the very fact that DFLers seemed so eager for the change made Republicans/Conservatives wary. Sabo was among the majority of candidates of both parties in the *Minneapolis Tribune*'s 1964 voters' guide who endorsed an end to nonpartisan legislative elections. Editorial writers around the state called for the change as well. Yet for years Republican leaders had declined to bring the question before the two chambers for a vote. Inaction in the face of so much support for change only served to make the issue more irritating to DFLers and more visible to the public.

"The DFL Party . . . will start its reign by approving party designation for legislators on future ballots," Sabo and Senate majority leader Nicholas Coleman told the *Minneapolis Star*'s Jim Talle in separate interviews less than twenty-four hours after the polls closed on November 7. Governor Wendell Anderson chimed in his concurrence during his State of the State message on January 3, arguing that returning to party designation amounted to "taking the blindfolds off" in the voting booth. By then, the issue had gained the aura of a foregone conclusion—so much so that a *Minneapolis Star* editorial faulted Anderson's speech for emphasizing the ballot labels question over more controversial matters.[30]

It took House and Senate committees a few weeks to make good on their leaders' party designation plan. But the delay was purely procedural. The change passed the Senate on a 52 to 11 vote on February 12; the House approved the change by 116 to 15 on February 15. Those lopsided bipartisan votes attest that the change's merits were no longer in question in 1973.[31]

A half century later, skepticism about party designation has returned in some quarters. Aligning legislators with national parties is sometimes blamed for increasing partisan tensions, sclerotic governance, and an unwillingness to reach bipartisan compromises at the Minnesota Legislature. One such critic is Gerald Knickerbocker, a Republican from Hopkins whose first term began in 1973 and who stayed in the House for twenty-two years. "Going to party designation helped the Democrats in the short term. But it wasn't good for the institution," he said in 2023, arguing that it contributed to a hardening of party lines. Another Republican, St. Cloud Representative Jim Knoblach, launched an attempt in 2018 to revert to the pre-1973 norm. It fell flat. Minnesotans, like other Americans, have evidently come to expect their legislators to run with familiar party labels and to caucus accordingly when elected.[32]

Developing Expertise

A word that was likely on Sabo's mind as he plotted changes in House operations in 1973 was "professionalization." It was a term he encountered with some frequency at National Legislative Conference meetings (he would attend eight of them in 1974 alone) and in its newsletters. Throughout the country, the legislatures that took office in the years after the redistricting revolution of the 1960s were an ambitious lot, keen to become equal partners with the executive branch of government in their states, as their constitutions envisioned. They wanted to set their own agendas, write their own bills, and craft their own budgets, independent of their governors. But in Minnesota and most states, they were still part-time bodies. They needed the help of larger, more able staffs.[33]

Sabo and his Senate counterpart Coleman set about enlarging two key offices that had been created in 1967. In the Senate, it was the Office of Senate Counsel, an in-house team of young lawyers who were attached to Senate committees and aided in preparing bills. In the House, it was House Research, which included fiscal analysts as well as lawyers. Both were strictly nonpartisan and valued by both parties, establishing a norm that would endure despite the increasingly polarized partisanship of the early twenty-first century. Expanding the reach of their operations to better serve every committee would take several years, as budgets grew. House Research was comprised of a director, eight analysts, three interns, and one administrative assistant in 1971; by 1975 it consisted of a director, fourteen analysts, six assistants, and four clerical staff. Some names stand out on those lists. Among them were James Nobles, who continued his nonpartisan contribution to state government as director for thirty-eight years of the state's Office of the Legislative Auditor; Eileen Baumgartner, who would serve as staff director of the US House Budget committee in the 1990s; and John Helland, who for nearly a half century was the Legislature's authority on environmental law and policy.[34]

Sabo well understood the value of keeping House Research nonpartisan. But he also valued what policy analysts could do for him and his caucus as they sought to be more than rubber stamps for the governor or their special-interest allies. That idea inspired the creation of House DFL Policy Research, a new office headed by Edward Dirkswager. Dirkswager was a St. Cloud native who had studied astrophysics at Yale and obtained a degree in religious education at the Catholic University of America in Washington, DC, before coming to work in Gerald Christenson's shop at the Minnesota State Planning Agency. Christenson recommended Dirkswager to Sabo as someone who could provide the supportive research that would help drive the caucus's priority bills forward. Dirkswager was tasked with building a five-member office. A similar budget was allocated to the minority Republican caucus for a research team of its own.[35]

The DFL research team's analyses did not include something that in later years would be a staple of such operations—public opinion polling. Rather, Dirkswager said, Sabo and Anderson—"mostly Martin"—decided which topics deserved the research team's attention. "Martin spent a great deal of time roaming the halls, knocking on office doors, talking to people," Dirkswager said. "He worked at it. He listened and observed. And since people saw that he wasn't trying to make a name for himself, they would trust him and confide in him." Caucus priorities sprang from those conversations.[36]

"Martin surrounded himself with amazing talent," remembered Roger Moe, brother of House member Don Moe and a second-term DFL state senator in 1973 who went on to become the state's longest-serving Senate majority leader. "I always considered it evidence that he was very comfortable with himself. He was very selfless about getting things done the right way. It was never about him."[37]

Sabo explained his thinking about staffing decades later. "I always thought that as speaker I should know something about more things than others, but there should always be someone who knew more about a subject than I did," he said. "I was lucky. We just had an incredible crew of very capable people."[38]

More Room and More Involvement

Closed-door, unrecorded committee meetings were a thing of the past in the new House. When speaking for public consumption, members of both parties said they welcomed the change. Their presence, comments, and votes in committee were now a matter of public record. Committee attendance and attentiveness improved. But privately, many legislators chafed at their new visibility—and lobbyists were especially unhappy. How could they have confidential conversations when legislators spent the bulk of each day "performing" in committees?

In most cases they could not huddle behind closed doors in House members' offices. There were no such spaces. Only the speaker, caucus leaders, and a couple of top committee chairs had private offices in 1973. Rank-and-file members had their desks on the House floor and the "bull pen" shared space on the Capitol's ground floor that was anything but private. They shared the services of a stenographic pool but did not have individually assigned assistants.

Discontent with that situation had simmered for years. It became more acute in 1973 as DFLers sought to keep their campaign promises about open meetings—and as House members saw the new arrangement that had been made for state senators. A Capitol remodeling project in 1972 had moved minority senators to the first floor of the State Office Building, across the street to the southwest of the Capitol, and given them private offices. Majority senators were afforded handsome, high-ceilinged office spaces on the Capitol's second and third floors, most of them just a few steps from the Senate floor.[39]

"We revolted," Bill Kelly said. "We decided we should no longer have to work out of our desks on the House floor. We needed space, staff, and the independence to do our work." Kelly and his like-minded colleagues found that Sabo was sympathetic to their complaint. "Most people who come to see their legislators are shocked to see the conditions in which we are forced to work," Sabo told reporters.[40]

Sabo engineered Kelly's appointment by Rules committee chair Irv Anderson to head a "space subcommittee" to devise a plan for individual House offices somewhere near the Capitol building. The five-member panel's composition signaled Sabo's serious intentions. It consisted of DFLers Kelly and Anderson, senior Republicans Rod Searle of Waseca and Tom Newcome of White Bear Lake—and Sabo himself.

In mid-July they were ready with a plan. The House would take over two (eventually four) floors of the State Office Building. The current residents of floors two and three—the state Commerce and Corrections Departments—would be sent packing to the new Metro Square building in downtown St. Paul. The space would then be remodeled in late 1973, in time for the first even-year regular session in nearly a hundred years in 1974. The project would nearly double the space that had been available to the House in the Capitol and would cost nearly $500,000—or five times more than had been spent the previous year to move minority senators out of the Capitol. That fact did not escape the notice of Republican candidates in 1974. For not the last time in Minnesota political annals, the effort to meet the office-space needs of a modern Legislature would provide the minority party with a campaign talking point.[41]

When asked in 1974 about the increase in office space, staff, and time spent at the Capitol by House members, Sabo was ready with a response that revealed his vision for the modern legislature. "I think it's clear we're going through some very fundamental changes in the Legislature," he told *Minneapolis Star* editorial writer Stephen Alnes. "[It is of] prime importance that the Legislature be much more involved in state government." He said he wanted the Legislature to more vigorously exercise its responsibility to set policy and oversee state operations. But, he added, he wanted legislators to avoid the temptation to administer state operations themselves. He was drawing a distinction that would sometimes appear blurry in other eyes, reported Dirkswager, whose next professional stop after heading DFL House Policy Research was at the newly reorganized Minnesota State Finance Department, part of the executive branch. He remembers that some legislators considered more time at the Capitol to be an invitation to meddle in state agency affairs.[42]

Playing a Quieter Hand

The 1973 Legislature ranks among the most consequential in Minnesota history. It produced 763 new statutes, not an all-time record but a tally that has not been surpassed since. The state's first minimum wage requirement, a new college student loan program, environmental requirements for large-project developers, and the state's first data privacy standards are just a few of the groundbreaking bills that became law that year. DFLers arrived in trifecta control of the Capitol with a long list of pent-up demands and desires, and leaders Sabo and Coleman were not inclined to restrain their colleagues' ambitions, with one exception: the leaders announced early that they would not support an increase in state taxes. The year's only tax change was a property tax cut for some Minnesotans, achieved by adjusting state aid to K–12 education in keeping with the 1971 overhaul of school finances.[43]

Sabo did not command the spotlight as any of those bills passed. He opted not to take the lead in briefing Capitol reporters on the progress of bills, allowing bill sponsors and committee chairs to speak for themselves. *Star Tribune* reporter Steven Dornfeld said that when sought by reporters, Sabo answered their questions respectfully and honestly but without flourish. Dirkswager said he was surprised by how little Sabo seemed interested in the content and frequency of caucus press releases.[44]

Sabo was not the legislator reporters called when hoping for a witty observation or clever phrase to embellish their stories. But as the 1973 session wore on, he was sought out by a select few of them for a different purpose. Arv Johnson of WCCO Radio, Gene Lahammer of the Associated Press, and William Fox of United Press International were avid bridge players. They passed time waiting for news to break with friendly games in the Capitol basement and were on the lookout for someone willing and able to play the fourth hand. On a few occasions, Sabo obliged them. The reporters learned that card games had been a favorite Sabo pastime since the long North Dakota winters of his childhood and that he kept his bridge skills sharp by joining with Sylvia in a couples bridge-and-dinner club that met monthly in members' homes.[45]

Sabo's positive relationships with reporters did not prevent his occasional unhappiness with news stories. His reaction to one of them on a cold winter morning caused him trouble. Former state Representative Tom Berg wrote in his 2012 book, *Minnesota's Miracle*, that Sabo was angered by a story he read in the local press. He left his Seward neighborhood home in a lather, hopped into his car, and began to back out of his unheated garage—forgetting that he had plugged his car's headbolt heater into the garage's outlet to ensure the car would start. Within seconds "he heard a loud crack. He looked up and noticed the electrical outlet, the cord, and a portion of his garage wall traveling with him. . . . He eventually made it to the Capitol and decided to deal with less controversial topics for the rest of the morning," Berg reported.[46]

Reforming Campaign Finance

Though Sabo no longer took the lead in making the case for legislation, his orchestrating hand was often at work in the background, encouraging bill sponsors and clearing procedural paths for measures he was keen to bring into law. Among them were three measures that helped to both fulfill the DFL's "openness in government" campaign promises and secure Minnesota's wider reputation as a state with a high-functioning democracy.

Freshman state Representative Joan Growe sponsored a major extension of the state's earlier open-meeting requirements, expanding the open-door rule to any state agency (save for the Legislature itself) or local government entity that "transacts public business in a meeting." Despite opposition from the League of Minnesota Cities and the Association of Minnesota Counties, Growe engineered the bill's passage on a strong bipartisan vote. In the Senate, another new legislator, Hubert H. "Skip" Humphrey III, was similarly successful. Together, these future state constitutional officers broke local governments of their bad habit of making decisions behind closed doors. Growe would go on to serve twenty-four years as Minnesota's secretary of state; Humphrey spent sixteen years as attorney general. Though their open-meeting law did not include a statutory requirement for the Legislature itself, it set a performance standard to which the Legislature's rules have adhered for more than a half century.[47]

Another freshman House member, Representative John Tomlinson of St. Paul, was tapped to carry a measure creating Minnesota's first statewide voter registration system. Until that bill became law, only the state's cities with populations in excess of 10,000 were required to preregister voters before each election. Among the provisions of the Tomlinson bill was the opportunity for the state's voters to register on election day. This "same-day" registration provision, the first in the nation when Governor Wendell Anderson signed it into law on May 24, 1973, is widely credited for ensuring that Minnesota would regularly produce nation-leading voter turnout levels in the ensuing years. Unlike Growe's bill, Tomlinson's measure encountered significant opposition from Republicans claiming that same-day registration was an invitation to fraud. That accusation persists despite fifty years of elections that produced no evidence of more than isolated same-day registration cheating.[48]

Meanwhile, Minneapolis Representative Tom Berg began work on a campaign finance and disclosure measure in March 1973, months before the nation's interest in that topic was heightened as the Watergate scandal engulfed President Richard Nixon. The idea of limiting campaign expenditures in exchange for partial public financing of campaigns had strong backing from the governor, who said in his 1973 State of the State address that "the way we are forced to finance our political campaigns" is "a deadly cancer infecting our free election system." But Republicans resisted the multipronged remedy Berg crafted and were particularly hostile to allowing tax dollars to flow to candidates for the Legislature under a formula driven by taxpayer designation on state income tax forms. That one-dollar checkoff provision did not raise taxes, but it allowed Minnesotans to direct which party's candidates would receive their one-dollar "donations" from the state treasury. Republicans "have an easier time raising money than the DFL, and there are more DFLers to use the check-off," *St. Cloud Times* political columnist David Hoium, a future Republican campaign operative, reported with uncommon candor in explaining the GOP position.[49]

It took Berg until March 1974 to find an accord with the Senate on what was hailed as a first-in-the nation step toward public financing of campaigns. Public money in a proportion determined by the checkoff dollars would be made available to candidates who agreed to spending limits, which ranged from $500,000 for gubernatorial candidates to $7,500 for state House candidates. The bill also required disclosure of campaign gifts by individuals above token threshold amounts and limited donations by political parties and independent expenditure groups. Later that same year—as the Watergate scandal led to Nixon's resignation—Congress passed similar legislation governing candidates for federal offices, including the presidency.[50]

That new system did not hold. In 1976 the US Supreme Court struck down spending limits for US House and Senate candidates and contribution limits for independent expenditures. Independent expenditures in American elections soon dramatically increased. Meanwhile, the failure to raise spending limits to keep pace with inflating campaign costs incentivized candidates for Minnesota's House and Senate to refuse public money and the spending limits that its receipt required.[51]

Nevertheless, the three pro-democracy measures Minnesota enacted in 1973–74 gave Sabo bragging rights as he attended National Legislative Conference meetings. He was chosen the conference's vice president in 1973, putting him in line to become its president in 1974—the year Sabo and other conference leaders planned to complete its merger with the National Society of State Legislatures and the National Conference of State Legislative Leaders. Sabo's group was the largest of the three and the one working hardest to promote the change.

"The merger will help us to do a better job of representing the states in Washington and would help us do a better job of self-education," Sabo told reporters in August 1974. His goal was for legislatures in Minnesota and around the country to function with such professionalism that they would no longer be perceived as amateurish—or worse—in comparison with governors or the federal government. He took pride in his chosen profession, and he was on a mission to instill the same pride in others.[52]

CHAPTER EIGHT

A SPEAKER FOR EVERYONE

"I REALLY VIEWED IT THAT, IF YOU WERE A SPEAKER, YOU WERE a speaker for everyone," Martin Sabo said years later of the Minnesota House position he held for six years. "I always described the speaker [as one who] had more capacity to shape things than anyone else but also had less personal freedom than anyone else. I think in every institution, if it's going to work, people have to give something of themselves to that institution."[1]

A significant chance for Sabo to put that leadership philosophy into practice presented itself in 1974, as his caucus faced the first election after returning to majority status in 1973. It was also the first election after their moves to party designation, annual sessions, greater openness in government, beefed-up legislative staffing, enlarged offices, and the enactment of a raft of progressive legislation. What could Sabo and his caucus do to persuade voters that they had been well served by that rush of change? Were voters paying attention to all that had happened at their state Capitol?

The answer to the latter question was unclear, not only in Minnesota but also around the country. For most of 1974 the nation had been riveted by unprecedented developments in Washington, DC. The Watergate scandal, which started as a petty break-in at Democratic National Committee offices in the Watergate complex in Washington in June 1972, had produced months of stunning revelations about presidential campaign dirty tricks and a subsequent cover-up. It led to President Richard Nixon's resignation on August 9, 1974. The drama continued a month later when the new president, Gerald Ford—who had been appointed to the vice presidency, not elected—gave Nixon a "full, free, and absolute pardon."[2]

Watergate gave many Americans their first real look at the dark underbelly of their nation's presidential campaigns, and they were both fixated and appalled. Candidates for other offices struggled to shift voters' attention to their own races. Republicans tried with limited success to distance themselves from Nixon and Ford.

In Minnesota that spring, Republicans gleefully watched Sabo and his Senate counterpart, majority leader Nicholas Coleman, make what the minority hoped would be a politically damaging blunder. Coleman's caucus—which was in year two of their four-year terms of office—tacked a 43 percent legislative pay raise onto an obscure government employees' pension bill in the legislative session's closing hours. The raise, intended to boost pay from $8,400 to $12,000 a year, had received no prior hearing or public discussion. Sabo and his DFL caucus went along with it, though they were on the 1974 ballot and vulnerable to the political fallout the eleventh-hour move produced. In the book *Minnesota's Miracle*, former state Representative Tom Berg reports that Sabo was unaware of the Senate's move until the session's last days—and that he learned about it while playing bridge with reporters in the Capitol basement. A tired and distracted Sabo told Senator Ed Gearty of Minneapolis that the House would "probably" go along, Berg reported. It did on March 28, on a 69 to 54 vote. Notably, fifteen of the votes for the increase came from Republicans. One of them was Republican minority leader Aubrey Dirlam, who had decided not to seek reelection in 1974 after thirty-four years in office.[3]

Governor Wendell Anderson was left out of the information loop before the bill passed. But in the ensuing days, the governor's office heard plenty. Gubernatorial staffers reported receiving a "flood of protest" from the public that swelled within a few days to more than 5,000 calls, letters, and telegrams. Anderson had said earlier in the session that he might support a pay increase if it was accompanied by a measure to reduce the size of the Legislature—something he knew legislators were unlikely to support. Now, in the face of an outcry in an election year, Anderson let it be known that he was considering a veto. Meanwhile, a barrage of Republican criticism had begun. The GOP state chair Bob Brown, a state senator from Stillwater, said the pay raise showed "how much out of tune the DFL Legislature is with the public, and it should definitely help the Republicans recapture the state House of Representatives."[4]

At that moment, Sabo could have retreated to a position of greater political safety. He could have backed off support for a pay raise for legislators and publicly called on Anderson to veto the bill. Six legislators who had voted for the bill—five of them DFLers—had already done just that. Instead, four days after adjournment, Sabo opted to publicly advocate for the best interests of his institution. He met with the governor to ask him to sign the increase into law. He then told reporters that he had done so, allowing that the House members who voted for the pay raise understood the political risks and believed they could justify the increase to voters. He expressed confidence in their judgment. He noted that legislators were now spending many more weeks at the Capitol than they did prior to 1973. Further, even at $12,000 per year, Minnesota legislators would still be paid less than the national average legislative salary of $14,000. What he did not say—but what he was surely thinking—was that low salaries were contributing to difficulty in attracting capable candidates for House seats.

Anderson's veto came on April 3, Sabo's pleas notwithstanding. Republicans lamented the loss of an issue they hoped would help them lift the Watergate gloom that had settled on their party. Sabo voiced regret too. He said he feared "that the public furor over the pay raise will forestall any adjustment of legislative salaries for several years," the *Minneapolis Tribune* reported. About that, he was prescient. Legislative pay in Minnesota would stay at $700 per month—$8,400 a year—until 1979, when it jumped to $16,500 during a period of high inflation in the United States. No extra compensation was granted to legislative leaders until 1979, when Sabo would no longer be its beneficiary.[5]

The memory of the public reaction to the 1974 pay raise lingered long thereafter. Low pay persisted at the Minnesota Legislature for decades, handicapping candidate recruitment and retention. In 2016 voters stepped in, adopting a constitutional amendment that took the power to set legislative salaries out of legislators' hands and gave it to a bipartisan council. That body's first action in 2017 was to give legislators a 45 percent pay increase, from $31,140 to $45,000.[6]

The Watergate Election

The depth of discouragement Minnesota Republicans felt in 1974 was evident when the candidate filing period for the state's 134 House districts ended in July. Thirteen Republican incumbents did not file for reelection. That number included minority leader Dirlam and all three of his assistant leaders. More telling: fourteen DFL incumbents, some of them from districts traditionally occupied by Republicans, faced no Republican opponent in the general election. Martin Sabo was one of the fourteen DFLers who had a free ride to reelection. That compared with only one Republican House member—future speaker Rod Searle—who had no DFL opponent.

Sabo was seeking his eighth term in heavily DFL District 57B in Minneapolis. The fact that "DFL" now accompanied his name on the ballot only enhanced his electability. Any Republican who had challenged him in 1974 would have done so expecting to lose. Yet the fact that no GOP loyalist could be found to "keep the leader busy" by giving him at least token competition in his home district speaks to the weakened condition of a political party that only a dozen years earlier had controlled the Minneapolis seat in the US Congress. Republicans still occupied two of the sixteen Minneapolis House districts after the 1974 election. But the party had begun what would be a long decline in the state's largest city.[7]

The absence of a reelection challenger left Sabo free to stump the state on behalf of other DFL candidates. He was free in one other respect as well: he gave up his insurance-selling career when he became House speaker. A Minneapolis newspaper's voters' guide published in October lists Sabo's occupation as "full-time legislator as speaker of the House." Being speaker meant his presence was required at more official meetings, making him eligible to collect more $25 per diem daily expense allowances than most legislators. But no other additional compensation accrued to his position. He was paid $700 per month, the same as any other legislator. Financial sacrifice may have been among the things on his mind years later when he spoke of his belief that leaders should "give something of themselves to that institution."[8]

Sabo's campaign trips, financed by DFL donors, took him to all corners of the state that fall. He often attended gatherings of campaign supporters at which he was asked to offer brief remarks. When he did, he took pains to point out differences with Republicans over ideas and policies, not personality or character. He tried to advocate for the DFL candidate without attacking the Republican. "Martin was really cautious about how he handled leadership," recalled Joe Graba, who was seeking his third House term in 1974. "He understood that as speaker, he had to lead both caucuses. He did not want to be seen as excessively partisan."[9]

While Sabo's rhetorical reticence in campaigning was sometimes attributed to an introverted nature, Sabo's friend Bill Kelly had a different take. Kelly said Sabo campaigned with an eye toward developing working relationships with whomever the voters elected. Kelly remembered Sabo saying, "We're not trying to make the Republicans look bad. We're trying to make government work better."[10]

On the eve of the 1974 election, Sabo predicted that voters might elect as many as ninety DFLers to the Minnesota House. That forecast suggests that even he was surprised by the results on November 5. The 1975 session would convene with 104 DFLers in the House, the largest majority since Conservatives had 104 seats in 1947. Liberals/DFLers had never before mustered so much House strength. The party also made a clean sweep of constitutional offices and elected five of the state's eight members of the US House. Governor Wendell

Anderson carried all eighty-seven counties as he won a second term, besting Republican state Representative John Johnson.[11]

It would have been easy for DFLers to claim that their success signaled an endorsement by the voters of all they had enacted in 1973–74 and a mandate to press on with more progressive change. In an interview with Gerry Nelson of the Associated Press three days after the election, Sabo sought to tamp down such talk. Look for fewer landmark bills in 1975 than in 1973, Sabo said. "I share the hope that we slow the process down somewhat, and that our agenda is not as large" as it had been two years earlier.[12]

Sabo seemingly took to heart an analysis of the election results that did not seem to register with some other DFLers. What is remembered as "the Watergate election" was a Democratic blowout in Minnesota not because independents and Republicans swung to the DFL—though a few undoubtedly did—but because dispirited Republican voters by the thousands simply did not vote. A telling statistic: Joan Growe won the secretary of state's office with 17,000 fewer votes than the losing DFL candidate had accumulated four years earlier. She unseated Republican Arlen Erdahl, who received 22 percent fewer votes than he did in 1970. The message of such numbers was not lost on Sabo. He understood that the big majority DFLers took into the 1975 session might not be long-lived.[13]

Shortening the Learning Curve

Newcomers seemed to be everywhere when the House convened on January 7, 1975. Fifty-two members—nearly 40 percent of the 134-member House—were first-timers. The House's sophomore class, forty-eight members strong in 1973, had dwindled to thirty-four. Still, that meant that a majority of the 134-member body had fewer than three years of legislative experience.

The newcomers had no memory of an all-male House. In 1975 the House's "women's caucus" had grown to seven members. One of them was Janet Clark of Minneapolis, who had unseated ten-term Representative James Adams in the September DFL primary. Adams, an electrician with strong labor backing, had campaigned alongside Sabo through many elections. But "Sabo was pretty neutral in that one," recalled the state senator from Clark's district, Jack Davies. "I probably was too," he added.[14]

"Martin cared about diversity" in legislative ranks, "but his attitude was gentle pushing. Make whatever forward steps you can without too much disruption," Davies said. It would have been uncharacteristic for Sabo to openly oppose the reelection of a longtime colleague. But it would have been uncomfortable for him to oppose Clark, a thirty-three-year-old former teacher who had out-hustled fifty-three-year-old Adams and won DFL endorsement at District 60's convention that spring. Sabo likely saw something he recognized in Clark's youthful energy and intelligence.[15]

How eager he was to bring more gender diversity to the House is less certain. Sabo was not regarded as a champion for feminism, but neither did he resist the ascent of women into formerly male-dominated positions. "The rise of more women candidates was something that was just happening in the world. The difference was, former leaders [in the Minnesota Legislature] would have discouraged it. Martin accepted it," recalled staffer Eileen Baumgartner years later. "Martin supported a lot of women candidates. He didn't bad-mouth women or stand in their way. He accepted that women had the ability to do the job."[16]

The Legislature's new members lacked the kind of institutional and policy memory that Sabo had acquired as an observant rookie in the back rows of committee hearing rooms in the early 1960s. His awareness of the steep learning curve they would face made Sabo receptive in mid-1974 when state planning agency director Gerald Christenson brought him an idea: why not start the 1975 session with a three-day seminar on long-term trends in the state's economy and society?

Christenson, a PhD educator and career public servant, was just forty-four years old in 1974, but among DFLers he already commanded the respect of an elder statesman. The son of a gasoline station manager in Litchfield, Minnesota, Christenson by 1974 had been a congressional chief of staff, an unsuccessful candidate for lieutenant governor, and, as planning agency director, the chief architect of the landmark school finance changes enacted in 1971. He had many more stops ahead of him as he sought for a half century to make government a more effective tool for improving people's lives. In that respect, Christenson and Sabo were kindred spirits.

At Christenson's urging, the Legislature in 1974 created a new position, state demographer. Christenson filled it with Hazel Reinhardt, who combined mathematical competence with dynamism as a communicator. (She would later become a vice president at Cowles Media Company, which owned the *Minneapolis Star Tribune*.) Christenson wanted to get legislators away from the distractions of the Capitol, allow them to hear Reinhardt explain the state's demographic trends, and give them a chance to discuss the significance of those patterns for state policy.[17]

Sabo enthusiastically backed Christenson's plan. It was a variation on something Sabo had initiated in December 1973—an overnight retreat at St. John's University in Collegeville for House members of both parties, with eighty members participating. While that meeting featured talks about the state's future from journalists Charles Bailey of the *Minneapolis Tribune* and Phil Jones of CBS News, policymaking wasn't its central purpose, Bill Kelly said. Rather, Sabo wanted to build better working relationships among legislators. "Martin's idea was, how do we work together better to make this place work better?"[18]

Christenson won assent from the other three caucus leaders as well, then took the lead in creating Minnesota Horizons. On three consecutive mornings, January 14, 15, and 16, at the St. Paul Technical College campus near the Capitol, legislators heard the presentation of seventeen briefing papers about the state's population, economy, natural resources, and well-being. Christenson and his staff raised money from foundations to arrange for the broadcast of the talks on public radio and television and to add slides and other audio-visual elements to the presentations. The series was widely praised and popular enough to be repeated in subsequent years. Since 2007 the event has been called the One Minnesota Conference.[19]

Minnesota Horizons 1975 was a swan song of sorts at the state planning agency for Christenson, who became commissioner of finance—a position second only to the governor in executive branch authority—in May 1975. Horizons provided legislators with valuable information, Kelly said years later, but that wasn't all. "It was a way to build expectations. It made me think, 'If I'm going to be here, I need to be serious. I need to strive for the best outcomes for the whole state. I'm not just here for myself.' Martin wanted us to set aside our own agendas and see ourselves as having a role in a larger system."[20]

The Politics of Compromise

The election of 104 DFLers in 1974 left no question that Sabo would be elected for a second term as House speaker on January 7, 1975. Nevertheless, how the House's Republican minority chose to handle the speaker's election that day is worth noting for what it says about how Republicans viewed Sabo as well as how they saw their own role in the DFL-dominated House.

Succeeding Dirlam as House Republican leader was Henry Savelkoul, an attorney from Albert Lea beginning his fourth term. His election as caucus leader signaled generational change and a fresh start for the depleted GOP caucus. Savelkoul, like Sabo, was a North Dakota native and had been a law school classmate of DFLer Tom Berg at the University of Minnesota. He was thirty-four years old at the start of the 1975 session and regarded as an ideological moderate. In the 1973–74 sessions, Savelkoul had worked with DFLers on environmental protection and election registration bills.[21]

Had tradition prevailed on the first day of the session, Republicans would have nominated and cast their votes for Savelkoul as their candidate to fill the speaker's chair. Instead, the minority caucus opted to make no nomination. Representative Rod Searle of Waseca, among the minority's most senior and most respected members, seconded the nomination of Martin Sabo. That made Sabo the first Minnesota House speaker since 1944 to be elected unanimously.

The Republicans' unusual move that day "indicates our desire to work with the majority," Savelkoul told Capitol reporters after Sabo's election. He added that there would be ample opportunity later in the session for Republicans to indicate their disagreements with DFLers. That was a backhanded way of saying that he was counting on Sabo to wield his gavel fairly during floor debates.[22]

Years later Sabo described another out-of-the-ordinary episode with Savelkoul that illustrated the trust the two men had developed. "We wanted to suspend the rules to speed something up" at the end of session, Sabo related. That motion required a two-thirds majority vote, something Sabo evidently could not easily muster at that moment with DFL votes alone. Savelkoul offered Sabo a deal. The minority would supply the requisite votes if Sabo would consent to coming to an imminent Republican caucus meeting to explain the major tax bill that would be on the House floor soon after the break. Savelkoul evidently considered no one in his caucus more knowledgeable than Sabo to fairly and accurately describe the complex measure that had been assembled by a conference committee.

"So while we (DFLers) were caucusing, I was in the Republican caucus going through the bill, and they were asking all good questions and getting the best answers we could (provide)," Sabo said years later. "They all voted no, but they still had confidence in what we told them, which was to the best of our ability accurate to what was in there."[23]

Savelkoul's invitation to that caucus meeting evinced a respect that had become mutual. Republicans in the mid-1970s "disagreed with us, but they were also very good folks to work with," Sabo said in 2015. "I always thought that we should maximize their input in the process," because "to the degree that we had a better product because of Republican suggestions, that was a plus for us as well as for them." For Sabo and Savelkoul, compromise was not to be feared. Compromise was what governance required.

Responsibility and Accountability

Experience—and a supersized DFL caucus—emboldened Sabo to break with tradition as he appointed committee chairs for the 1975 session. He had a vacancy to fill in one of the institution's most powerful and politically sensitive committees, Taxes. Representative Ray Pavlak of South St. Paul, the House Taxes committee chair in 1973–74, had resigned after the 1974 session to accept appointment as a district court judge. If Sabo hewed to "seniority rules," he would have been compelled to give the gavel to the committee's most senior DFLer, Representative Bernard Carlson of Cloquet, a paper mill maintenance worker first elected with Sabo in 1960.[24]

Instead, Sabo appointed a third-termer who had not previously served on the committee, Bill Kelly. The move raised a few eyebrows. While acknowledged as bright and hardworking, Kelly was seen as one of Sabo's most loyal lieutenants. If Sabo put him in charge of Taxes, the gossips said, Sabo must have exacted a promise for something in return—perhaps a tax break for Minneapolis.

Years later Kelly said that he and Sabo had no such arrangement. "He didn't talk to me about a plan for the committee. He never asked me for anything special for Minneapolis. He never second-guessed or tried to dictate anything to his committee chairs. That wasn't his style," Kelly said.

Sabo also retained his own seat on the Taxes committee, on which he had served since 1967. "He always knew what was going on" in the committee, Kelly said. State tax policy had become a Sabo specialty. "But he offered only subtle guidance, if that. He had this whole issue of expectations. He expected his committee chairs to do their best. He held that if you took a responsibility, you were accountable and responsible for how you performed. You'd work your ass off to avoid disappointing him," Kelly said.

Accountability, Sabo-style, meant that errant members were sometimes asked to visit the speaker's office. "He would make them sit there for a time, until he was ready," Kelly said. "Then he would say, 'That's not what we need to have here. I don't expect it to happen again.' It generally didn't."[25]

With the Kelly appointment, Sabo was shifting away from automatic rewards for seniority and toward recognition of merit in House appointments. The same could be said about two other 1975 committee chair appointments. Sabo combined three previous committees into one new Local and Urban Affairs committee and gave that gavel to Tom Berg of Minneapolis. And he put Harry Sieben of Hastings in charge of the Government Operations committee. Like Kelly, Berg and Sieben were both attorneys starting their third terms and had earned reputations as capable and energetic lawmakers.

"He did a fantastic job of putting people into committee chair positions that matched their skills as well as their interests," remembered Ted Suss, a rookie DFL House member in 1975 representing a southwest-exurban district. "Berg, Kelly, Carl Johnson (Education), Joe Graba (K–12 Finance)—these people were fantastically qualified."[26]

Suss was a twenty-five-year-old veteran of the US Marine Corps when elected in 1974. He had relatively little contact with the House speaker during his campaign, meeting him only briefly during a state DFL convention seminar offering new candidates practical campaign advice. But within days of his election, Suss was invited to meet with Sabo at the State Office Building. "I remember being very honored," Suss said. The one-on-one meeting was a screening session, one of many the speaker was conducting, Suss learned. Sabo was pondering 1975 committee assignments. Suss made a case for appointment to the Education committee. Sabo honored the request and in so doing gained an ally. "I felt that he wanted to mentor me," Suss said.

Sabo also arranged for the deployment of the talented people at House Research to aid specific committees. That's how Eileen Baumgartner became Kelly's reliable researcher, number cruncher, and tax policy advisor from 1975 through 1978. She had originally moved from the state planning agency to House Research to work on education policy. But her preference was tax policy, and Sabo wanted her in that role too.

"Martin always wanted to keep an eye on the numbers," Baumgartner said years later. Another future staff member, Mike Erlandson, called Sabo a "one-man budget committee." He was seeking not only a reliably balanced state budget, but also a fair distribution of the state and local tax burden. He knew that overreliance on regressive sales and property taxes meant that lower-income Minnesotans would pay a larger share of their incomes to the state than upper-income earners would. A desire to shift more of the tax burden onto those with more ability to pay drove Sabo's thinking.[27]

"He wanted to give the little guy a chance," Baumgartner said. "Fairness was a paramount value in his mind." Sabo saw state tax policy as "the one place where you can equalize opportunities for people. He cared so much about giving more power to weaker people."[28]

The Insurance Salesman

A belief that state government should give a lift to low-income people also drove Sabo's growing interest in two other complex policy matters: housing and health care. Ed Dirkswager, the first head of the House DFL Policy Research office, said he came to think of those topics as "Martin's issues." Sabo had seen hundreds of units of low-income housing in his district lost in the 1960s with freeways built, commercial properties expanded, and residential blocks redeveloped. As an insurance agent, Sabo had also seen health insurance become unavailable and/or unaffordable for growing numbers of Minnesotans.

Sabo wanted state government to craft remedies for those problems—preferably remedies that left some responsibility for decision-making with local governments or nonprofit entities. "His attitude was, 'St. Paul doesn't know everything. Let's leave some decisions to the local people,'" Dirkswager said.[29]

As speaker, Sabo was not often able to be the chief author of bills. But he could—and did—assure that housing and health care measures he valued had a clear procedural path forward when he deemed them ready for enactment. He could also slow them down if he believed they needed more work. He left no doubt about his preferences. James Solem, then the state planning agency official carrying the housing portfolio, was working with Minnesota Housing Finance Agency director Jim Dlugosch to develop a federal-state low-interest loan program for low-income homeowners in 1975 when he was advised by someone in the governor's office, "You need to talk to Martin." Sabo's experience in the blue-collar Seward neighborhood in Minneapolis had shown him that federally backed loans were being denied to homeowners who could not afford to bring their entire homes up to modern building code standards for the sake of a new roof, windows, or heating system. Sabo wanted any new state program to explicitly relieve loan recipients of a duty to bring their properties fully up to code.

Sabo was already well versed in the House version of the housing loan bill when Solem called on him. Solem tried to convince Sabo that the language he favored was not needed for the program to function as intended. Sabo would not budge. "I want to see the language," he insisted, arms folded as if to say, "This bill will go nowhere unless the language I want is included." Solem took that message back to Dlugosch. Sabo got his wish. Added to the bill: "No loan under this subdivision shall be denied solely because the loan will not be used for placing the residential housing in full compliance with all state, county, or municipal building, housing maintenance, fire, health, or similar codes and standards." The result, Solem said years later, was that Minnesota's federally insured home-improvement loan program became the largest in the nation and endures fifty years later. (Solem succeeded Dlugosch as executive director of the Minnesota Housing Finance Agency in 1978 and served until 1994.)[30]

Sabo pumped the brakes on a health insurance bill soon thereafter, punting it to an interim study commission. In his 1975 inaugural message, Governor Anderson proposed the creation of "an effective, practical state program to insure every Minnesota citizen against the most severe effects of catastrophic illness." Anderson likely did not realize that he was opening a messy can of worms. Sabo did. He knew that a careful interface would be needed between any new state program and existing health insurance products to prevent a rush away from private insurance that would prove unaffordable for taxpayers. Sabo told Capitol reporters in April that he recommended a pause for further study during the summer. He was in a position to make that recommendation stick and to assemble a study team that included Dirkswager, Kevin Kenny from House Research, Larry Fredrikson from Senate Research, and John Turner of Northwestern

National Life Insurance Company in Minneapolis—a future company president.[31]

Under Sabo's watchful eyes, they came up with a state-funded, high-risk insurance pool to be administered by a new nonprofit membership entity, the Minnesota Comprehensive Health Association (MCHA). Its members were all entities licensed to sell insurance in Minnesota, save for self-insured employers, whose exclusion was required by federal law. The high-risk pool provided affordable coverage to individuals with preexisting conditions and other high-cost health care needs. It operated until 2010, when the federal Affordable Care Act supplanted such state programs. The MCHA is one of several state ventures credited for giving Minnesota one of the lowest shares of uninsured people in the nation in the decades before 2010.[32]

The Legislative Audit Commission

Both as speaker of the Minnesota House and 1974–75 president of the National Legislative Conference, Sabo was on the lookout for ideas for strengthening the legislative branches of state governments relative to executive branches. That explains his interest in an idea that came from the Loaned Executive Action Program (LEAP), an advisory group of Minnesota private sector leaders assembled by Wendell Anderson early in his first gubernatorial term. The LEAPers had plenty to say about how state government budgeted and accounted for its spending. Among their recommendations: move the auditing of executive branch spending out of the executive branch. Put it instead in the legislative branch, under a nonpartisan office akin to the General Accounting Office in the US Congress.[33]

That proposal led in 1973 to the creation of the Office of the Legislative Auditor, to be overseen by the new Legislative Audit Commission, a bipartisan, bicameral body composed of legislative leaders and major committee chairs. The new office was granted auditing authority over state agencies and programs that had previously been watched by the state's public examiner, a gubernatorially appointed position created during the administration of Governor John S. Pillsbury in

1878 in response to graft and corruption in local governments. The 1973 measure shifted authority to audit local governments to the independently elected state auditor, abolishing the public examiner position. The head of the new Office of the Legislative Auditor would be appointed for a six-year term and could be removed only for cause, not political whim.[34]

From the start, "the tone was set by Sabo," said James Nobles about the team of government watchdogs that, beginning in 1981, he would lead for most of the next forty years. Nobles was a House Research staffer in 1973, assigned to the Government Operations committee. He watched with keen interest the actions Sabo was engineering to establish a more thorough and independent system of state agency oversight. "Martin made a point of saying, 'We are not politicizing this office. We are only moving it into the Legislature,'" Nobles recalled years later. Sabo underscored that point by inviting the longtime head of the public examiner's office, Robert Whitaker, to take the helm at the newly created office. Whitaker, who was nearing the end of a long career, made the move with some hesitation, Nobles said. He was fearful that the office was about to be weaponized for partisan purposes. But Sabo was true to his word, and Whitaker stayed in that position until he retired in 1977.[35]

A news release issued by Republican leader Savelkoul when he was appointed to the Legislative Audit Commission early in the 1975 session attested to the reputation for partisan neutrality the office had already acquired. "The Audit Commission has gained a reputation for requiring a high degree of accountability from those who spend state money. It has fulfilled its watchdog role with determination and high purpose," Savelkoul's release said.[36]

The new office was scarcely two years old when Dirkswager and a cadre of DFL legislators, including Bill Kelly, saw its potential to do more. Dirkswager enlisted Nobles early in 1975 to help prepare legislation authorizing the Office of the Legislative Auditor to review program performance as well as spending. It could seek to answer the question, "Is this program producing the results the Legislature intended?" They came up with a plan for a program evaluation division within the office, separate from its financial audit division. Under their design, the Audit Commission could assign topics for investigation but did not have authority to interfere in the investigations themselves.

Dirkswager and Nobles took that arrangement to Sabo and, with his blessing, to the Legislature, where it was approved. "It's one of the signature improvements Martin made in state government," Dirkswager said. The move did not come without early tension, as some legislators wanted Legislative Audit Commission members and staff to sway the office's work, Nobles said. But those initial battles were won by Sabo's allies. The result is an office that has grown in stature and retained a reputation for nonpartisan reliability for a half century, despite increasing partisan tensions elsewhere in state government. The office's website in 2025 proclaims its political independence with words Sabo might have written: "Reports are not approved or disapproved or even reviewed in advance by the commission. Findings, conclusions and recommendations are solely the responsibility of the Office of the Legislative Auditor."[37]

Ashes to Ashtrays

Sabo seemed to be everywhere as the 1975 session charged through an agenda that turned out to be more consequential than he had advertised at its outset. News reports from April and May credit him for spearheading a compromise between metro transit and rural highway interests; orchestrating a state takeover of teacher retirement plans in Minneapolis, St. Paul, and Duluth for the sake of a property tax reduction in those cities, over the opposition of teachers' unions; promoting the creation of a commission to set state salaries; seeking a comparative study of spending by the state's cities; and generally having a hand in nearly every legislative pot.[38]

Make that a foot. Sabo made a point of spending a portion of nearly every working day walking the halls in the State Office Building that in 1975 had become House territory. With a cup of coffee in one hand and a cigarette in the other, he sought one-on-one and small-group conversations with every legislator—not just committee chairs and not just DFLers, Ed Dirkswager said. "He wanted to avoid anyone thinking that he had a kitchen cabinet" to whom he listened exclusively. His meanderings brought him both useful information and personal loyalty, as members perceived Sabo as someone who knew and cared about them. "It was amazing to learn in later years how many people felt close to Martin," Dirkswager said.[39]

The building of those relationships was aided by Sabo's evident disinterest in drawing attention to himself. "He wasn't a glory hound," Dirkswager said. "He was just very intent on good public policy." If putting other people in the spotlight produced sound outcomes, Sabo was satisfied.

Sabo also sought out the people in the House's "little university"—House Research—to discuss ideas about improving government. Nobles, while assigned to the Government Operations committee, got a call from Sabo asking him to discuss the merits of adding expiration dates—"sunsets"—to legislation authorizing programs, compelling their periodic review. Nobles considered the idea unnecessarily disruptive and said so in a memo. He was surprised to receive a call from a familiar voice saying, "Hey Jim, I read your memo. Can you come over and talk about this?"

Nobles met Sabo in his corner office, explained his position on the question, and waited. "Martin sat and smoked and listened. I thought maybe I should jump in and say a little more. But I decided, no, he's thinking. When he was ready, he asked a question and I said more, and we paused again. I learned a whole new cadence of talking and listening that day. He showed me that the pace of interaction is important. The pauses were a sign of respect from a guy who wanted to be connected to good ideas."[40]

Respect for Sabo evidently crossed party lines. A news report on a Republican-sponsored bill to increase Minnesota's legal drinking age from eighteen to nineteen mentioned a move by Sabo to cancel an evening committee hearing that was scheduled to discuss the measure. Sabo told reporters he did so in adherence to House rules about avoiding evening hearings, not because of his personal views about the bill. What's notable was the care taken by the bill's sponsor, eight-term Republican Representative Ralph Jopp, not to complain about Sabo's move. "I don't want to irritate the speaker. I want to get the bill passed," Jopp told reporters. He did, in February 1976, with Sabo voting no.[41]

Among the 1975 bills remembered a half century later is the Clean Indoor Air Act. Sponsored by second-term DFL Representative Phyllis Kahn, it was a first-in-the-nation ban on tobacco smoking in any public place that does not offer a designated nonsmoking area. Kahn, a Yale-educated PhD biophysicist who represented a Minneapolis district adjacent to Sabo's, took seriously the landmark 1964 warning from the US surgeon general about smoking's toll on health and wanted state policy to do so too.

At the start of the 1975 session, Kahn announced her intention to sponsor both a smoking ban statute and a rules change banning smoking on the House floor. She took the latter proposal to the House Rules committee, where she encountered the speaker. Sabo "pointedly lit a cigarette and began smoking," the *Minneapolis Star*'s Betty Wilson reported in a front-page story headlined, "Legislative

Representative Phyllis Kahn (center) and others at a meeting in 1975.

Smoking: She Huffs, He Puffs." Kahn remembered him "blowing perfectly formed smoke rings at me." The response to Wilson's story was so anti-smoking that Sabo decided to join forces with Kahn as a cosponsor of her bill governing public spaces outside the Capitol.[42]

Kahn thereafter credited the attachment of Sabo's name with the ease with which that bill became law. Perhaps out of gratitude, she altered her proposed smoking rule for the House itself. Her new version banned smoking everywhere in the semicircular House chamber except for the dais at the front, at which Sabo presided and chief clerk Ed Burdick and his staff worked. "Even though I ask for justice . . . I see nothing wrong with justice tempered by mercy," Kahn explained during the floor debate on the proposed smoking ban.[43]

But Bill Kelly was not as merciful—and he was close enough to Sabo to be willing to risk displeasing his friend for the sake of his health and that of the House staff. Kelly proposed an amendment to Kahn's rule that stripped its exception for the speaker's platform. It sailed through the House on an 89 to 34 vote. "The speaker lit one final cigarette before the ban took effect," noted *Tribune* reporter Jack Coffman.[44]

Kelly succeeded that day. But if he was hoping to persuade his friend to kick his injurious habit, he would be disappointed for several more decades.

Friendly Competition

The "Minnesota Miracle" tax and school finance moves in 1971 were so sweeping that some legislators likely expected they had set the state's tax policy for a generation. But property taxes started climbing rapidly again in 1975, as did inflation. When the ten-member House-Senate tax conference committee got to work on the final version of the 1975 tax bill, Gerry Nelson of the Associated Press reported, forecasts for 1976 showed property tax increases of 15 to 20 percent in the offing, after a 15 percent increase in 1975. Sabo understood that such large increases were neither good policy nor good politics—and to him, those two aims were one and the same.[45]

As House Taxes committee chair, Kelly held the gavel for the House in the conference committee. But Sabo had appointed himself as one of the five House conferees, and he made sure that the staff members he trusted most on fiscal matters—Ed Dirkswager and Eileen Baumgartner—were close at hand. Similarly, the Senate's conference committee team was led by Senate Taxes chair A. J. "Tony" Perpich. But majority leader Nicholas Coleman sat with him at the negotiating table, and he relied for numbers on William Riemerman from Senate Research.

The committee was tasked with reconciling competing schemes for keeping a lid on property taxes. The House tax bill followed the lead of Governor Anderson and a tax study commission that had been created in 1971. It provided what Anderson, in his 1975 inaugural message, called "income-adjusted property tax relief" and Sabo and Kelly dubbed the "circuit breaker." It would eliminate existing property tax credit programs and replace them with one that would send aid directly to property taxpayers whose bills "overload his income, just as an electrical overload trips a circuit breaker and cuts off current," Betty Wilson of the *Minneapolis Star* explained. The House's plan consolidated previously enacted state property tax credit schemes into a single income-based plan, sending relief to any taxpayer whose property tax bill exceeds 1.5 percent of his or her income, up to a maximum of $425.[46]

The Senate, guided by Coleman and his ally Senator George Conzemius, chair of the Health and Welfare committee, chose a different approach. The Senate intended to ease property taxes via a state takeover of county welfare costs, which would thereby reduce county property tax bites. It was a variation on the 1971 school finance scheme that had the added benefit in legislators' eyes of bringing greater uniformity to welfare administration. The Senate was also interested in sending taxpayers a one-time rebate in 1976—an election year in which both the House and Senate would be on the ballot.[47]

Those ideas and the research that buttressed them were in contest at the conference committee. So were the persuasive powers of the ten legislators—nine DFLers and one Republican, former Senate

Taxes chair Jerome Blatz—who faced each other across the committee table. Capitol reporters focused most keenly on Sabo and Coleman. Though different in style, personality, and background, the two DFL leaders both wanted to make state government an ally of average people. And both had a firm grip on the levers of power within their respective caucuses.

It's hard to assess the extent to which Sabo and Coleman saw themselves as rivals, though gossip among Capitol reporters featured that narrative. The two leaders were in concert on most issues and exhibited a respectful professional relationship. But they were not known to be personal friends or close working partners, as Sabo and Wendell Anderson were. It may have mattered that Coleman's urban-Irish-Catholic background was a stark contrast with Sabo's rural-Norwegian-Lutheran roots. Likely more significant were events at the DFL state convention in 1970, when Coleman was one of Anderson's competitors in an intense contest for the party's gubernatorial endorsement. Already then, Sabo was part of Anderson's camp.

Rivalry between the House and Senate was also an ingredient in that conference committee's proceedings, as it has been in many high-profile end-of-session negotiations through the decades at the Minnesota Capitol. Dirkswager attested that the House staffers at that 1975 conference committee were spurred by a desire to best their Senate counterparts.[48]

"Eileen and I would put together for Martin all the data I could acquire about future revenues and expenditures," Dirkswager said, citing Sabo's focus on keeping the state budget in the black. The House staffers were on their own in applying national economic forecasts to Minnesota's projected state revenues. The state would not hire its first state economist until later that year. "We always wanted Martin to know more than Nick in conference committee. That was just good old competition. We wanted to beat Riemerman!"

Sabo likely encouraged that spirit. He relished friendly competition. As was his wont, Sabo was often quiet during conference committee meetings, allowing the more voluble Coleman and Kelly to hold forth. But observers who interpreted his quiet negotiating style as meekness were mistaken, said Baumgartner, who watched Sabo in such legislative bargaining sessions for more than two decades.

"Because he was quiet, people thought he was humble. That's not the case at all. He had a very strong ego. But that's not something you could see from the outside," Baumgartner said about her long-time boss. He listened carefully and absorbed information, especially numeric data, with remarkable facility, Baumgartner added. "When you briefed him, he always got it right away."[49]

Sabo favored the circuit breaker's approach because of its simplicity and because it targeted relief directly at Minnesotans who were struggling to pay their property tax bills. The Senate's alternative spread relief money more widely and indirectly through the state, reaching affluent homeowners and businesses as well as those with lower incomes. That feature was touted as a virtue by Coleman and Conzemius. "I see nothing much wrong in giving a business property tax relief," Conzemius told reporters. Sabo disagreed, calling Conzemius's argument "incredible" and fretting about the state budget's future capacity to shoulder welfare costs, which were rapidly increasing in the 1970s as the population in need of residential long-term care grew.[50]

After five fruitless meetings of the tax conference committee—and with the constitutionally required adjournment date four days away—Sabo decided to bend. He was loath to adjourn without property tax relief enacted, knowing that the large DFL majorities would stand accused of an inability to govern. He badly wanted to get the circuit breaker concept into state law. But he was willing to do so without tearing down existing tax relief programs—at least not right away. News reports said that in the wee hours of Saturday, May 17—with a Monday adjournment looming—Sabo offered a "no losers" plan under which all homeowners would get a credit for 40 percent of their tax bill up to a $325 maximum. Only after that credit was applied would a "circuit breaker" kick in, offering additional relief based on income and paid via a rebate check in October, before the year's second deadline for paying property taxes. Sabo's plan also called for state takeover of 90 percent of county medical assistance costs, a boon to larger counties where such costs were high.[51]

That did the trick. The tax bill was among several major measures approved by the House and Senate during a sprint to adjournment at midnight on May 19. Sabo's endorsement was sufficient to attract a big 124 to 8 vote for the measure in the House. In the Senate, where the deal was perceived as more Sabo's than Coleman's, the vote was a more tepid 39 to 28. Republicans criticized the measure and the DFL Party as antibusiness since the tax bill did not direct relief to owners of commercial-industrial property. That complaint about business property taxes would be a staple Republican talking point in Minnesota politics for the next quarter century. But the "circuit breaker" also would endure. It's known in 2025 as the Property Tax Refund Program.[52]

The Session's End

A legislative session that was expected to produce smooth sailing under the control of an all-DFL crew wound up with a turbulent finish, *Minneapolis Star* analyst Jim Shoop reported a few days after the 1975 session's adjournment. Governor Wendell Anderson was granted only about half of twenty major legislative requests, and one major spending bill went unfinished when the session's midnight deadline was reached. "Throughout the session, the DFL problem was chiefly in the Senate, where Majority Leader Nicholas Coleman labored mightily to keep his troops in line," Shoop wrote, citing Senate DFL divisions on bills involving gun control, highway financing, and workers' compensation as examples.

By contrast, he noted, "speculation that the more than 40 new members of the House would be difficult to control never materialized." Sabo, Shoop said, was "in clear command on most issues."[53]

Jimmy Carter and Walter Mondale at the Democratic National Convention, New York City, July 1976.

CHAPTER NINE

DOMINOES FALL

ELECTIONS MATTER—AND SO DO APPOINTMENTS TO PUBLIC offices. At several junctures in Minnesota history, political careers were upended and the state's policy trajectory was altered by someone's appointment to a judgeship, a military office, a cabinet post, or a seat in the US Senate.

Two such consequential appointments occurred in 1976. On July 15, Democratic presidential nominee Jimmy Carter appointed Minnesota US Senator Walter "Fritz" Mondale as his running mate, a choice ratified by the Democratic National Convention that evening. And on November 10—one week after the Carter-Mondale ticket had won the presidential election, requiring Mondale's resignation from the Senate—Governor Wendell Anderson revealed his intention to be the next occupant of Mondale's Senate seat. He would resign on December 29, Lieutenant Governor Rudy Perpich would take over as governor, and Perpich would immediately appoint Anderson to fill the Senate vacancy.[1]

Nearly a half century later, what is remembered as Anderson's "self-appointment" is considered a colossal political blunder. It misread and disregarded an electorate that loathed self-dealing on the part of elected officials. Anderson's move was a major contributor to DFL election reversals in 1978. Hence, it's perplexing to look back at the summer and fall of 1976 and find that some of the DFL Party's most respected political strategists urged Anderson to put himself in the Senate. Among them was House Speaker Martin Sabo.

We can second-guess Sabo's thinking. Sabo was closely allied with Anderson—so much so that Sabo's public comments about Anderson's future in 1976 might have reflected Anderson's views as much as Sabo's own. But those comments also reveal Sabo's notion about how one builds a long career in elective office. That's what Sabo desired for himself, and he knew Anderson hoped elective service would be his life's work as well.

If Anderson "wants to remain in public life as an elective official, there probably are limitations on how long he could stay on as governor—but not as senator," Sabo told *Minneapolis Star* reporters Betty Wilson and Eric Pianin in early August, soon after the Democratic National Convention adjourned.[2]

Sabo was alluding to a tradition about gubernatorial tenure that had prevailed in Minnesota through 118 years of statehood. Through that span, no Minnesota governor had served longer than six years. From 1858 until 1962, governors had been elected to two-year terms. While no constitutional limit exists on the number of terms a governor could serve, only three—John Pillsbury, Theodore Christenson, and Orville Freeman—had stayed in office for a full six years. Freeman, the state's first DFL governor, was defeated in 1960 when he tried for a fourth term. That history undoubtedly influenced Sabo's thinking. He likely believed that, despite Anderson's sweeping victory in 1974 and his continued strong showing in opinion polls, Anderson's governorship was nearing its natural end.[3]

Sabo may have been unaware of some additional history that should have been deemed at least as pertinent. Between 1933 and 1978, nine American governors had elevated themselves to the US Senate, employing some version of the gambit Anderson contemplated. Eight of them had been defeated when they subsequently stood for election for a full six-year Senate term.[4]

By October Sabo and Anderson were on notice that Minnesotans did not like the self-appointment idea. The *Minneapolis Tribune*'s Minnesota Poll advised on October 10 that 55 percent of those polled opposed a maneuver by Anderson to put himself in the Senate to succeed Mondale. That sentiment was nearly as strong among DFLers as among Republicans and independents polled. Only 23 percent of respondents said they favored the move.[5]

But a different Minnesota Poll carried more weight in the governor's office, recalled Andrew Kozak, who served Anderson as an assistant and went on to head a prominent Minnesota lobbying firm, North State Advisors. In June 1976 the *Tribune*'s poll found a solid 56 percent of respondents rated Anderson's performance as either "excellent" or "good." Those results were virtually identical to the ones the poll found a year earlier and also in 1974, when Anderson's reelection bid swept the state. The poll left Anderson and others in the office believing he could overcome any disapproval engendered by self-appointment. Only one senior staff member disagreed, Kozak remembered. It was Tom Kelm, Anderson's longtime chief of staff and the son of the Democratic-Farmer-Labor Party's founding chairman, Elmer Kelm. Anderson had relied on Kelm's shrewd political insights through nearly six years in office—but not this time.[6]

Another administration figure who disliked Anderson's intention was Gerald Christenson. As commissioner of finance—the second-most powerful post in the state's executive branch—Christenson had been at work since the fall of 1975 upgrading the state's budgeting processes and fiscal forecasting capacity. That important work needed a governor's staunch support. Christenson was undoubtedly loath to lose Anderson.

Christenson, in his privately published 2005 memoir, *A Minnesota Citizen*, described meeting with Anderson as it was becoming clear that Mondale was likely to leave the Senate.

> I thought the best senator might have been Don Fraser. [Fraser had been Minnesota's Fifth District US representative since 1962.] . . . But Wendy was not close to Fraser, so I knew he wouldn't appoint him. But he loved Martin Sabo, the speaker of the House. He and Martin tracked on everything. I said, "Wendy, why don't you appoint Martin Sabo. Martin thinks like you do; he'll vote like you would. You have a strong friend there. You stay as governor and appoint Martin Sabo."

> Later, it became clear that Wendy was starting to move toward self-appointment, and I asked to meet with him. When I came in, the first thing he said was, "I thought seriously about what you said, and Martin would make a great senator, but I don't know if he can be elected statewide. He has trouble raising money, he comes across as being too serious, and he's not good on television, so I think Martin would have trouble."[7]

Anderson's critique of his friend's political weaknesses likely would have stung, had Sabo heard them. But the assessment Anderson shared with Christenson was not far off the mark. Sabo was not a prodigious fundraiser. He had never needed to raise a significant war chest for his own campaigns. They had been run largely on shoe leather, with enough backing from the well-oiled Minneapolis DFL machine and organized labor to pay for brochures and a smattering of advertising. As a legislative leader, he played a supporting role as the DFL Party took the lead in recruiting candidates, raising money, and employing volunteers—a level of support latter-day legislative leaders have not always had. It was also true that Sabo preferred serious talk about policy ideas, not gossip or political palaver, and he often seemed less than forthcoming when television cameras rolled. His fellow DFL legislators appreciated that about Sabo, but voters might not.

Nevertheless, Christenson evidently wasn't the only DFL insider who thought Anderson should appoint Sabo. A few days after the election, the *Minneapolis Tribune*'s Steven Dornfeld reported that "sources" believed Sabo was the most likely Anderson appointee, if the governor decided against installing himself in the Senate.[8]

What Sabo thought about such talk is not clear. But he did not behave in 1976 like a politician who expected to seek or occupy statewide office anytime soon. He made several campaign appearances around the state with DFL House candidates, as he had done every year since 1970. But his most visible trip during that campaign season had not been to Duluth, Moorhead, or Rochester. It was to Kansas City, Missouri, in September to assume the presidency of the National Conference of State Legislatures—the organization he had helped to create via a three-way organizational merger two years earlier. He was accompanied to the NCSL annual meeting by seventy-three other members and staffers from the Minnesota House, giving Minnesota the second-largest delegation at the meeting and triggering a front-page story in the *Minneapolis Tribune* detailing the conference's cost to state taxpayers.[9]

State Representative Ted Suss, a first-term DFLer from Prior Lake, remembers feeling honored to be selected to attend—and surprised when he stepped into an elevator at the conference hotel and found Minnesota House minority leader Henry Savelkoul and several other Republicans from Minnesota. What are all these Republicans doing here, he wondered. Suss asked Sabo at the next opportunity.

"Martin said, 'When you keep the opposition happy, they are a lot less hungry,'" Suss remembered years later. "He laughed as he said it. I knew he didn't invite them because he wanted them to be less aggressive. He wanted them to have the same opportunity we had to grow in understanding of the issues. He believed that if we freeze out the minority, we'll lose what they can contribute to public policy."[10]

Sabo defended Minnesota's large contingent to inquiring reporters in much the same way. He said participation in the conference would prove "very useful" for a legislature that was striving for best practices stewardship of state and local government. He noted that the meeting included a wide array of workshops and briefings about issues relevant to Minnesota lawmaking. It was a conference agenda he had helped craft. Sabo came across as a legislative leader whose focus was on building his institution, not winning higher office.

The Contest for Majority Leader

It might have been Mondale's coattails, or the high presidential-year voter turnout (73 percent in Minnesota), or the quality of candidates in the DFL field. For some or all of those reasons, the 1977 Legislature convened with a DFL House majority as lopsided as it had been in January 1975: 104 to 30. In the half century that has elapsed since then, no House majority has been as large.

When legislative majorities are supersized, observers note, the fissures within those majority caucuses tend to become evident. That happened in the days following the 1976 election when DFLers assembled to elect caucus leaders. Sabo's hold on the speakership was unquestioned and unchallenged. But Irv Anderson was facing a challenge for majority leader, the caucus's number-two post, from Neil Haugerud, a farmer, former Fillmore County sheriff, and fifth-term legislator from southeastern Minnesota. Anderson's gruff, abrupt nature and unpolished performances during floor debates had irritated his colleagues. But the last straw for several House members was Anderson's proposal to give the Rules committee—which he chaired—the power to approve committee chairmanships and conference committee members. Those were prerogatives of the speaker.

Martin Sabo reelected as speaker in 1977.

Tellingly, the most prominent Haugerud backers were DFLers closely associated with Sabo—Bill Kelly of East Grand Forks, Tom Berg of Minneapolis, and Ray Faricy of St. Paul. Sabo told reporters he was officially neutral in the Anderson-Haugerud contest. But he also made clear that he disagreed with Anderson's proposals for the Rules committee. Characteristically, Sabo voiced concern not for his own power, but for the smooth functioning of the House. According to the *Minneapolis Tribune*, Sabo said Anderson's plans "could lead to the kind of disorder that has characterized the operation of the Senate, where the leader of the DFL majority has few formal powers."[11]

Anderson evidently detected that in proposing to usurp some of the power of the House speaker, he had gone too far. In the days before the Monday, November 8 meeting at which caucus leaders would be elected, Anderson withdrew those proposals. He also let it be known that he favored higher salaries and more generous expense allowances for legislators. And he boasted that he was "a very good friend" of the next governor, Rudy Perpich—implying that he could offer the caucus the same close relationship with the governor's office that Sabo had provided while Wendell Anderson was in the Capitol's executive suite. That was enough to secure another term as majority leader. Irv Anderson defeated Neil Haugerud on a 55 to 47 vote.[12]

Might the result have been different if Sabo had voiced a preference for Haugerud? And might that have made a long-term difference for the Legislature? Those "what-if" questions entertained legislative observers for many years thereafter, as Irv Anderson's career trajectory went from high to low and back again, always accompanied by intra-caucus turmoil. Anderson was denied the speakership in 1980 by a rare alliance of urban DFLers and Independent-Republicans. Voters in his International Falls district turned him out in 1982 and returned him to office in 1990. He was chosen as speaker in 1993, then ejected from the post by his own party in 1997. He retired for good in 2007 and died the next year, at age eighty-five.

Sabo knew full well Anderson's strengths and weaknesses. He likely admired the loyalty Anderson engendered among legislators from northeastern Minnesota, then a DFL stronghold. He appreciated Anderson's close relationship with organized labor—an alliance Sabo shared. He may have concurred when Anderson pointed out that his relationship with Rudy Perpich could be an asset to the House. By 1976 Sabo had worked closely with Irv Anderson through four fruitful years. Observers said while the two leaders were not buddies, they had also avoided any public rift. Sabo likely had confidence that he could make the relationship work again—and less confidence that, even with a Sabo endorsement, his caucus would unite around Haugerud.

Sabo surely knew that by saying he was neutral in the Anderson–Haugerud contest, he was making Haugerud's election less probable. In so doing, he likely believed he was promoting DFL caucus unity. Ironically, Sabo may also have made caucus unity harder to achieve in future years.

Martin and Rudy

Precisely as orchestrated by Wendell Anderson, Minnesota's gubernatorial baton passed to Rudy Perpich on December 29, 1976. Perpich played his role according to Anderson's design. But the personal touches Perpich brought to the day—a polka mass at the Roman Catholic Church of the Assumption in St. Paul, an extended open house for all comers in lieu of the traditional formal dinner and inaugural ball—signaled a significant stylistic change at the top of state government.

Perpich, a forty-eight-year-old dentist who had been a state senator for eight years before becoming lieutenant governor, was Minnesota's first Catholic governor, first governor from the Iron Range, and first governor of Eastern European descent. He was a font of ideas—some brilliant, some baffling—and he was unrestrained in sharing his thinking and emotions with Minnesotans. He was high-energy, bighearted, impulsive, and—at least initially—undisciplined. During his first weeks in office, his staff had to admit on several embarrassing occasions that they had no idea where he was. Perpich was wont to jump into a car without notice and conduct impromptu listening sessions in Greater Minnesota coffee shops, seeking average-Joe-and-Jane input about matters including taxes, a power line controversy, and taconite-related pollution in Lake Superior.[13]

In a desire to make government an ally of average people, Perpich and Sabo were well matched. But in leadership style, the new governor and the House speaker were a study in contrasts. As a result, observers whispered, the potential for each to irritate the other was high. The fact that Perpich was personally close to Senate majority leader Nicholas Coleman—as Sabo had been to Wendell Anderson—provided ample subtext for such speculation.

Thus to some who watched Minnesota lawmaking from the Capitol basement, it was a surprise that the 1977 session was among the most orderly and harmonious in Minnesota's modern era. If Sabo faulted Perpich's uninhibited comments to reporters, or Perpich disliked Sabo's inscrutability, they kept their critiques to themselves.

An episode on a radio talk show in Hibbing—the heart of the Iron Range and Perpich's hometown—revealed the respect Perpich had for both Sabo and the separation of powers between the state's executive and legislative branches of government. On April 25, WMFG radio's *Candid Comment* show featured former state Representative Carl D'Aquila, a Republican who, while still in his twenties, had represented an Iron Range district for two terms in the late 1940s. D'Aquila, who made a career in radio and television after leaving the Legislature, had long been a critic of Perpich and his brothers Tony and George, both of whom also served stints in the state Senate.

D'Aquila accused Perpich of supporting a bill that would raise the tax on taconite production, impose a tax on tailings not dumped on land (an attempt to curb dumping in Lake Superior), and raise the property tax on unmined taconite. The bill was seen as punitive by northeastern Minnesota's dominant industry. Among the bill's sponsors was House Speaker Martin Sabo.

D'Aquila had barely finished uttering his claim when the station had a caller on the line—Governor Rudy Perpich. He fired back at D'Aquila in full-throated Iron Range fashion, calling him "the worst possible liar in this state." Perpich supported a different bill that contained more modest taconite tax increases and directed the proceeds to Iron Range schools and communities.

If D'Aquila "had the best interest of the Range at heart, he would never tell anyone that I am supporting the Sabo bill. If you go around telling that to people, legislators are going to believe that and the Sabo bill will go through without any changes," Perpich said on the air.

D'Aquila then challenged Perpich to play political boss and direct Sabo to withdraw his bill. The governor's response was telling: "You mean to tell me that I'm going to tell people they can't introduce a bill? Where the hell is this, Russia? Or what? How can you say that I can tell Marty Sabo what he can introduce? This is a free country, Carl."[14]

Sabo might not have expressed himself in the same fashion. But he would have appreciated Perpich's sentiment.

Tax Tensions

Just as Perpich respectfully disagreed with Sabo on taconite taxation, Sabo respectfully cast doubt on several of the ideas that came in rapid-fire fashion from Perpich. "My impression is that it won't happen," Sabo said when asked about Perpich's proposal to make Southwest State University in Marshall part of the University of Minnesota. (It didn't.) He voiced quiet hesitation when Perpich proposed sending the university an additional $20 million appropriation for health research. He let others shoot down Perpich's proposal to turn over enforcement of the Occupational Safety and Health Act to the federal government.[15]

None of those disagreements produced obvious tension between the speaker and the governor. But their disparate views about state income taxes and the state's commitment to provide property tax relief generated evident friction. Sabo's views about tax policy had not changed since 1971, when he was one of the architects of the substitution of income taxes for school and city property taxes known as the Minnesota Miracle. Sabo considered a progressive income tax, with rates structured to increase with income levels, the foundation of sound tax policy. Based on ability to pay, the income tax also had the virtue of serving as a counterweight to regressive sales and property taxes, which take a higher proportion of the incomes of lower-income people than more affluent ones. Sabo's goal was to equalize the total state and local tax burden so that every Minnesota taxpayer's burden was approximately the same share of his or her income.

Perpich was not hostile to those ideas. But he was bothered by Minnesota's growing reputation for income taxes that were uncompetitively high and complicated compared with other states. In January 1977 the new governor proposed a $100 million income tax cut as part of a simplification scheme. Sabo immediately objected. Any money available for tax relief should "be used to maintain stability in the property tax," Sabo told reporters. Income tax simplification could be accomplished at a much lower cost, he added.

Those comments were the start of a prolonged tug-of-war over tax policy between Perpich and Sabo—with Sabo sometimes aided by House Taxes chair Kelly, whose views were aligned with the speaker's. The House prevailed over the governor during the 1977 regular session, sending Perpich a bill that added new, higher-rate income tax brackets for upper-income Minnesotans and boosting property tax relief measures by $163 million. Perpich signed the bill but told reporters only a few hours after the Legislature recessed for the year that he was considering calling a special session for the sake of income tax simplification. The governor predicted that cost-saving measures in state agencies he planned to impose would be sufficient to allow the state to afford an income tax cut.

Sabo learned about Perpich's special session idea from a reporter who called him at home the evening after the session's adjournment. "I'm not enthused," Sabo said in terse response, undoubtedly restraining a temptation to use stronger language.[16]

No special session materialized in 1977, but Perpich did not abandon his desire for income tax relief. In November Perpich and Kelly faced off in print with dueling "pro-con" essays in the *Minneapolis Star*. Perpich faulted the Legislature for allowing Minnesota's income taxes to climb to the fourth-highest in the nation. In some middle-income brackets, the state's taxpayers paid the nation's highest rate, he said. "It's not good policy to have the highest income tax in any categories because people begin to think we are the highest, period! This attitude creates a bad tax climate that can become detrimental to the state."[17]

Kelly countered with the argument that by relying on the income tax, Minnesota had built a tax system that was both fair and stable—that is, unlikely to lead to disruptive deficits and cuts in government services. "A reduction in income taxes could damage this fair tax system by forcing us to place more emphasis on the less fair real estate tax in the years ahead. . . . Small reserves in the state treasury should not be spent during this time of uncertainty. We should not risk either the fairness of our tax system or the well-being of our residents to achieve a minor, short-term tax cut." The byline was Kelly's, but the ideas were pure Sabo.[18]

Perpich was unpersuaded by the House position. He restated his call for income tax relief when he appeared before a joint session of the Legislature on January 24, 1978. His message was front-page news that day, but so was a story that would have a bigger impact on Martin Sabo. Its headline: "Rep. Fraser to Seek Senate Seat of HHH, Will Not Run for House."[19]

The Death of a Giant

Former Vice President Hubert Humphrey's death on January 13, 1978, was not a surprise. Minnesota's senior US senator had been battling bladder cancer for eighteen months, enduring grueling surgery and chemotherapy. It had been clear for weeks that the treatments were not working. Humphrey's passing was met with genuine sorrow throughout the state, with Republicans joining DFLers in praising Humphrey's service to Minnesota and the nation.

The death was also met almost immediately with speculation about who would fill Humphrey's Senate seat for the nine months until the next general election, when state law required that the seat be on the ballot. The power to appoint a senator belonged solely to Governor Rudy Perpich.

Three names topped the handicappers' lists—Donald Fraser, Nicholas Coleman, and Muriel Humphrey, Hubert Humphrey's widow. The analysis: If Perpich wants to reward a DFLer who is already well established in Washington and has been planning a Senate campaign for months, he'll go with Fraser, a sixteen-year veteran of the US House representing Minneapolis. A Fraser appointment would also shore up Perpich's standing with metro-area DFLers, which could boost Perpich's own election bid in 1978. But Fraser had become a champion for maintaining the Boundary Waters Canoe Area in northeastern Minnesota as a protected national wilderness, free of motorboats—and that made him anathema to the northern Minnesota tourism industry. A Fraser appointment would bring Perpich more grief from his friends than he likely cared to endure.

The prognosticators looked next to Coleman. Coleman and Perpich had been friends since they were freshmen state senators in 1963. As Wendell Anderson's rival for the governorship in 1970, Coleman had engineered Perpich's endorsement for lieutenant governor. That move was crucial to Perpich's ascension into the governor's office. On more than one occasion in 1977, Perpich reportedly had assured Coleman that "if there's a vacancy, you're going to Washington."[20]

Coleman may have been aiming to curry favor with Perpich in mid-December when he surprised his own Senate Taxes committee chair—and the House speaker—by endorsing Perpich's proposal for an income tax cut. Taxes chair William McCutcheon—a future St. Paul police chief—sided with Sabo and Kelly in urging fiscal restraint, knowing that the state budget was barely in the black and a new budget forecast was several months away. But Coleman said he was ready to make an income tax cut a high priority in 1978. He may have anticipated that well before he would need to make good on that promise, he would be working in Washington, not St. Paul.[21]

But when Perpich was confronted with the possibility that he would be on the same 1978 DFL general election ticket as an appointed Senator Coleman, he hesitated. Only a few years earlier, Coleman had been through an attention-getting divorce, leaving his wife and the mother of his six children to marry a *Minneapolis Star* journalist, Deborah Howell. Perpich believed Coleman's still-recent personal history would not play well with voters.

That led Perpich to the third name on pundits' lists and the safest choice, Muriel Humphrey. Appointing widows to complete the elective terms of their late husbands was a well-established practice in American politics. This sixty-five-year-old recent widow was widely known and admired by Minnesotans. Her persona was that of a political helpmate and homemaker. That image was incomplete. More than many voters knew, Muriel Humphrey had been among Hubert's closest policy and career advisers, playing that role since before their marriage in 1936. Like her husband, Muriel Humphrey was a staunch advocate for racial justice and government help for the downtrodden. Perpich may have expected that she would accept the Senate seat as a caretaker and announce immediately that she would not be a candidate in the fall general election. But she would make no such promise. She indicated that she wanted to retain the option of running in the fall for the remaining four years of Hubert's term. That position may have given Perpich pause. But—likely due to his own leaks—word was already out that he planned to appoint her. It was too late for him to change course. Perpich made the appointment on January 25. Muriel Humphrey would become the only woman in the hundred-member US Senate of 1978.[22]

Martin Sabo was not on Perpich's list. Sabo was more than qualified to serve in the US Senate. He had just completed a one-year term as president of the National Conference of State Legislatures, a role that took him to Washington on several occasions, including a meeting with President Jimmy Carter in the White House in February 1977. His record as both a lawmaker and a leader of a lawmaking body was long and strong. His personal life was free of scandal, his work ethic was unquestioned, and his name recognition in Minnesota was as high as that of any legislator.[23]

But Perpich had not warmed to Sabo. Perpich said in later years that when he interviewed candidates for appointment to various positions, he asked himself, "How do I feel about this person? Would

I feel comfortable walking to the other side of this table and hugging this person?" He likely would not have found the upright, taciturn North Dakota Norwegian particularly huggable.[24]

It's also possible that Perpich and the rest of the state Capitol crowd already understood that Sabo was in hot pursuit of a different opportunity. If the political dominoes were to fall in a way that would remove incumbent US Representative Don Fraser from the 1978 Fifth District ballot, Sabo was expected to be a candidate to succeed him. This time, the professional speculators in the Capitol basement got it right. Less than forty-eight hours after Fraser's January 23 announcement that he would not seek reelection to the US House, Sabo summoned reporters to his bungalow home at 3129 East Twenty-Second Street in Minneapolis and launched his campaign for the Fifth District seat.[25]

A New Campaign

In January 1978 Sabo exhibited none of the hesitation that he had experienced before running for Minnesota House speaker in November 1972. His mind was made up. And his family was behind him. A letter to Klara Sabo in North Dakota from Sylvia dated January 18, 1978—two days after Humphrey's funeral—allows that Martin "is now having to look at what he has to do next. It may be that Fraser, our congressman, will go for Humphrey's Senate seat and Martin is the likely person for the congressional seat," Sylvia informed her mother-in-law. "We have talked with Karin and Julie of the situation. Karin is very eager to try a change and Washington D.C. makes her happy. . . . We will back Martin up whatever he wants to do."[26]

Sabo knew the value of timely action in party endorsement contests. News reports said Sabo began calling Minneapolis DFL leaders to solicit their support for a congressional bid immediately after Humphrey's death. If he could secure enough early support, he calculated, other ambitious wannabes would see him blocking their paths and decline to run. The gambit paid off with at least a few potential candidates, the *Minneapolis Star* reported on January 25. Already state Representatives Phyllis Kahn and Linda Berglin let it be known that they would yield to Sabo.

Why was Sabo so eager in this pursuit? Years later he opened a window on his thinking. He noted that incumbent members of the US House from seats dominated by one party, as the Minneapolis–Columbia Heights–Fridley–St. Anthony seat was, tended to have long tenures. Those coveted seats don't often open to nonincumbents. Fraser had held the seat for sixteen years; his predecessor, Republican Walter Judd, represented Minnesota's Fifth District for twenty years. Opt to wait for "the next time," and the wait could be long indeed.

Sabo also had a sense that an unwritten time limit existed for an effective speakership in the Minnesota House, and that in year six of his tenure he was approaching that deadline. Until that time, only two speakers in state history had served longer—Lawrence Hall in the 1940s and Lloyd Duxbury in the 1960s. They each held the post for eight years.

The risk for him, as Sabo described it, wasn't running out of political backing. It was running out of forbearance with the many trivial demands a speaker confronts. "I think there's a limit on how long you can be speaker, more so than say Senate majority leader," Sabo said. "I maybe could have lasted for a couple more years. But pretty soon, you get a little less sensitive to people with the small issues, to put it politely. You need to have patience on that job, and I think there's a time when that might run out. I think I could have been there for a little while longer, but not much longer."[27]

To continue his chosen career, Sabo concluded, he needed a new lawmaking venue, preferably one that lauded long service. The US House with its seniority-based rewards system nicely filled the bill.

A change of venue in 1979 also suited Sabo for personal reasons that he did not mention to reporters. His daughters Karin and Julie were fourteen and twelve years old, respectively, in 1978. Karin was about to start high school and was eager for a change of venue. Like most members of Congress in those years, the Sabos planned to move to Washington if elected. Martin and Sylvia undoubtedly believed that moving the girls to a new home and new school would be less disruptive for them in late 1978 than it might be at a later juncture.

"Sylvia deserves a lot of credit" for Martin's career success, observed former state Representative Joe Graba years later. "She played a major role, running the household well so that Martin was free to do what he loved as a legislator." The Sabos lived frugally in the modest bungalow house they bought soon after their marriage, with Sylvia putting in stints as a part-time nurse at Fairview Convalescent Home and Prospect Park Nursing Home to supplement Martin's legislative salary.[28]

As the daughter of a small-town merchant who became a Lutheran pastor, Sylvia was accustomed to a life of community service—and she enjoyed it, her sister Margaret Bostelmann attested years later. She was happy to play the role of political hostess and enjoyed participating in the Rotunda Club, a group of legislators' wives, and the Dome Club, which included spouses of both genders of both legislators and state constitutional officers.

Sylvia had a gift—as did their mother—for remembering people's names and faces, Bostelmann said. "Our parents were so available for leadership roles. It wasn't anything other than the ordinary for them to take on some church or community project. They never felt that leadership was an imposition on them. They passed those values along to us," Bostelmann said.[29]

Shifting Political Winds

One might surmise that the 1978 session was among the shortest even-year sessions in state history because the House speaker was waging a congressional endorsement campaign that spring. The Fifth District DFL endorsing convention was set for April 29. The Legislature adjourned for the year on March 24, just sixty-seven days after the 1978 session convened.

But it likely wasn't the congressional election calendar that kept the 1978 session short. Rather, it was growing perception among at least some DFL House members that they were about to encounter stiffer political headwinds than they had experienced in the last three election cycles and that they should get busy campaigning. (The state Senate was not on the ballot that year.) Perpich shared that concern. He told reporters he favored adjournment by St. Patrick's Day, March 17. Legislators missed his deadline by a week but were still able to hit the campaign trail by April Fool's Day.[30]

They were right to be worried. At an annual DFL fundraising dinner on April 8, Muriel Humphrey announced that she would not be a candidate after all in the coming November's special election to complete her late husband's US Senate term. A lively, potentially divisive contest had already emerged for that seat on the DFL side, with Fraser winning significant support from state convention delegates even before Humphrey's departure from the race. Coleman was also testing the waters, as was an anti-abortion conservative-populist from southwestern Minnesota, state Senator Marion "Mike" Menning. (He would soon switch parties.) And businessman Robert Short, a DFL party maverick and critic of Fraser, was signaling an intention to bypass the party endorsement process and enter the DFL primary.

Meanwhile, Independent-Republicans (the state GOP's official name since 1975) were sorting out assignments among the strongest array of statewide candidates they had fielded in a number of years. David Durenberger, a former chief of staff to Governor Harold LeVander, yielded to party leaders' pressure to leave the governor's race and switch to a bid for Humphrey's Senate seat. That cleared the IR gubernatorial field for retiring First District US Representative Al Quie. Durenberger was not well known around the state, but he was a telegenic moderate who made a favorable impression on the stump. For the other Senate race, versus Wendell Anderson, the IR Party was rallying behind Twin Cities retailer and Republican activist Rudy Boschwitz, the son of refugees from Hitler's Germany whose personalized television commercials for his Plywood Minnesota retail chain had given him wide name recognition. DFLers were stunned by a March 19 Minnesota Poll that put Boschwitz slightly ahead of Anderson, 48 to 45 percent.[31]

Awareness that voters were not responding as warmly to DFL candidates as they had only a few years earlier likely affected the House's willingness to battle with Perpich over tax policy in 1978. Sabo and Kelly realized their calls for fiscal restraint and property tax relief could not compete politically with the allure of the income tax cut Perpich wanted. "Folks like to spend money and cut taxes," Sabo told reporter Betty Wilson when she asked about Sabo's softening position during the session's final days. "I like to do that too."[32]

Sabo and Kelly held out as long as they thought they could for a larger boost in aid to schools (which serves to reduce property tax burdens) and for income tax credits targeted at working families rather than rate cuts for upper-income earners. Their effort only partially paid off. A split-the-difference compromise came closer to the House's position on aid to schools but included cuts in upper-end income taxes that had been increased only the previous year. It was an all-DFL compromise, yet it won the support of both Republican minority leaders. Sabo acknowledged his unhappiness with the tax cut bill, but he was silent when it was discussed one last time in the tax conference committee and then voted for it.[33]

State Representative Pete Petrafeso, a DFLer from St. Louis Park, told reporters that day that House DFLers feared that if they did not support an income tax cut, Perpich would campaign against them in the fall. Was that fear well founded? Maybe not. But Sabo would not have been sure—and Sabo knew that as a candidate for Congress in the fall, he would be in a poor position to fight back if his party's governor publicly criticized DFL legislators.[34]

End of the Session

When the tax and school aid deals were done, the session was done—and so was Sabo's eighteen-year career as a state legislator. Action on legislation ended in the wee hours of March 24. A ceremonial meeting later that day officially closed the session.

Emotions ran high in the House chamber on March 23, the last full day of business. Sabo's impending departure from the House was not the only exit on members' minds. Republican leader Henry Savelkoul had also announced he would not run again. An attorney from Albert Lea, Savelkoul was one of several legislators in the 1970s who found the demands of annual sessions to be more than their families and careers could stand. "All the traveling, recruiting candidates—I just got burned out, frankly," Savelkoul said decades later.[35]

When Sabo needed a break from the speaker's dais, he customarily invited one of several senior DFL members to wield the gavel in his absence. At one point on March 23, he signaled for Savelkoul to come to the dais and take his place. It was a rare gesture of tribute by one adversary to another. When Sabo returned to the chamber, he warmly shook hands with Savelkoul as House members cheered.[36]

"Martin was someone I could work with on a collegial basis," Savelkoul said. "He was the sort with whom you could go out and have a beer and figure out how to make things work." As a result, he said, despite the deep minority status that Republicans had in the 1977–78 House, major bills carried a bipartisan stamp. "Nearly all the spending bills were approved on nearly unanimous votes," he recalled.

Another rare moment was caught by an Associated Press photographer during the afternoon ceremony on March 24. It was a close-up shot of Martin Sabo wiping a tear from his right eye. The caption said he was about to bang the House gavel for the last time.[37]

A Recap of Reform

For weeks a sense had pervaded the Minnesota House that a major chapter in institutional history was coming to a close. That sense was also conveyed by *Minneapolis Tribune* reporters Steven Dornfeld and Steve Brandt in a February five-part series entitled "The Changing Legislature." It summarized much that had happened since the late 1960s to help Minnesota's legislators become better informed and more open and responsive to their constituents. Annual sessions, open meetings, recorded votes, party designation, private offices, lobbyist expenditure disclosure, more in-depth research, more interaction with constituents—all had come to pass in the late 1960s and early 1970s, mostly on Sabo's watch.[38]

The newspaper series also called attention to the cost of those changes. The biennial budgets of the House and Senate swelled from $6.2 million in 1967–68 to $33.9 million in 1977–78. The number of staff employed during sessions went from 218 to 577 in the same period. Many of those staffers—too many, the series implied—were engaged in work that boosted incumbents' prospects for reelection.

The human cost of annual sessions was described as well. The series noted that several talented legislators had left office after only a few terms, citing as the reason for their departure an inability to manage the growing time demands of legislative service. Several other legislators said they believed the demands of state lawmaking and oversight were great enough to warrant a switch from a part-time to a full-time legislature. Sabo disagreed. But, he added, "No longer can being a legislator be a secondary concern of someone who serves. It must be the primary concern." Nearly fifty years later, a debate continues over whether Minnesota's legislators should meet year-round or for only a portion of each year.[39]

The series tacitly asked readers whether the changes that had been wrought at the Legislature were worth their cost. A similar question was being asked around the county in 1978 by a growing faction of conservative Republicans. When in June 1978 California voters overwhelmingly approved Proposition 13 to limit property taxes, an anti-taxation political wave started that spread quickly to other states, including Minnesota. It was suddenly in vogue to fault governments at all levels for fiscal imprudence and excessive taxation and to question whether any improvement in governmental institutions was worth its cost.

Those who engineered the modernization of the Minnesota Legislature had a strong argument to make in the 1978 campaign about the value of what they had done. They could defend beefed up staffing as necessary to making sure that legislators understood the growing complexities of state government's many portfolios. They could cite the need to avoid costly unintended consequences in legislation.

They could have explained the value to constituents of adequate support staff, meeting space, and legislator compensation. They could have connected the changes at the Legislature to a desire to situate Minnesota's governing institutions close to the people, thereby keeping democracy strong.

But the legislator arguably best able to make that case on behalf of Minnesota House members was otherwise engaged. Martin Sabo was running for Congress.

CHAPTER TEN

THE WAY TO WASHINGTON

MARTIN SABO MAINTAINED THAT POLITICS SHOULD BE A MEANS to an end—sound governance—and not an end in itself. He held that when deciding how to govern, political considerations should be secondary to principles like fairness, prudence, effectiveness, and transparency. Yet Sabo respected politics and the activists who were its practitioners at the conventions of the Democratic-Farmer-Labor Party—even in 1978, when it became evident that not all of them shared his sentiments.

Sabo was a very impressive congressional candidate. At age forty, he had been in the Legislature for eighteen years, his party's leader in the Minnesota House for ten years, and House speaker for six years. He helped engineer sweeping changes in government finance and legislative operations, making taxes fairer and state government more open and responsive to Minnesotans. He had twice been elected president of national legislative organizations, winning wide recognition and acclaim.

"Without question, he is the most effective legislator over here," another Minneapolis legislator told the *Minneapolis Star*'s Robert Whereatt. "Marty knows every bill that goes in. He knows every bill that goes out." That praise came not from a DFLer, but from future Republican Governor Arne Carlson, then a House assistant minority leader who represented a Minneapolis district adjacent to Sabo's.[1]

It may have come as a surprise to Carlson and others unfamiliar with the internal workings of the Minneapolis DFL Party that Sabo was not a shoo-in for its Fifth Congressional District endorsement. Instead, he was one of four candidates vying for the party's blessing on April 29 at the venerable Leamington Hotel in downtown Minneapolis. And though Carlson attested that in Republican eyes Sabo was "a hardcore partisan," all three of Sabo's rivals were challenging him from the left. Their contest was indicative of a gap in ideas and identity between party activists and elected officials that was increasingly evident in both of Minnesota's major political parties. In the DFL, grassroots movements centered on racial and gender justice and opposition to the Vietnam War had widened that gap.

Most formidable among Sabo's rivals for Fifth District endorsement was Lois Gibson, president of the Minnesota chapter of Americans for Democratic Action (ADA). In the late 1970s that organization was past its prime nationally, but it remained respected in Minnesota for its DFL pedigree. As Minneapolis mayor, Hubert Humphrey was among the ADA's founders, and in 1949–50, then-Senator Humphrey was its national president. Gibson, fifty-one, was a New York native who had moved to Minnesota in 1966 and had been active in arts and Jewish women's organizations as well as DFL politics. In 1973 she had run unsuccessfully for the Minneapolis City Council in Ward 11, a middle- and upper-class part of the city in which a moderate Republican such as alderman Walter Rockenstein could win election in the 1970s.[2]

Gibson's campaign theme was "In the Fraser tradition." The intended implication was that she—and not Sabo—was philosophically aligned with sixteen-year congressman Donald Fraser, a staunch liberal on matters including civil rights at home, human rights abroad, and environmental protection everywhere. In fact, Gibson's positions were almost identical to Sabo's on major issues, including the one that was increasingly a litmus test for candidates in both parties, abortion. Sabo and Gibson were both firmly pro-choice. When reporters pressed Gibson, she could cite only a few policy disputes with Sabo. He was in favor of allowing a limited amount of state aid to flow to parochial schools for such things as transportation costs. She was not. He was in favor of streamlining municipal government in Minneapolis by eliminating the park and library boards. She was not.[3]

Rather than emphasizing issues, however, Gibson's campaign stressed her gender and her grassroots pedigree. She boasted about the fact that her political alliances included few elected officials. Without naming Sabo, she distinguished herself from a class of "good ol' boys" in politics, depicted in her campaign literature as crusty, cigar-chomping poker players holding cards labeled "special interests," "favors" and "fed. projects." She cast herself as one of a "new kind of representative, one who does not get in line and wait, in the 'I'm next' tradition." She would be "someone who won't play the game just to get into the club." She judged—with considerable accuracy—that in the wake of Watergate and Vietnam, many voters in both parties were mistrustful of the nation's political establishment.[4]

That message could best Martin Sabo, Gibson naively claimed in early April as legislative district conventions met to select delegates to the Fifth Congressional District convention. "It's beyond my wildest dreams!" she exuded as she reported a strong preliminary delegate count. Sabo, a more seasoned vote-counter, disputed Gibson's hype. But he exhibited no complacency. As soon as he extricated himself from his legislative responsibilities at the state Capitol, he set about campaigning for party endorsement with the convention version of door-knocking, the tactic he knew best. Systematically, he phoned or met individually with as many delegates as possible.[5]

He described his face-to-face, high-touch approach to campaigning when he addressed the April 29 convention. "I've enjoyed these past weeks—the opportunity of visiting with many of you and trying to answer your questions and give you the opportunity to get to know me a little bit better and to get to know you," he said. "In that process, I've learned a great deal. I pledge you one thing as a candidate: to continue that process in the future, so both you can get to know me a little bit better, but more importantly, so that I can continue to learn from you."[6]

As the convention drew nigh, several developments seemed to conspire against a quick win, which required passing a 60 percent vote threshold. Two more candidates emerged: Methuselah Bradley, endorsed by the convention's Black caucus, and Tom O'Connell of the Farmer-Labor Association, a vestige of the Farmer-Labor Party that had merged with the Democratic Party in Minnesota in 1944. O'Connell's group held true to the Farmer-Labor Party's socialist traditions. He argued for nationalization of oil companies and other key industries.

On the eve of the convention, Gibson was endorsed by the Hennepin County chapter of the Minnesota Women's Political Caucus. It was a bipartisan group founded in 1972 in Minnesota, with ties to national feminist organizations whose leaders included Arvonne Fraser, Don Fraser's well-known wife who was then head of the Office of Women in Development in the US State Department. The group's Hennepin County chair, Nadine Strossen, made clear that the group saw the Sabo–Gibson contest as an opportunity to flex feminist political muscle. Strossen told the *Minneapolis Tribune* that "the real issue" is, "Do you assert your power by jumping on the bandwagon of a powerful male candidate? Or do you show your power by making it difficult for him to get endorsement unless he addresses feminist issues?" She would have been hard-pressed to identify issues of relevance to women on which Sabo had not already staked out a position feminists favored. Her critique evidently was about degrees of emphasis—and about gender itself.[7]

In addition, some 30 of the convention's 139 delegates were known to be anti-abortion—and the leaders of that cohort announced their intention to vote "uncommitted," at least in the early balloting, to register their objection to the candidates' pro-choice stances. With all of that in play, Sabo and his convention floor team braced themselves for a multi-ballot day on April 29.

The Sabo team undoubtedly brightened after the first ballot. As expected, Sabo's vote total fell short of the 89 votes needed for endorsement. He mustered just 61 votes. But the "uncommitted/pro-life" total was only nine, well short of the expected thirty-plus that had been ballyhooed. "A lot of the pro-lifers are also experienced political workers, and they didn't want a locked-up convention," one delegate told the press. Better still, O'Connell and Bradley appeared to be drawing more support from Gibson than from Sabo. O'Connell's first-ballot total surpassed Gibson's, 32 to 29. From that position, the Sabo team deduced, Gibson was unlikely to be able to make the contest a prolonged two-way tussle leading to a deadlocked convention and an open primary in September. It might take a few more ballots, but Sabo was on the way to endorsement.[8]

It came after the third ballot. Sabo reached 79 votes on the second ballot and 84 on the third before both O'Connell and Gibson withdrew and backed Sabo. That was followed by a near-unanimous standing vote endorsing Sabo. Gibson's statement of support for Sabo ended speculation that she might refuse to "abide by the endorsement" in party parlance and continue her candidacy in the September 14 primary.

Caucus-to-Convention

Might Sabo have been tempted at some point to walk away from the courtship of party-insider delegates and take his bid for Congress directly to DFL primary voters? Not likely, say those who knew him well—though with his superior name recognition and capacity to raise money in 1978, he would have been a hands-down favorite to win had he done so. Throughout his career, Sabo was a proponent of Minnesota's party-based, caucus-to-convention system of selecting candidates for elective office. He believed that one-on-one interaction between a candidate and the people who devoted time and treasure to a political party provided valuable preparation for public service.

That conviction was put to the test in 1992, and it's worth getting ahead of our story to describe that year's convention experience. Sabo was running in 1992 for his eighth term in the US House. His endorsement by Fifth District DFLers at their May 9 convention was expected to be a routine matter. Instead, a leader of the Minnesota Women's

Political Caucus, Lisa Niebauer-Stall, blocked Sabo's endorsement through six ballots. Redistricting had given Sabo new territory, moving the Fifth District to the northwest into Robbinsdale, New Hope, and Crystal and west into Golden Valley and St. Louis Park. He had dozens of new delegates to court. That change plus unhappiness with a perceived anti-female bias in Washington after the confirmation of Justice Clarence Thomas to the US Supreme Court had created an opening for Niebauer-Stall.[9]

What ended the impasse in the wee hours of Sunday morning May 10 was a question put to both candidates before the assembled delegates: Will you abide by the endorsement? In other words, will you end your candidacy if your opponent is endorsed? Niebauer-Stall said no, she would make no such promise. Sabo answered yes.

Martin Sabo speaking at DFL state convention in 1978.

His answer both stunned and impressed the weary delegates. Sabo was saying that he respected their judgment so much that he was prepared to end his reelection campaign and his congressional career—even though he was on the verge of chairing a major US House committee—if 60 percent of the assembled delegates preferred his little-known opponent. He was entrusting those delegates with his career. They rewarded his trust on the seventh ballot, endorsing him at 3 a.m. Sabo's promise would not have been credible had it come from many other politicians. But through thirty-two years in public life, Sabo had built a reputation as a man who keeps his word. That, too, made a difference in the small hours of May 10, 1992.

Niebauer-Stall kept her word too. She ran against Sabo in the September 15, 1992, primary election. She received 28 percent of the vote, compared with Sabo's 67 percent.[10]

Competition

Given his well-honed sensitivity to the direction and force of Minnesota political winds, Sabo likely recognized early that those winds were shifting in 1978. Republicans were better positioned to make gains than they had been since Harold LeVander was elected governor in 1966. LeVander had won that year in good part because DFLers were divided, having wounded each other in a brutal gubernatorial primary between Governor Karl Rolvaag and Lieutenant Governor A. M. "Sandy" Keith.

A similarly fractious intraparty contest was shaping up in the spring and summer of 1978. US Senator Muriel Humphrey announced on April 8 what Governor Rudy Perpich had hoped she would say in January: she would not be a candidate for election to serve the remaining four years of her late husband's Senate term. That decision left Don Fraser in a strong position to win the DFL Party's endorsement for the seat at the June 3 convention.

But Humphrey's withdrawal also ushered in the candidacy of a well-known, well-heeled party maverick, Robert Short. Short's previous foray into elective politics had been as Karl Rolvaag's 1966 choice to replace Sandy Keith as lieutenant governor. But he was better known as a self-made, self-promoting Minneapolis entrepreneur. Short had built a successful trucking business and had acquired a chain of hotels (including the DFL's frequent gathering spot, the Leamington) and sports teams including the Minneapolis Lakers and the Washington Senators. He outraged Senators fans in 1972 when he moved the team to Arlington, Texas, and rechristened it the Texas Rangers.[11]

As Short announced his Senate candidacy three days after Muriel Humphrey's withdrawal, he emphasized his differences with Fraser on three emotionally charged issues—guns, abortion, and protection of the Boundary Waters Canoe Area—and his intention to bypass the DFL convention and take his campaign directly to voters in the September 12 primary. Short's candidacy seemed tailor-made to divide DFLers geographically. His pro-gun, anti-abortion, anti–BWCA protection stances were anathema in much of the metro area but popular in Greater Minnesota, particularly on the Iron Range.

Sabo faced only token opposition in the Fifth District primary election. But, as had been his pattern since 1960, he spent nearly every afternoon and early evening that summer systematically knocking on doors throughout the district to meet potential voters, often in the company of small teams of volunteers. He undoubtedly detected the heat the Fraser–Short contest was generating and recognized that a Short win could dampen DFL turnout in the pro-Fraser Fifth District or even send some unhappy voters into the Republican column on the ballot.[12]

Sabo was also up against something he had not faced through eighteen years in elective office: a well-funded Republican opponent. Michael Till, the head of pediatric dentistry at the University of Minnesota, won Independent-Republican backing at a five-ballot convention on April 22 that cleared the field of other Republicans. Till, forty-three, was a political moderate whose views did not align with the emerging right wing of the national Republican Party. He favored national health insurance, wanted abortion kept legal, supported the Equal Rights Amendment, and wanted more federal assistance directed to the elderly poor. Those positions served him well as he asked the district's moderate-minded voters to consider his candidacy. Though Till was a newcomer to Minnesota elective politics, he was not a political neophyte. He had been a legislative assistant to a congressman from Pennsylvania early in his career; more recently, he had been a lobbyist for the Minnesota Dental Association. The relationships he made doing that work gave Till a leg up on fundraising. Campaign finance reports filed in October (a new requirement, imposed in the wake of the Watergate scandal) showed that Till had raised nearly $110,000, topping Sabo's tally by nearly $35,000.[13]

The result was a congressional contest that attracted more notice than Fifth District voters had witnessed since at least 1962, when Fraser unseated Walter Judd—and more than they would see again for several decades. Till had the means and the savvy to mount a prime-time television ad campaign in August that achieved two of his goals. The week-long ad blitz boosted Till's name recognition in the district from 8 percent to 44 percent, his campaign told reporters. And it put Sabo on the defensive on two perennially sensitive issues, taxes and legislators' pay.[14]

During his last term as speaker, Sabo had helped engineer a pay raise for legislators that included higher pay for leaders of legislative caucuses, who are expected to work full-time. By constitutional requirement, that pay increase could not become effective until the following session, in 1979. Throughout his six years as House speaker, Sabo was paid the same annual salary as any other legislator—$8,400. But the need for him to participate in meetings when the Legislature was not in session made him eligible for more per diem, or $48 daily expense payments, than the typical legislator received. And a 1977 rules change allowed the House speaker, majority leader, and minority leader to collect per diem payments five days a week, or $240 per week, for business conducted away from the Capitol, including in their districts.

Sabo was taking full advantage of that new provision while running for Congress in the summer of 1978, the *Minneapolis Tribune* reported on August 3 in a story that topped page one and featured

Sabo's photo. The story implied that taxpayers were paying Sabo for time spent campaigning for Congress. He justified the expense payments by noting that he spent a portion of nearly every workday at the Capitol attending to House administration.[15]

The story included a scolding from Representative Rod Searle of Waseca, the respected dean of House Independent-Republicans. He called automatic weekly expense payments "inappropriate," especially in a campaign year, when "it's very difficult to draw the line between constituent service and campaigning." When reporters asked Sabo how he would draw that line, Sabo had a sour reply: "Maybe we could develop a system under which we close down government for six months."

Sabo undoubtedly had grown weary of both his meager compensation for legislative work and the not-so-subtle inference by Capitol reporters and others that any legislative pay was excessive or tainted by self-interest. With expense payments, legislators in 1978 typically were paid $17,800, or about $2,000 less than the state's 1979 median income. Sabo's state salary plus expenses in 1978 may have reached $20,000. By comparison, members of the US House in 1977 were paid $57,500. In hindsight, any suggestion that Sabo was overpaid as a legislator seems laughable. But so does overreliance on per diem to compensate legislators—a practice that persists a half century later.[16]

Campaigning on Taxes

Till's other advertising shot at Sabo noted that the DFL House speaker had failed to push hard for major state tax relief in 1977–78. The charge was fair. Sabo eventually agreed in 1978 with a modest income tax cut, but he dragged his feet all session, preferring to beef up state aid to low-income property taxpayers and to safeguard the state's unstable budget surplus rather than reduce income taxes.

Nationally, Republicans had begun a chorus of complaint about federal income taxes that would culminate in 1981 with enactment of one of the largest tax cuts in the nation's history, giving the preponderance of relief to the nation's wealthiest taxpayers. Till was enamored of the idea that cutting taxes would stimulate the economy sufficiently to improve the lot of average Americans and generate enough tax revenue to keep government programs solvent—all without causing inflation, he claimed. Minnesotans who followed his campaign were witness to a preview of the "supply-side economics" theory that would be touted by Ronald Reagan in his 1980 presidential campaign. Till called for a 10 percent reduction in federal taxation in year one and, as a goal, an additional 10 percent cut in each of the subsequent two years. "We can absorb a 10-percent cut without losing vital services," he assured, telling voters that mere efficiency improvements would keep programs functional. He refused to say whether, or which, spending reductions might be required.[17]

Till had never crafted a public sector budget. Sabo had a major role in designing and enacting five of them over the previous ten years. He understood how simplistic and unrealistic Till's proposals were—and who would be ill served if Till's ideas were enacted.

For the first time in his eighteen-year political career, Sabo was waging a relatively high-visibility campaign. Sabo vs. Till wasn't as attention-getting as was Anderson vs. Boschwitz or Short vs. Durenberger that year. But the Fifth District race was generating enough notice for the *Minneapolis Star* to ask Sabo to respond in some detail to Till's tax proposal. He relished the opportunity. It allowed him to describe the two guiding principles that drove his thinking about government finance: balanced budgets and progressive taxation. Both would make government better serve the people who need government most, he believed.

"I don't know anyone who doesn't like to cut taxes. But I have to be responsible," Sabo told the *Star*'s Robert Whereatt. "I can't tell people their taxes will be cut and we'll get more programs"—not without major deficit spending. Sabo allowed that he favored reducing Social Security taxes, which fell disproportionately hard on lower-income Americans. He wanted to use the progressive federal income tax to pay for the nonpension portion of Social Security outlays. He also believed that defense spending was bloated; now that the Vietnam War had ended, it could be modestly reduced.

But "it is inaccurate to tell people that there will be large, huge, massive cuts in federal spending. That is simply unrealistic," Sabo said. He explained that federal, state, and local spending were entwined in several ways. Cutting federal spending would inevitably push more burden for necessary government services onto state and local governments, which relied more on sales and property taxes. Those are regressive taxes, costing lower-income people a proportionately larger share of their incomes than wealthier earners paid.

"What you end up with is a massive shift from the progressive income tax to the [regressive] property tax. That clearly is not a good trade-off," Sabo said. "That is not the way tax policy in this country should go."

He said more about how best to hold down property taxes in response to the *Tribune*'s Voters' Guide, published on October 31. "Local property taxes can best be controlled by maintaining an adequate system of support for local governments from the federal government and the states," he said. "Aid to cities such as federal revenue sharing should be continued and strengthened," not cut.[18]

That nuanced message was not what Americans were hearing from other candidates in 1978. On June 6 California voters had surprised the nation with their overwhelming approval of Proposition 13, a statewide cut in and limit on property taxation. From that election day forward, anti-tax messages echoed in campaigns around the country. The *Star*'s Whereatt alluded to as much, noting: "It's like swearing in church or spitting into the wind. There are some things that rational people just don't do. You do not tell voters in an election year that you cannot support a massive federal tax cut. You do not tell voters you are against huge slashes in the federal budget. But Martin O. Sabo, a DFLer, is telling people that he is against those things."[19]

About that "O"

Martin's middle name, Olav, or his middle initial appeared consistently on legislative ballots during elections from 1960 to 1976. Early in his career, he might have believed that using his distinctively

Norwegian middle name could be an asset in what was then a heavily Scandinavian part of Minneapolis. It may also have simply been his bow to the full-name formality of the era. But Sabo did not often cite his middle name as he toiled at the Legislature, and the Capitol press corps did not often mention it either. He was called simply "Martin Sabo." (Those who called him "Marty" did not know him well.)

Reporters took note, however, when he filed for election in 1978 as "Martin Olav Sabo." Under the subhead "Ya, Shure, Yew Betchew," the *Minneapolis Star* took a teasing jab at Sabo for employing his full name "for some reason or other" on the congressional ballot. The implication was that use of his full name was a ploy, intended to curry favor in the congressional district. Unfazed, Sabo continued to use his full given name when he filed for office for the rest of his career.[20]

Legislators' Jitters

While Sabo was honing his congressional campaign message, several dozen House DFL "Watergate babies" were groping for a message that would help them sustain their political careers. Elected for the first time in either 1974 or 1976, the members of this relatively youthful legislative cohort found themselves navigating rougher political waters than they had previously sailed. Watergate had receded in voters' memories. Wendell Anderson, Rudy Perpich, and Don Fraser were now in voters' sights.

Six years earlier, when the top of the Democratic ticket was in trouble in Minnesota, Martin Sabo and state party chair Richard Moe had offered legislative candidates a simple, appealing message about openness in government that helped them stand apart from presidential nominee George McGovern. But in 1978 Sabo had his own campaign to run and Dick Moe was in Washington, serving Vice President Walter Mondale as chief of staff. When it came to messaging, DFL candidates in 1978 were largely on their own.

"We were rudderless," remembered Ted Suss, a second-term representative from Prior Lake. "I don't think there was a caucus effort to keep us on message. In fact, we didn't have a caucus message. Never once was there a communication from the caucus that said, 'Here's our message. Here are the things the DFL majority has done that are good for Minnesota.'"[21]

Richard Cohen was a twenty-eight-year-old first-term House member from St. Paul's upscale Highland Park area. He had won in 1976 by nearly a thousand votes. But as he knocked on doors in the summer and fall of 1978, he sensed that this year would be different. "It was a sour year," he recalled decades later. Too many voters brought up unpopular votes he had cast for a legislative pay raise, a pension upgrade, and a new professional football and baseball stadium. His Independent-Republican opponent, insurance agent John Drew, was attacking Cohen for those votes.

Sabo had been loath to advise legislators representing swing districts to vote against potentially unpopular bills. "Martin's view was, be responsible. Run government as you think you should. Don't worry about the politics. As long as you also work for your district, you'll be fine," Cohen said. "Well, that's not always true."[22]

Suss told a similar story. He once struggled with how to vote on a bill he knew would be unpopular with his constituents. Sabo supported the measure. "Martin called me into his office and said, 'You should vote how you want to vote. But think of how you will feel if you voted against a good bill because you thought you had to in order to win reelection, and then you lose anyway.' His message was: 'Do the right thing and let the chips fall where they may.' That summed up his philosophy."

A pair of twenty-nine-year-olds serving their third terms, Russell Stanton of Marshall and Robert Vanasek of New Prague, were among the members of the House DFL caucus campaign steering committee. Several months before the election, they tried to warn the committee about the political headwinds they were encountering. "We could feel the vibes at the door," Stanton said years later. Their concerns were dismissed. One more-senior committee member, Jim Rice of Minneapolis, accused Stanton of being a "whiner, always running scared." That was easy for Rice to say from the security of one of the most heavily DFL districts in the state. Stanton's district in the state's southwestern corner had a different partisan complexion.[23]

Sabo did not participate in those meetings, Stanton recalled. Neither did he travel outside the Fifth District to campaign for House candidates, as he had done in the previous four election cycles. "Martin's energies were focused on running for Congress," Stanton said.

His absence left a void. Sabo had been the glue that held his large caucus together. When he departed, fissures quickly appeared over who would replace him. Irv Anderson, majority leader in 1977–78, was positioned to assume the top job. But Anderson's abrupt, abrasive style cost him support, particularly among younger legislators. Stanton was "one of the leaders of a House faction hoping to prevent Majority Leader Irv Anderson from becoming speaker," the *Minneapolis Tribune* reported.[24]

"There was a lot of division within the caucus," Stanton said. "I had the sense that the leadership wasn't focused on winning the election."

In fact, few political observers in the state that summer and fall thought that DFLers were at risk of losing control of the state House. Since the 1974 election DFLers had enjoyed the largest House majorities in state history. They entered the campaign season with 99 of the chamber's 134 seats—a 64-seat advantage over Independent-Republicans. It seemed unfathomable that a margin that large could be erased in a single election.

Cohen's alarm about the negative reception he received as he campaigned prompted him to do something he believes no previous Minnesota House candidate had done. He commissioned a poll. University of Minnesota political scientist John Sullivan lived in Cohen's district and offered to conduct a random-sample measure of district voters' opinions on the impending election. The results confirmed Cohen's impression. The poll found him losing to John Drew.

What Cohen did with those results says much about attitudes and relationships within the House DFL caucus that fall. Cohen chose to not share the findings with Irv Anderson or the caucus steering committee. He feared unpleasant repercussions for him "if word got out that Cohen thinks he's going to lose."[25]

The Final Push

Sabo sailed to an easy primary victory on September 12, winning more than 80 percent of the vote against two token opponents. But any joy that news brought him drained away as the primary night gave way to a bitter morning-after for DFL insiders. Their endorsed candidate for Humphrey's US Senate seat, Don Fraser, lost to Robert Short by fewer than 3,500 votes. Short's support came largely from Greater Minnesota and was overwhelming on the DFL-dominated Iron Range.

Sabo had known and admired Fraser for more than twenty years. He had attended DFL meetings in Fraser's home in southeast Minneapolis while he was still a student at Augsburg College and Fraser was a state senator. He likely recognized Fraser's serious-minded approach to public policy as a trait they shared. It had to rankle Sabo to watch Fraser, a career public servant, fall to a well-heeled maverick who had never held elective office.

But personal disappointment was not what most troubled Sabo and other metro-area DFL candidates in the days after the primary. Rather, they worried about their voters' unhappiness with the top of the party's ticket and how that sentiment would affect them.

"At door after door in the days after the primary, Democrats told me, 'I'm just not going to vote this time,'" recalled Wes Skoglund. He was seeking a third term in the state House and was already aware before the primary that voters in his southeastern Minneapolis district were critical of Wendell Anderson and Rudy Perpich. After the primary "they were really mad at Bob Short" for what they believed was an unfair campaign against Fraser. "It was a storm. People in my district knew and loved Don Fraser. Some told me they were going to vote for [Republican Dave] Durenberger. But some just weren't going to vote" in the general election.

That would spell trouble in November, Skoglund knew. He reported as much to DFL campaign officials. "When we complained, we were ignored. We were afterthoughts," he said.[26]

Sabo's exchange with one unhappy voter two weeks after the primary occurred in the presence of *Minneapolis Tribune* reporter Jim Parsons, giving Parsons a vivid story lede. After a brief conversation at the door with homeowner Sue Feinstein, she followed Sabo up the street to demand, "What are you going to do about Bob Short?" She wanted him and other DFL leaders to publicly disavow the primary winner, not cozy up to him, as Walter Mondale and Muriel Humphrey had already done.

"Well, I don't think you are going to find many Democrats recommending that people vote for Short's opponent," Sabo unflappably replied before continuing down the street. Parsons lingered with Feinstein long enough to learn that though she customarily voted for DFL candidates, she was undecided this time—about the Fifth District race as well as the top of the ticket.[27]

Despite that unsettled context and Mike Till's October media blitz, Sabo stuck with his tried-and-true formula to finish the campaign. He opted against hiring a full-time campaign manager and maintained his modest budget. (The October 23 campaign finance report showed him spending $58,609 compared with Till's $104,960.) With a small army of volunteers at his side, Sabo doubled down on door-knocking in vote-rich precincts. He personally pounded scores of lawn signs in supporters' yards. He was generous with his time when journalists asked for interviews. "Nothing beats personal contact, especially with the candidate or someone who believes in the candidate," he said. Parsons reported that the candidate conveyed serene confidence.[28]

Still, it must have been gratifying—and maybe a relief—when both Minneapolis daily newspapers gave him solid endorsements days before the election. The *Star* called him "an expert in the art of government, tough and pragmatic with just a touch of idealism." The *Tribune* described him as possessing a "becoming confidence, in himself and in Fifth District voters." That editorial added, "He is particularly strong in his knowledge of federal-state-local relations." The editorial's writer had spotted what would be a Sabo specialty for the remainder of his career.[29]

The newspaper endorsement that might have pleased Sabo most came not from the big dailies, but from Augsburg College's student newspaper, the *Echo*. It said about Augsburg's alumnus of the class of 1959: "Sabo has done more for Minnesota in the areas of education and housing than any other legislator we can recall. The education aids formula and one of the finest state housing agencies in the nation were the result of his excellent legislative leadership. . . . The country, as well as Minnesota, needs men like Martin Olav Sabo."[30]

The Minnesota Massacre

"Republicans Lead Major Races" was the *Minneapolis Tribune*'s page-one banner headline the morning after the November 7 election. Senate candidate Dave Durenberger led the statewide ballot, defeating Robert Short with 61 percent of the vote. Rudy Boschwitz ousted Wendell Anderson from the US Senate by garnering 57 percent. Rudy Perpich's first stint as governor ended with Al Quie getting 53 percent of the vote. (Perpich would be back in the 1980s.)

In a yearbook-style display, the *Tribune*'s front page featured mug shots of "Minnesota's vote leaders." In the top row next to photos of Republicans Durenberger, Boschwitz, Quie, and Third District Representative Bill Frenzel was the image of just one DFLer—Martin Olav Sabo. He had carried the Fifth District decisively with 62 percent of the vote.[31]

Sabo had survived the election that Republicans dubbed "the Minnesota massacre," a name that has stuck through the ensuing five decades. But many of Sabo's allies in the Minnesota House were not as fortunate. Bill Kelly, the Taxes committee chair who may have been Sabo's most devoted lieutenant, was among the losers that night. Russ Stanton lost to future Republican gubernatorial candidate Cal Ludeman in southwestern Minnesota. Several dozen DFL "Watergate babies" were defeated, including Richard Cohen, Wes Skoglund, and Ted Suss. The final count in the House was a tie, 67 DFLers, 67 Independent-Republicans. The House would convene in January 1979 with no majority and, courtesy of a mutually unsatisfying deal, a strained power-sharing arrangement that would last for less than a year. Republican Rod Searle was the next speaker; DFLer Irv Anderson was the new Rules committee chair.

When asked to comment on the House tie, Sabo mildly noted a few days after the election, "I always think the legislature works better if there is a majority for one side or the other."[32]

Those restrained words understated Sabo's feelings as he absorbed what the voters had wrought. "Martin was shell-shocked after the election," Cohen said years later, describing a conversation he had with Sabo after Cohen's defeat was clear. "He had been so sure that we'd be fine. His entire theory of legislative politics had been demolished."[33]

Like Thomas P. "Tip" O'Neill, the US House speaker who would welcome Sabo to Washington days after the election, Sabo held that "all politics are local." Mind your district—be visible, go to meetings, respond promptly to constituent calls, bring home the bacon when state money is doled out for infrastructure or programs—and one need not worry about reelection, Sabo believed.

Nicholas Coleman (right) with Martin Sabo in 1979.

That formula did not work in 1978, teaching DFL leaders a bitter lesson and spurring changes in the way Minnesota legislators campaigned. Future legislative elections would feature much more involvement by caucus leaders in candidate recruitment and messaging. Particularly in swing districts, candidates would make more use of direct mail, broadcast advertising, and, eventually, social media to reach voters. Door-knocking would continue to be widely practiced but would no longer be relied upon as the sole or primary means of reaching voters. Henceforward, legislative campaigns would become more costly, with candidates more dependent on big-donor support, including from sources outside Minnesota. And few candidates in closely contested races would adhere to Sabo's rule about declining to speak ill of one's opponent. Attack ads became much more commonplace. Those changes would not come all at once. But a new direction was set in 1978 that within a few years would make Sabo-style campaigns seem antiquated.

"Martin was a brilliant legislative leader, in terms of both policy substance and the relationships he developed," Cohen said in summation of Sabo's Minnesota legislative career. "But his political acumen was from a different era."

CHAPTER ELEVEN

CONGRESSMAN SABO

IT'S NATURAL TO THINK OF MARTIN SABO'S CAREER AS HAVING two parts, the first eighteen years in the Minnesota House, the last twenty-eight years in the US House of Representatives. But Sabo's congressional service can also be seen as a continuation of all he had learned and accomplished as a state legislator. He may have understood it that way himself.

"I did not consider running for Congress to be running for higher office," he told an academic interviewer in 2006. "I considered it at best a lateral move, and maybe less. . . . I would not trade my time in the Legislature for any of the time in Washington."[1]

Sabo's goal—to make government a better servant of average people—was fixed throughout the decades. Many of the issues he tackled in Washington—housing, health care, progressive taxation—were the same ones he had championed in St. Paul. His stewardship of the public purse continued, animated by his understanding that government is less able to meet people's needs if it is hobbled by debt.

Several of the people he called to his side as he built his congressional staff in 1979 had been aides and allies in Minnesota. David Bieging, an unsuccessful DFL state House candidate from Stillwater in 1972, worked in St. Paul after law school as an administrative assistant to DFL majority leader Irv Anderson and next in Washington as a special assistant to Vice President Walter Mondale, reporting to Mondale's chief of staff, former DFL state chair Richard Moe. He became the first chief of staff in Sabo's congressional office. Eileen Baumgartner, the agile number cruncher who had most recently been a nonpartisan aide to the House Taxes committee, moved to Washington to become his legislative director. ("He called me the day after the election" to offer her the job, Baumgartner said years later. "I would have killed him if he hadn't.") John Haynes, who had worked alongside Sabo and Baumgartner to develop the Minnesota Miracle funding formulas in 1971, also joined Sabo's congressional staff, moving to the Cannon House Office Building from the US Senate office of departing Senator Wendell Anderson.[2]

Joe Graba took charge of Sabo's Minneapolis office. Graba, a former biology teacher and a reliable Sabo ally during three terms in the state House, had left the Legislature after the 1976 session to serve as deputy commissioner of education. That job ended with the first Perpich administration. It was a fortuitous development for Sabo, who was delighted to have his able, amiable friend in charge of congressional services in the district.

Graba would stay only two years. He went next to work for another friend and political ally, Roger Moe, when Moe became state Senate majority leader in 1981. Graba's successor in Sabo's shop also came from the Minnesota House. Kathleen Clarke Anderson had been a House committee clerk during Sabo's years. She became a mainstay in Sabo's Minneapolis congressional office, serving as his local eyes and ears for nearly a quarter century.

Mr. Sabo Goes to Washington

New members of the US House often aspire to serve on committees with real clout but have to settle for something more mundane in their first few terms. But Martin Sabo was not just another freshman. His record as a three-term speaker of the Minnesota Legislature and a founder and recent past president of the National Conference of State Legislatures set him apart. He was a known quantity to several members of the majority caucus's fifteen-member steering and policy committee, which worked with Speaker Thomas P. "Tip" O'Neill to make committee assignments. Those whom Sabo did not know, Walter Mondale did, and Bieging's Mondale connection opened doors for Sabo to get acquainted.

As he had done in every previous election in his life, Sabo started door-knocking—making systematic one-on-one calls on steering committee members. He found a ready backer in the Midwest regional representative on that committee, Bill Ford of Michigan. A less-expected ally was House Rules committee chair Richard Bolling of Kansas City. Sabo discovered that at the start of his political career in 1948, Bolling had come into the orbit of Hubert Humphrey and Americans for Democratic Action. Bolling correctly judged Sabo to be part of Humphrey's political lineage.[3]

Given Sabo's tax policy expertise—and that of Baumgartner and Haynes—his first choice was assignment to the House Ways and Means committee, which has jurisdiction over revenue raising. However, a more senior member of the Minnesota delegation, Eighth District Representative James Oberstar, was angling for a spot on that committee. Sabo yielded, out of respect both for the institution's tradition of seniority preference and for Jim Oberstar, who had spent a dozen years in Washington as a congressional aide before being elected in his own right in 1974.[4]

Instead, Sabo switched his sights to the Appropriations committee, the discretionary-spending counterpart to Ways and Means and one whose coveted seats were rarely awarded to freshmen. Sabo analyzed the situation in late 1978 and saw the potential for a change in that custom, but not necessarily in his favor. The nation's most populous state, California, had lost several Democratic members on the committee, "and the only people going for Appropriations from California were freshmen," he recalled years later. One or more of those first-termers would be tapped for Appropriations, he surmised, minimizing his own chances.

"I'd quit working for it," Sabo said. "All of a sudden, I was pleasantly surprised. I got a call that I was on." The news was reported on January 16, 1979. Sabo later learned that Bolling "apparently made a hard push for me." The Rules committee chair liked the fact that Sabo represented a relatively safe district and hence would likely be around for the long haul and "able to take some tough votes," Sabo said.[5]

Subcommittee appointments were announced a few days later, and Sabo was pleased again. His two—Housing and Urban Affairs, and Transportation—dealt with federal spending on those topics and a few more. Baumgartner, who staffed Sabo's work on the housing panel, said that in those years it also oversaw budgets for smaller agencies as diverse as the National Science Foundation, the National Aeronautics and Space Administration (NASA), and the Environmental Protection Agency. The mix made the work more interesting, she said. John Haynes took the transportation subcommittee staff assignment and soon found himself immersed in the arcanery of urban transit funding. It would become a Sabo specialty.[6]

"Our entry to Congress was enjoyable," Baumgartner said. Sabo "loved being there. There was a lot more volume of work, but it was easier than the work he'd been doing in St. Paul—because he wasn't as responsible for the outcome, not at first anyway."[7]

Sabo's committee assignments put him on a track toward significant responsibility and possibly—someday—a House leadership role. It had taken Sabo eight years in the Minnesota House to become minority leader, and that was considered a rapid rise. The leadership escalator in the US House moved even more slowly and less reliably. But he had made an auspicious start.

Building Relationships

For Martin and Sylvia, the decision to move their family to Washington was easily made. Most members of Congress in those years made that choice, and many likely would be surprised and dismayed to learn that a half century later such moves have become uncommon. The Sabo family was ready for a larger house—they chose a handsome, newly constructed, brick-fronted colonial model in suburban Vienna, Virginia—and new schools for Karin, fourteen, and Julie, twelve. Sylvia resumed her nursing career by first enrolling in the University of

Virginia's continuing education program to update her requisite certification. For a time she worked in a lamp shop, interacting with customers as she had learned to do in her father's grocery store.

With perhaps a tinge of regret, the Sabos sold their home in the Seward neighborhood in Minneapolis. "Martin would always say there's no place like Seward," his sister-in-law Margaret Bostelmann said. The Sabos often described the neighborhood as "pious and politically progressive," with a bent toward the Norwegian Lutheran culture of nearby Augsburg College. They would not find anything as culturally familiar in the DC suburbs.[8]

Sylvia and Margaret's parents had retired in Minneapolis and spent winters in warmer climes. During Martin's first years in Washington, his in-laws' home would be his landing pad when returned to the city on weekends and during congressional recesses. Often his weekend trips back to Minnesota involved only one night away from his wife and daughters. He grew impatient if he found himself with too much downtime away from them. Later, when those daughters were young adults, Martin and Sylvia bought a condominium in Minneapolis to serve as their home base.[9]

Martin was undoubtedly pleased by his family's enthusiasm for their move. But his primary motive for relocation was the advantage it brought to his work. He arrived in Washington with a deep appreciation for the value of strong relationships among members of a legislative body. He saw human connection as a lawmaking tool. He held that living close at hand with other members of the US House would help him build relationships, which in turn would help him succeed.

"When I came, most members moved their families here," Sabo told an interviewer as he prepared to retire in 2006. "There was more socializing. Both within and across party lines, people got to know each other better. The work week was longer, so there was more time for informal meetings." He lamented the change in those patterns that began with the GOP takeover of the House in 1994. The new norm—members spending only three nights a week in Washington, with families left behind in their districts—was making bipartisan governance more difficult, he said. "Now there isn't time for people to talk to each other. The whole atmosphere is more separate. Anytime people don't know each other, there's a certain edge that develops that doesn't exist if people know each other."[10]

During the workweek when Congress was in session, Sabo adhered to a daily routine that included time for relationship building, said Michael Erlandson, who spent nineteen years in Sabo's congressional office, fourteen of them as chief of staff. At midafternoon, Sabo would announce to his staff that he was "going to the library." In fact, Erlandson said, they knew he was going to the House gym, often to play a little pick-up basketball with other male members of Congress. After matches that may have been more notable for trash talk than athleticism, those imitation jocks—Republicans and Democrats—would retire to the steam room. The relationships Sabo developed in that setting may not have sprung up anywhere else. For example, Erlandson said, Sabo became a good friend of Barney Frank, a loquacious House member from Massachusetts. Frank was two years' Sabo's junior, a Jew originally from New Jersey, a Harvard graduate, and the first openly gay member of Congress.[11]

Sylvia was Martin's companion and asset as he set out to become well acquainted with his new colleagues. She joined the congressional wives' club and was soon much involved in organizing annual luncheons and creating fundraising cookbooks. She enjoyed hosting small gatherings in their home and joining other couples for evenings of card games. Her skill at baking Scandinavian pastries won her acclaim. The growing maturity of their daughters—and the family's improved financial status—afforded the Sabos more opportunity for evening socializing in Washington than they had enjoyed in Minnesota.[12]

"I don't think there's any question that Martin preferred serving in the Legislature to Congress. He never enjoyed a job better than being speaker of the House," attested Erlandson. "That said, he loved the energy of Congress. He liked the [congressional delegation] trips. He liked going to events with Sylvia. And he loved his colleagues."[13]

Play Ball

Martin Sabo also loved baseball. He may have resented Bob Short almost as much for moving the Washington Senators to Texas in 1972 as for defeating Don Fraser in the 1978 US Senate DFL primary. As a new resident of the greater Washington, DC, area in 1979, he no longer had a local major-league team to follow—though his devotion to the Minnesota Twins never wavered.

Sabo soon discovered that he had an opportunity to play ball himself. House Democrats were looking for a second baseman for their squad in the annual match between House Republicans and Democrats that had been played for fun and charity since the early 1960s. Though well past his prime playing days in North Dakota town ball, Sabo was an eager recruit. The activity offered a happy intersection of Sabo's love of baseball, desire to better know his colleagues, competitive spirit, and preference for good clean fun. In 1987 he became the Democrats' team manager. He would hold that post for eighteen years.[14]

The games presented players with ample opportunities for bruises, muscle strains, and trash talk and Washington reporters with a chance for some good-natured ribbing of the politicians-cum-athletes. "Sabo hits right, throws right and votes left, according to the official game program published by *Roll Call* newspaper," the *Star Tribune* reported. *Roll Call* was among the game's sponsors.[15]

The players typically donned the uniforms of their home districts' major league baseball teams. In 1982 Sabo wore a Twins uniform bearing number 6, the retired number of Twins hitting star Tony Oliva. Sabo and Oliva had developed a connection. Sabo had helped Oliva's family in Cuba obtain visitor visas. Steve Berg of the *Minneapolis Star and Tribune*—himself a Minnesota Twins fan—allowed: "On a soggy night in Foggy Bottom, Martin Olav Sabo, the congressman from Minneapolis, proved what a lot of baseball fans back in the Twin Cities already know: Nearly anyone these days can wear a Minnesota Twins uniform." Berg then reported a strong performance by the forty-four-year-old rookie second baseman, including a flashy infield catch of a fly ball hit by Texas Representative Ron Paul and a run scored after being hit by a pitch at the plate, followed by two stolen bases. The Democrats won that match seven to five.[16]

Such triumphs—on and off the field—were rarer for Democrats after Republicans gained control of the House in 1994. The GOP fielded a more athletic crew than Democrats could muster, despite Sabo's exertions as a talent scout among newly elected Democrats. "They average about 10 years younger than us," Sabo said in 2006. He shared his coaching advice: "Swing the bat and try and hit the ball. Don't make it too complicated."[17]

Representative Mike Doyle of Pennsylvania told a *Star Tribune* reporter, "My first day in Congress, I'm in line for a picture, and this guy walks up to me and says, 'Can you throw?' I said, 'What are you talking about?' He says, 'Can you throw a baseball? I'm Martin Sabo, and I coach the Democrats.'" Doyle succeeded Sabo as the Democrats' coach in 2006. Sabo's record as a coach: five wins, thirteen losses.[18]

Doing the Work

As he had done two decades earlier in the Minnesota House, Sabo made himself a student of the rules, traditions, and governing responsibilities of the US House. "We are elected to do a job," he said at the end of his tenure, explaining his approach to the work. "That job is being in Washington . . . not simply passing an occasional law, but to be involved in significant oversight, significant committee hearings, and significant amount of communication back and forth with other members. For a legislative body to work, you have to have good committees functioning." Politicking took a back seat with him, as he thought it should for any serious member of Congress. "There's plenty of time for doing politics and still to do our jobs," he said.[19]

That head-down, shoulder-to-the-wheel approach to congressional service did not win him much external attention during his first few terms. But it was noticed and appreciated inside the House and would serve him well over the long haul. So predicted Representative David Obey, a Wisconsin Democrat whose district abutted

Minnesota and who also served on the House Appropriations committee. Though Sabo's age contemporary, Obey had served ten years longer in the House and was thus positioned to be both Sabo's mentor and his friend. Eileen Baumgartner described Obey as "Martin's big brother" in the House.[20]

"Martin is straight Midwest," Obey told reporter Steve Berg in 1983. "He is a very plain, unadorned person; there's no pretense about him. But he's got a lot of savvy. . . . He's very much the antithesis of the cheap-shot artists that populate this place. That's the only way you can be effective here over the long haul." The headline on Berg's story reinforced the prospect of Sabo's durability. "Sabo Set for Long Haul in House," it said.[21]

Characteristically, Sabo declined Berg's invitation to talk about his political aspirations. "I'm not one who believes in planning for 10 or 20 years ahead," he said. "You try to deal with your opportunities as they come along." But it was already clear that Sabo would likely spend the rest of his political career in the US House. Running for statewide office—governor or US senator—did not appeal to him. His long suit was oversight and management of the heart of the federal government, its budget. He aimed to climb in seniority toward ever-greater fiscal responsibility. Already in 1983 he ranked second to the chair of the House Appropriations committee's transportation subcommittee, a position of considerable clout in dispensing federal money to highway and transit projects, such as the upgrade of US Highway 12 to Interstate Highway 394 in Hennepin County.

If Sabo's climb someday was to go higher, to House majority leader or speaker, he did not encourage such talk, Berg reported. But Berg heard it from Sabo's colleagues on both sides of the aisle.

"I've always been a great fan of Martin Sabo," vouched Republican US Representative Bill Frenzel, who had served with Sabo in the Minnesota House before being elected to the US House from the west-suburban Third District in 1970. Frenzel complimented Sabo's humility and practicality, while nevertheless calling Sabo's position on issues "obsoletely liberal."[22]

Another Minnesota Republican, US Representative Vin Weber of the Sixth District in southwestern Minnesota, wasn't even sure about that. "We Republicans always thought he was more conservative than he was," Weber said years later.[23]

Sabo's interest in achieving a balanced budget may have created that impression. Few other urban liberal Democrats were as conspicuously supportive of ending the annual budget deficits that had become habitual in the federal government. Sabo saw no inconsistency in his support for both more public-assistance spending and balanced budgets. He understood that if debt service was allowed to consume an ever-larger share of federal revenues, government's capacity to support the needs of the poor and middle class would diminish. Discretionary spending of the type he favored would disproportionately suffer, he knew, since it would always be more politically vulnerable than spending on defense or middle-class entitlements.

Defense spending was politically charged, Sabo knew, and not just because keeping the nation's military well financed was popular among members of Congress with military contractors and installations in their districts. Particularly in the wake of the Vietnam War, defense spending was also distinctly unpopular in some liberal circles, and those circles were present in Minnesota's Fifth District, to which few federal defense dollars flowed. "Politics of the Fifth District, probably you'd get in more trouble voting for a defense bill than anything else," Sabo said years later, explaining why he initially turned down several opportunities for appointment to the powerful Defense subcommittee of the House Appropriations committee before accepting the assignment in 1987, at the start of his fifth term. "I felt badly I had not done it" earlier, he confessed.[24]

Sabo likely recognized that a grip on the nation's defense budget would be an asset for him, should he have a chance to take on even more responsibility for the national purse. What's more, he knew, that chance would be more likely to come if other House members saw and trusted him as someone schooled in defense spending. Sabo kept his spot on the transportation subcommittee, let go of housing, and dug in on such arcanery as missile defense systems, fighter aircraft fleets, and military housing and health care. Transportation and defense budgets would be his specialties for the remainder of his House career.[25]

Two years after Sabo said yes to the defense subcommittee, he was rewarded as one of five members of the Appropriations committee assigned to the House Budget committee. It was a coveted assignment. The Budget committee is charged with drafting each year's budget resolution, which sets spending targets in more than twenty categories throughout the federal government. It functions as an overseer and coordinator of both the Appropriations and Ways and Means committees. Its chair, elected by the majority caucus, ranked among the half dozen top caucus leaders. In 1989 that seat was filled by a California Democrat who, like Sabo, had earned a reputation for fiscal responsibility, so much so that his nickname was "Mr. Budget." His name was Leon Panetta.

Chairman Sabo

The 1992 election was a changemaker for Sabo—and not just because the primary challenge posed by Lisa Neibauer Stall in the newly redesigned Fifth District (described in the previous chapter) jolted Sabo into mounting a campaign unlike any he had run before. He stepped up fundraising, hired a pollster, aired television ads, and dispatched key aides such as Eileen Baumgartner to Minnesota to assist the campaign. In other words, he finally did what colleagues in swing districts did routinely in every election. Making those changes didn't come easily to him. "Martin hated fundraising," said his longtime aide Erlandson. "Fortunately, for most of his career, he didn't have to do much of it." He spent campaign funds frugally, often having sums left over that he could donate to other candidates.[26]

On November 3, 1992, Sabo won an eighth term in a seven-person contest, capturing 63 percent of the vote. American voters that day also elected a new president, William J. "Bill" Clinton. Almost immediately the grapevine among House committee staffers reported to Sabo chief of staff Baumgartner—and she reported to Sabo—that Panetta would likely be Clinton's choice to head the Office of

Management and Budget in the executive branch. That would create an opening for a new Budget committee chair.[27]

Baumgartner approached Sabo. "'Would you be interested in running for budget chair?' Sure, he'd be interested," Baumgartner recalled years later. Shortly thereafter, she told him, "'It's going to happen. You'd better get ready; it's going to happen soon.'"[28]

Sabo promptly started systematically knocking on the doors of the "voters," in this case the other 255 members of the incoming 1993–94 Democratic caucus. He discovered he would face an opponent when he called a more conservative member, John Spratt of South Carolina, to ask for support. Spratt replied that he intended to run for Budget committee chair as well but had not started seeking commitments from House members. That last bit of information undoubtedly made Sabo smile. He liked being ahead of the competition.

Martin and Sylvia stayed in Washington during the 1992 Christmas holidays—a rare move for them—so that Martin's quest for commitments of support from his colleagues could press on. He spent long hours listening to the spending concerns of his colleagues before asking for their support. Erlandson was tasked with helping Sabo count votes. It was an exacting and exhausting assignment. Sabo insisted on hearing from three different sources that a colleague intended to support him before he would add that colleague's name to his running count.[29]

Baumgartner was riding herd on both the staff and her boss. She related that on the Friday night before the election, Sabo was attempting to leave the office and meet Sylvia before he had made calls to potential supporters whom Baumgartner believed were persuadable. "'You know, you need to make those calls.' He said 'I'll do it Monday morning.' I said, 'Martin, they're moving us [to a new office suite] this weekend. I don't know if we'll have phones Monday morning. Make the calls now.' Our press secretary was sitting there laughing. He said, 'Oh, Martin, I'm so glad to see that the whip cracks upward too.'"[30]

The Sabo team's effort to obtain a credible vote count allowed him to walk confidently into the January 6, 1993, caucus meeting at which secret ballots would be cast. Sabo defeated Spratt on a 149 to

112 vote. That was two votes fewer than he and Erlandson expected. Sabo appeared unruffled and gracious when speaking to reporters, pledging to support the new president's program. In private, however, Sabo was agitated, Erlandson said. "Who were the two liars? It drove Martin crazy!"[31]

The Politics of Fiscal Policy

Sabo was not alone in making deficit reduction a priority in 1993. President Clinton arrived in the White House as a former Arkansas governor, accustomed to the balanced budget requirement under which US states routinely operate. He also heard loud and clear the message voters sent in the three-way 1992 presidential election. Clinton won handily, earning 370 of the 535 electoral votes. But third-party candidate Ross Perot captured 19 percent of the popular vote, holding Clinton's share to 43 percent. Perot's signature campaign theme was criticism of persistent deficit spending by Congress and the swelling national debt, which since 1980 had climbed from about 30 percent to more than 60 percent of the nation's annual gross domestic product. The Texas businessman's call for fiscal responsibility was heard sympathetically in the districts of many House Democrats, some of whom emerged from the 1992 election unnerved by a perception that the nation's political winds were shifting. The new House Budget committee chairman found more support than he expected among his fellow House members for putting the federal budget back in the black.[32]

That sentiment propelled the first step in 1993 budget-setting, the enactment of a blueprint budget resolution to guide the decisions of spending subcommittees in the remainder of the year. The House resolution cut spending $63 billion more than Clinton's own budget had proposed. "They thought they had gone as far as they could go," Baumgartner said of the original Clinton budget, which Leon Panetta had engineered. "Leon didn't realize how much the caucus in the House had changed."[33]

The resolution also called for a significant tax increase, which was anathema to Republicans. In all, the measure aimed to achieve a half-trillion-dollar reduction in the deficit by 1998. It won House approval on March 18, 1993, by a 243 to 183 vote, with only eleven Democrats voting "no" with the Republicans. That much Democratic unity was seen as a major victory for Clinton—but credit also flowed to Sabo. A *Minneapolis Star Tribune* analysis called Sabo "essential" to the resolution's approval. "He capitalized on his familiarity and trust among liberals and conservatives alike," the newspaper reported, adding, "this was his first opportunity on the national stage to demonstrate the insider skills that made him successful during 18 years in the Minnesota House."[34]

Passing a starting-point resolution was one thing; passing an actual budget would be another. There would be few, if any, bipartisan deals struck in the thirteen House appropriations subcommittees. Republican minority leader Newt Gingrich insisted that his caucus's role was to oppose and defeat Democrats, not help them govern. "The Republicans essentially walked away from that process," Panetta said years later. "Democrats would have to pass the budget on their own." Thus ensued many meetings among Democrats on Capitol Hill and at the White House during the spring and summer, hammering out a difficult consensus on what became known as the Deficit Reduction Act of 1993. In those sessions, Panetta said, "Marty was an ally. He would come to the White House for the leadership meetings. I can't tell you how encouraged I was when I would see Marty's face, because I knew there would be a strong voice at the table for doing what's right. He understood the politics, but he also really cared about getting the job done."[35]

A final bill was ready for House and Senate votes in early August. It made upper-income earners shoulder a larger share of the federal tax burden while giving a break to lower-income earners via an increase in the earned income tax credit. The bill increased income taxes for high-income individuals and high-earning corporations, raised the gas tax, lifted the income cap on withholding taxes for Medicare, and increased the share of Social Security benefits that were subject to taxation. It also made $255 billion in spending cuts over a five-year period, with the bulk of those cuts falling on the military and Medicare.[36]

Sabo appreciated the progressive tilt of the tax policy the budget bill contained. But he was never content, in 1993 or any other year, when a major budget bill was assembled exclusively by one party, his own or the Republicans. "Martin believed that a bill that couldn't get any support from the other side of the aisle was a bill that was troubled," remembered Sabo aide Erlandson. "When you need to negotiate your entire position to keep your own caucus together, you have nothing left to bring to the other side to negotiate. You wind up with a weaker bill and more partisanship in the institution. That ate away at him."[37]

The 1993 package's long implementation time meant its full fiscal effect would not be seen until 1998, when the federal government experienced its first budget surplus in thirty years. It was a major achievement and a rare one. But its political effect was felt much sooner and was not positive for Democrats. Republican opposition to the bill's tax increases was ferocious, giving Democrats in swing districts a bad case of jitters. House and Senate Democratic leaders allowed as many of their number as they could spare to vote against the bill—but they were determined that the bill would pass. Speaker Tom Foley and his leadership team—Sabo among them—leaned hard on some reluctant members to vote "yes." The vote in the House on August 5 followed party lines and reached the bare minimum needed for enactment—218 to 216. In the Senate the next day, Vice President Al Gore cast a tie-breaking vote, giving the bill a 51 to 50 send-off to the president's desk.

In the House, a Republican alternative bill containing deeper spending cuts and no tax increases was defeated with a much more lopsided vote, 138 to 295. That alternative's front man, Representative John Kasich of Ohio—the Republican ranking member on Sabo's budget committee—had to conclude that the spending cuts he had been touting were even more unpopular in the House than were the tax increases in the Democrats' bill.

But that did nothing to stifle Republican criticism of the tax increases Sabo had helped engineer, nor did it stop Kasich from seeking bigger budget cuts. Allied with a Minnesota Democrat, Representative Tim Penny of the First District, Kasich came closer to success with a proposal to cut an additional $37 billion, mostly in Medicare spending.

Minnesotans might have been surprised by Penny's emergence as a fiscal policy ally of Kasich, not of Sabo. As a college student at Winona State University, Penny had been an intern on Sabo's legislative staff in 1971. A dozen years later, when Penny and his young family moved to Washington to begin his congressional career, Sabo helped Penny find rental housing in the Sabos' neighborhood, provided him rides to work, and invited him to pick-up basketball games in the House gym. Those games didn't last long for Penny. Norm Dicks, a burly House member from Washington state, collided with Penny and broke a bone in Penny's foot.

"I didn't turn out exactly as he had hoped," Penny said years later about his relationship with Sabo on fiscal policy. "But I never heard him utter an unkind word about any other member of the House, including me." When Penny retired in 1994 after six terms, Sabo was among the colleagues who spoke at Penny's retirement party.[38]

The Penny-Kasich budget proposal went down on a 213 to 219 vote, with Sabo leading the opposition. Sabo made clear that he did not oppose more cuts in Medicare spending, as that plan envisioned. His disagreement was over how the funds thus saved would be used. He wanted to employ them to support the start-up of expanded health insurance coverage for the working poor, under a plan being touted by First Lady Hillary Rodham Clinton. That plan was still alive in November 1993; ten months later it was declared politically dead in Congress. The expansion of health insurance coverage for lower-income Americans would not be accomplished for another sixteen years.[39]

Kasich, a future governor of Ohio and Republican presidential contender, must have been extremely busy rounding up support for his alternative measure during the days before the House votes on August 5. That makes all the more remarkable the letter to the editor he found time to write and send to the *Minneapolis Star Tribune* on or about August 2. Published on August 4 and headlined "Sabo at the Budget Helm," the letter said Sabo "has worked hard to ensure that Republican committee members are treated fairly." He "deserves praise for the manner in which he has presided over the committee this year. He is truly a gentleman."[40]

Such cross-party public testimonials were rare then. Thirty years later, they have all but vanished from American politics. Kasich affirmed in 2024 that his opinion of Sabo had not changed. "Martin was a great professional. He had a job to do, I had a job to do, and we did it together. We saw things differently, but it never resulted in any animosity whatsoever. He never tried to shut anybody down. He was a good man."[41]

November 1994

"The whole country was nuts on the subject of taxes," Eileen Baumgartner said years later, explaining the political heat that attached to the Deficit Reduction Act of 1993 well into 1994. She and Sabo tried to take down the temperature by arming House Democrats with "Dear Colleague" letters and information packets about various aspects of the budget bill. Those plain-language letters, sent over Sabo's signature on newly designed "House Budget Committee Democratic Caucus" stationery, were put in colleagues' hands at the start of long weekends and congressional recesses to arm them with talking points they could use to rebut critics in their home districts.[42]

House Republican candidates were countering with anti-tax talking points of their own. Their ideas jelled six weeks before the 1994 congressional election into a policy-and-practice reform package called "Contract with America." Signed by more than three hundred GOP House candidates, its ideas were largely those Republicans had touted for years. But their packaging and well-publicized push from fiery minority leader Newt Gingrich gave them widespread attention and succeeded in nationalizing House races in a manner seldom seen before. It promised to balance the federal budget while both cutting taxes and increasing military spending.

Sabo and Baumgartner promptly issued an analysis that attempted to point out how unrealistic—and damaging—the Republican plan would be. To balance the budget in five years while shielding military spending from cuts, other outlays would need to be cut by at least 20 percent, their analysis said. What's more, the GOP's proposed tax cuts would primarily benefit affluent Americans, Sabo pointed out—much as had federal tax cuts enacted in the 1980s. "Republicans are gambling that voters won't blame them for the record of the 1980s, when Ronald Reagan made virtually the same pledge and the nation sank deeply into a debt that is now constricting programs for everyone from inner-city children to farmers," the *Minneapolis Star Tribune* reported.[43]

Their message was not working, Baumgartner sensed. Though she was a budget analyst by trade, twenty years of working for elected officials had made Baumgartner an astute political prognosticator as well. All during the summer and fall of 1994, she sensed that the forty-year reign of Democrats in the House majority was coming to an end. It was a feeling she shared with fellow congressional staffers and, undoubtedly, with her longtime boss. "The country had changed. . . . The country wanted something different," she recalled years later.[44]

Though Sabo won reelection in 1994 with his customary solid margin—receiving 62 percent of the vote—Democratic members of the US House around the country faired far worse. Republicans made a net gain of 54 seats in the 435-member House and 8 seats in the 100-member Senate and took the majority in both chambers for the first time since 1953. Sabo's opportunity to chair a House committee had vanished, never to return for the remainder of his career.

Some commentators blamed the 1993 tax increases for the Democrats' losses in 1994. In an interview a dozen years later, Sabo rejected that analysis. "I thought there were many other things that were more important" to public unhappiness than were the tax increases, he said. "I thought our failure (to act) after the high visibility of health care, to not be able to do anything, contributed more to our loss of control." A controversial crime control bill may also have been a factor, he said.

So were the tactics of "a group of Republicans who were very aggressive about trying to get out of the minority, and their strategy was to tear down the institution."

But, he added, "sometimes there's just a mood that we want to change things."[45]

The Blue Dogs

House rules limiting tenure on committees allowed Sabo two years as ranking minority member on the Budget committee. Its new chair in 1995 was John Kasich. Sabo and Kasich, friendly competitors on the House basketball court and in the committee room, had switched roles. Sabo explored offering the committee or the entire House a Democratic alternative budget, much as Kasich had done for Republicans in 1993. But "we could not figure out how to do one with the whole caucus," Sabo said years later. The caucus was split between urban liberals and a smaller, mostly rural faction of fiscal conservatives that jelled in the wake of the 1994 election. The latter group was dubbed "Blue Dog Democrats," so named because one of them claimed they had been "choked blue" by liberals in their caucus and were organizing to defend themselves. Representatives Collin Peterson of Minnesota's Seventh Congressional District and David Minge of Minnesota's Sixth District were among its members.[46]

In a quiet way in the fall of 1995, so was Martin Sabo. He consulted with the group to make sure the alternative plan they were developing was workable. "I eventually went in conversations with them, and we got enough modifications to their plan that I supported their version," Sabo said. "They were viewed as a small splinter group that would have maybe gotten twenty or twenty-five votes." When Sabo got through with it, upward of half of the 204-member Democratic minority caucus was behind the bill. "We got what we thought was a pretty responsible budget," Sabo said. It would have created a balanced budget over a span of seven years, not the ten years President Clinton was proposing, while avoiding the deep cuts in social programs Republicans sought. But it called on Clinton to accept larger spending cuts than he favored and Republicans to abandon plans for a major tax cut.[47]

Neither Clinton nor Gingrich were prepared to compromise in November 1995. The result was two government shutdowns, November 14–29, 1995, and December 16, 1995–January 6, 1996. During those periods, Sabo was one of eight Democrats involved in talks with Republicans that aimed to resolve the impasse. He also served as one of several Democratic spokespeople, including appearances on NBC-TV's *Meet the Press* Sunday morning show and CNN's *Larry King Live*. Sabo faulted Republicans for insisting on cutting taxes. "A rather strange way to get a balanced budget is to borrow more money to go deeper in debt to pay for a tax cut," Sabo said on CNN a few days before Christmas. "That's what Republicans are doing."[48]

On December 7 Clinton adopted the Blue Dog notion of a seven-year timeline for achieving a balanced budget, along with some of the subcaucus's ideas for spending restraint. That move was not enough to avert the longer and more politically damaging shutdown. Baumgartner chalked up the shutdown to Republican political miscalculation. "They thought the president would suffer for it," she said. In fact, by January 1996 polls showed that voters blamed Republicans for the negative consequences of shuttering government services. They were the ones to capitulate. The Blue Dog compromise was not fully embraced, but it had played a constructive role. Sabo's contributions had won respect for the Blue Dog proposal and likely contributed to the caucus's endurance as a voice for fiscal restraint. It had fifty-four members at its peak in 2009, when Democrats controlled the House; in 2024, with Democrats in the minority, its membership was down to ten.[49]

Transportation

House rules required that Sabo's time on the House Budget committee ended with the 104th Congress. In 1997 he was back on the House Appropriations committee and a leading Democratic voice on the Transportation and National Security subcommittees. There, he could leave his mark on the meat-and-potatoes of government work—the stuff he valued. "He just settled in there and made seniority work for him—and for us," observed former Vice President Walter Mondale in 2006 as he summed up Sabo's career.[50]

Sabo once remarked that when he listened to other committees, "all the exotic issues they were dealing with, it sounded sort of interesting." But when "I watched at the end of the year, nothing ever happened in any of those. Our bills had to be there, they had to pass, and they became law."[51]

He put considerable time and energy into the creation and implementation of the Department of Homeland Security after the attack on Washington and New York on September 11, 2001. "They'd shoved a dozen troubled agencies into one department," Erlandson said. "Martin wondered how to make them better in the process." That question dogged him as he attended every relevant hearing and boned up on the intricacies of the agency's work. "He always went to hearings with his own questions as well as questions the staff prepared for him," Erlandson said. "The staff would listen to him and ask, 'Why didn't we think of that?'"[52]

Becoming the ranking Democrat on the transportation subcommittee allowed Sabo to excel in the perennial congressional competition to "bring home the bacon"—in this case, money for roads, bridges, and transit. A 1997 analysis by the *Star Tribune* found that during the previous four years Sabo had secured nearly $88 million for Twin Cities transit projects, including a $12 million start for the region's first light rail line. He had "delivered the goods again," the newspaper reported.[53]

He did so again when funds were needed to restore the 1883 Stone Arch Bridge near downtown Minneapolis and build a new pedestrian/bicycle suspension bridge over Hiawatha Avenue, which became difficult to cross after light rail trains began running alongside that thoroughfare in 2004. In tribute to his effort, the Minneapolis City Council in 2005 named the Hiawatha crossing the Martin Olav Sabo Bridge.[54]

Cyclists heading east on the Martin Olav Sabo Bridge.

Sabo undoubtedly appreciated that accolade. But he may have taken as much pride in preserving routine bus service and holding down bus fares as he did in any new bridge or rail line. He was a protector of funding for mass transit operations around the country, knowing that such subsidies prevented fare increases. Tim Penny said that as part of the so-called Porkbusters group of House fiscal conservatives in the early 1990s, he attempted to reduce an appropriation for Metro Transit in the Twin Cities. He encountered unexpectedly fierce opposition from Sabo, he recalled. "In Penny's district they may call this pork, but in the Twin Cities, we call them buses," Sabo reportedly said as he beat back Penny's amendment.[55]

Sabo's hands on federal financial levers also allowed him to be helpful to his district when unusual needs arose. Greg Ortale, the former president of the Minneapolis convention bureau Meet

Minneapolis, told of one such instance. In 1998 the city had landed the Plenipotentiary Conference of the International Telecommunications Union, a major international conference hosted by the US State Department for the first time since 1947. Its organizers required the reservation of a large share of the city's hotel rooms for a full thirty days. When many attendees opted to attend far fewer than thirty days, the city's hotels "were about to take a serious hit," Ortale said. Vance Opperman, a leading DFL donor and cochair of the local host committee, suggested seeking help from Sabo. Soon Ortale, Opperman, and Dick Graham, the convention bureau's executive director, were on their way to Washington to meet with the congressman.[56]

They were surprised when Sabo arrived at their meeting wearing a baseball uniform. He had come from a practice session with the Democrats' charity baseball team that he managed. "Martin was so casual about it. He listened carefully and promised to look into it. A couple of days later, we had more than enough to take care of the hotels," Ortale said.[57]

Equity and Democracy

Not all of Sabo's legislative ventures were successful. Sabo demonstrated notable persistence with one that was not. Beginning in 1991 and in each remaining year of his congressional career, Sabo introduced a corporate tax measure he called the Income Equity Act. It would have denied corporations tax deductions on any executive compensation that exceeded twenty-five times the amount the business was paying its lowest-paid worker.

Sabo knew full well that his idea was not likely to become law. But he insisted on proposing it anyway, issuing a release and offering reporters interviews on the subject each time. He was not trying to penalize executives, he said. His aim was to raise wages for workers at the lowest rungs of corporate pay ladders. That effort went to the heart of Sabo's philosophy about government's rightful role as an ally of average people. He wanted to mitigate the tendency of unfettered capitalism to make the rich richer while the poor become more numerous. That trend is destructive of the basic fabric of American society, Sabo maintained. Over time, he argued, it would destroy democracy.[58]

"Government has a responsibility to combat income polarization," he told *Star Tribune* reporter Jessica Thompson in 2001. "The people who are benefitting the most from our economy at the top need to be somewhat concerned about what happens to those at the bottom end of the economic scale." He was making the same argument fourteen years later: "Unless the corporate leadership, businesses in general, deal with this issue, you're not going to solve it . . . it's got to be something that happens within corporate culture in this country to pay people throughout their companies a better wage."[59]

Sabo was not a socialist. He was not attempting to dictate executive compensation in the private sector. "He's merely capping the taxpayer's liability in this game," noted a *Star Tribune* editorial that urged Congress to take Sabo's point seriously. It never did. By 2006, when Sabo retired, the gap between CEO and worker pay had grown four times larger than it had been when he first introduced his bill in 1991.[60]

CHAPTER TWELVE

THE LIBERAL DECENTRALIST

IN MID-MARCH 2006—JUST PAST HIS SIXTY-EIGHTH BIRTHDAY and just seven weeks before the Fifth District DFL convention would meet to endorse its 2006 candidate for the US House—Martin Sabo decided to retire.

"He thought about it for a fairly long time," said aide Michael Erlandson. But Sabo did not announce his decision to anyone on his staff, including Erlandson, until shortly before he stood before reporters in Minneapolis on March 18 to wipe a tear and declare that twenty-three campaigns for elective office were enough. He would not stand for reelection.[1]

Was he tired? "A little," Erlandson said. Was he discouraged? "I don't think so. His patience had worn thinner, I'd say." He was surely bothered by the fact that the budget surplus he had worked hard to create in the late 1990s had been erased in the early 2000s by recession, a tax cut, and a war he opposed.

Was he ill? "No," Erlandson said. "Clearly he was slowing down, but he could easily have served a couple more years." It was a question reporters posed as well, knowing Sabo's affinity for tobacco. The *Star Tribune* reported that Sabo "said his health and energy levels were good. Sabo quit smoking cold turkey two years ago after 45 years of a two-pack-a-day habit."[2]

Rather than citing any of those things, Sabo explained his decision as a gut feeling that "the time is right." He had done what he intended to do in elective office. He was at peace with his accomplishments. Now it was time for someone younger to shoulder that responsibility.

He soon had that someone in mind—Erlandson. The staffer said he did not discuss the possibility of running for the House with his boss until a few days after the March 18 announcement. When he did, Sabo offered his enthusiastic backing. When Erlandson filed his candidacy at the secretary of state's office on July 6, Sabo was at his side. But that show of support—and Erlandson's service as DFL state chair from 1999 to 2005—were not sufficient to win either DFL endorsement or the September 12 DFL primary. Both went to Keith Ellison, a state representative from north Minneapolis. Ellison succeeded Sabo and became the first Muslim member of the US House. In 2018 Ellison was elected Minnesota's attorney general.[3]

When Ellison took office, he joined the House majority. Democrats were back in charge in 2007, just as Sabo was cleaning out his spacious office in the Rayburn House Office Building. House members who had been his peers on the Appropriations committee—Nancy Pelosi and Steny Hoyer—were the new speaker and majority leader, respectively. Had he known that he could spend one more term in the majority as the chair of a major committee—or even been a candidate for one of the top jobs—might he have opted to not retire? Erlandson does not think so. "He'd 'been there, done that' with regard to chairing a committee," he said. "He was at peace with his time in Congress."[4]

Sabo moved home to Minneapolis, to the downtown condominium he and Sylvia had purchased some years before. They went to their six grandchildren's events. He attended Minnesota Twins home games, Trinity Lutheran Church services, and civic meetings. In 2011 DFL Governor Mark Dayton appointed him to the ballpark authority that oversees Target Field, then the new home of the Minnesota Twins. He was a board member of Growth & Justice in Minnesota; cochair of the National Transportation Policy Project at the Bipartisan Policy Center in Washington, DC; a leader on the Committee for a Responsible Federal Budget; and, as always, an active alumnus at Augsburg College. The Sabo Center for Democracy and Citizenship at his alma mater seeks to instill in students Sabo's passion for democratic engagement and government service.[5]

And when invited to do so, Sabo explained his thinking about how state and federal governments ought to work for the betterment of all of their citizens, and how they were falling short. Here is some of what he said:

- "I call myself a liberal decentralist," Sabo said in an oral history interview in 2015. He latched onto that label "not because of ideology, but from experience on how government works best. It's a mistake to think that decisions on how best to run programs should be top down, whether from Washington, the state or the school district." When possible, Sabo wanted to empower local governments to make decisions about what government does and how it functions. He suspected that large state or federal bureaucracies were inefficient and less than optimally effective.

  For example, he said, "I don't think the federal government has the capacity to run education from Washington. I don't know that the Minneapolis Central [School District] Office has the capacity to run individual schools. . . . It's a mistake to think that decisions on how best to run programs should be top down. It's also a mistake to forget the important but limited role of government in providing services that can't be, or aren't, provided in other ways."[6]

- State attention to affordable housing lagged in the decades after Sabo left the Legislature, he said in 2007. The result has been concentration of poverty and the societal ills it brings that he believed could have been avoided.

  "I thought what we did in the 1970s eliminated all the reasons for there not being dispersal of low-income housing for families throughout the metropolitan area. . . . But from the 1980s on, we've had increased concentration of low-income housing for families in the central cities and some suburbs. Somehow, that issue was not dealt with. That's one of the reasons we're having problems in the central cities today. It should not have happened."[7]

- Sabo held that to function well, governments should avoid excessive debt and chronic deficits. Yet he rejected calls for a constitutional amendment requiring a balanced federal budget. "I think that'd be a disaster," he said in 2015, noting the need for a robust federal response in times of national emergency. But a balanced budget requirement is "a plus at the state level," he said. "Everything drags on in Washington . . . the committees basically don't work. The conference committees end up being in the hands of a handful of leaders who, in the end, are not nearly as smart, or their staff is not nearly as smart, as they think they are. It's not very good."[8]

  He held out hope for a long-term "grand bargain" between the two political parties that would bring debt down to more sustainable levels. In that spirit, in 2013 he agreed to cochair the Minnesota branch of the national Campaign to Fix the Debt. His Minnesota counterparts were former Republican US Senator Rudy Boschwitz and former Independence Party gubernatorial candidate (and Sabo's former House colleague) Tim Penny.[9]

- "I think the growing gap between the top and the bottom in this country is a very fundamental problem. Clearly, we should very significantly increase the minimum wage. But that's only part of (what's needed). The capacity of labor to organize is incredibly important. That's been weakened over the years. The industrial workers of this country didn't become middle class because government mandated it. It's because government put in the process where they could organize and bargain collectively." Protecting that process is vital, Sabo argued.[10]

- "I think government is there to try to help people." Sabo continued. Providing financial security for retirees and the disabled is among government's fundamental responsibilities, he maintained. The solvency of Social Security and Medicare must be prioritized. "I think Social Security is great. The sooner we fix the long-term Social Security [funding] question—which some modest modifications could take care of—the better." He scoffed at those who argue that Social Security is a twentieth-century idea that won't long endure in the twenty-first century. "It's going to be around.

It's important to have it there, with a defined benefit and a lifetime guarantee. . . . With the disappearance of regular pension plans, you need to have something that is guaranteed for a lifetime."[11]

But Sabo would not go so far as to shield Social Security and Medicare from cost reductions as part of larger budget-balancing plans. "To my friends on the left who say we can spare the entitlement side and cut enough from discretionary spending, they should think about food safety programs and environmental programs and regulatory agencies and education and everything else that would absolutely get clobbered if we tried to shelter entitlements from any cuts."[12]

Saying Goodbye

Many of those words were spoken in a gravelly voice with the halting cadence of someone who was slightly winded and laboring for each breath. A tube supplying oxygen from a portable tank was attached to Sabo's face in September 2015 as he answered questions posed by his old friends and former colleagues Joe Graba and Edward Dirkswager as part of an oral history project. Sabo was afflicted with chronic obstructive pulmonary disease. It was a progressive condition that was sapping his strength and making him appear older than his years.

"He put off using oxygen for as long as possible," said his elder daughter, Karin Mantor. Even after oxygen use became unavoidable, he did not let it make him housebound. He still appeared at family events, Twins games, church services, and a Norwegian American men's club.[13]

"He never stopped paying attention to policy and politics," Erlandson said. "Our conversations were 50 percent about sports and 50 percent about politics or policy." Sabo was quick to comment if an Augsburg College team had defeated a team from Erlandson's alma mater, St. John's University in Collegeville. In 2016 he shared with Erlandson his support for Hillary Clinton's presidential campaign and unhappiness about the direction Donald Trump was taking the Republican Party. "He was a student of what was going on in Minnesota and Washington until the very end."[14]

The end came on March 13, 2016, at Abbott Northwestern Hospital in Minneapolis, where he had been hospitalized for a week with difficulty breathing. At his side in his last hours were family members including Sylvia, Karin, and Julie. The day before they had serenaded him with "Take Me Out to the Ballgame." His sister, Anna Marie Heusers, survived him; his mother, Klara Haga Sabo, had died in 1996 at age ninety-four.[15]

Tributes poured forth from around the country. The *New York Times* praised him for a "quiet Scandinavian demeanor" that "conveyed a sense of civility during increasingly partisan times." Lois Gibson, the challenger he defeated for DFL endorsement to launch his congressional career in 1978, said in a letter to the editor of the *Star Tribune*, "I know the party did the right thing. Sabo was an outstanding congressman."[16]

For its own part, the *Star Tribune* noted that it had become fashionable in America to disdain "career politicians." The editorial board wrote that "Sabo was a 'career politician' . . . so deeply committed to representative democracy that he made doing it well his life's work. That commitment deserves appreciation, not denigration. This state and nation are better for it."[17]

Legacy in Lives

"Martin Sabo planted seeds in people," Sheletta Brundidge said. "I'm one of his seeds. I'm part of his harvest."

Seventeen years had passed since Sabo left office; seven years had passed since he died. Yet the mention of his name during a chance encounter among acquaintances at a St. Paul post office was enough to prompt a fulsome recounting of an experience with Sabo that had happened twenty-five years earlier.[18]

Brundidge is well known in the Twin Cities as a comedian, radio talk show host, public television and newspaper commentator, podcaster, and advocate for racial justice and Black businesses. Less known is that she is a native of Texas and that her first connection with Minnesota was made in Washington, DC, as an intern in the office of Representative Martin Sabo. A University of Houston student, she was the recipient of a fellowship named after the late US Representative Mickey Leland, who had died in a plane crash while on a congressional trip to Ethiopia in 1989.[19]

"When I was assigned to Martin's office, I had to look for Minnesota on the map. Why Minnesota? Why not Texas?" Brundidge said. She soon learned that Leland and Sabo had been friends—and that she had landed well.

"I had a better experience than the other Leland Fellows," she said, relating that she was the only Leland Fellow and the only Black intern among several others in Sabo's office. "I got a chance to go to major meetings. I went to weekend lunches, breakfasts, places, and spaces where other interns couldn't go. I went to the State of the Union speech. The rest of the Leland Fellows were watching it on TV. All that was part of Martin's plan.

"Martin embodied Minnesota Nice. He took the time to talk to us. He made sure that the staff interacted with us. He made me feel so welcome. It was not just 'Hi, how are you?' He got to know our families, our siblings' names. He was so intentional about being inclusive."

Brundidge counts that experience as her first professional job. It provided her with a model that she has sought to follow ever since, she said. "Martin's staff loved him. I saw a team of people who would run through a brick wall for him," she said. The experience eased her path years later to a permanent home in the Twin Cities.

"Times have changed. People have not," Brundidge observed. "The heart of that man was good and true. He walked the walk. I felt that."

What Sabo Knew

If Martin Sabo had still been a member of the US House on November 29, 2022, the vote on Representative Ilhan Omar's post office–naming bill would not have been unanimous, Sabo's longtime chief of staff vouched. "He would have been the one dissenting vote on the bill to name this place after him," Mike Erlandson said, to the appreciative chuckles of assembled Sabo family, friends, and admirers. They knew well Martin's discomfort when he was the object of what he considered excessive attention and praise.

Nevertheless, Erlandson told the crowd (including this author) in the sleek art deco lobby on March 18, 2024, Sabo likely would have warmed to the idea of being associated with a US post office. He was a champion of basic government services, the sort that average people rely on throughout the nation, from cities like Minneapolis to remote hamlets like Alkabo, North Dakota. He liked to be associated with the sort of people employed by the post office—hard workers who exercised brain and brawn each day for the public good, and who, thanks to their union's persistent bargaining, had decent wages, benefits, and pensions.

Sabo also might have enjoyed seeing his name attached to this building in particular. The place formerly known simply as the Minneapolis Post Office is an architectural masterpiece. It's a large, handsome expanse that, when it was new in 1933, must have been welcomed as a signal of civic optimism during tough economic times. It testifies to the ambition of Minneapolitans to reclaim their city's prosperity and resume its growth. Situated downtown near the Falls of St. Anthony, the Martin Olav Sabo Post Office is a temple of public service at the region's historic economic epicenter. There, it tacitly asserts that government has been and continues to be as necessary as commerce and industry in building a good life in the Upper Midwest. Sabo would have concurred.

The human span of Sabo's forty-six years in public life was reflected that morning in the Sabo Post Office. His daughters and sister-in-law were present—undoubtedly keenly missing Sylvia, who died in October 2022. So were former legislators, members of Congress, members of the Minneapolis City Council, members of his staff, and friends and admirers.

The physical span of his work was invoked. Sabo's ability to "bring home the bacon" gave Minneapolis a light rail transit network, the Midtown Greenway, makeovers of the Stone Arch and Hennepin Avenue Bridges, new facilities at the Minneapolis Veterans Administration Medical Center, parking garages, bicycle lanes, pollution cleanup, and more.

Already, Sabo's visage had been cast in bronze and permanently installed in two public spaces in the Twin Cities in gratitude for his sponsorship of federal funding for local projects. At the University of St. Thomas in St. Paul, a 1997 plaque on an outdoor pillar salutes Sabo for obtaining $15.5 million in federal funds for a new science and engineering center on campus. "Without his efforts, the center would not be a reality," the inscription says. And at the Diana E. Murphy Federal Courthouse in downtown Minneapolis, a 2022 plaque salutes Sabo for securing funding for "countless projects," including the 1997 court headquarters.[20]

At the post office, Ilhan Omar, first elected to Sabo's former seat in 2018, praised Sabo's commitment to balancing the federal budget while still championing spending on government services that would "give everyone the chance not just to get by, but to get ahead through hard work." Representative Betty McCollum, who has served the St. Paul–dominated Fourth District since 2000, told of Sabo's kindness to her when she was a rookie member of Congress. He liked to joke that since they represented the Twin Cities, "I was his twin sister," McCollum said with a wistful laugh.

The listeners seemed especially still as Senator Amy Klobuchar described Sabo's commitment to civility in public affairs—the absence of which in American politics was keenly felt in 2024. Klobuchar said that Sabo once told her—not boastfully, but as advice to a protégé—"I don't recall ever making a negative statement about a colleague." The memory of those words, and their value, have grown for Klobuchar through three terms in the US Senate, she said. She has come to appreciate what Sabo knew: if American democracy is to endure and flourish, its practitioners must treat each other with respect. For him, kindness and fairness were more than lessons he learned in Lutheran Sunday school. They were essential disciplines for those intent on making democracy work.

Ways, Means, and the Ultimate Goal

How to assess Sabo's legacy? It's much more than a rail line or a bike path, more than his name on a post office, a bridge, or an academic program at his alma mater. It's even larger than the public policies he helped craft and enact, significant though many of them were. It lies more fully in Sabo's effort to make local, state, and federal governments more responsible and responsive to the people they are intended to serve. That work produced its most notable achievements in the Minnesota Legislature of the 1970s, transforming an archaic, unambitious institution into a potent instrument for the betterment of Minnesotans' lives. The work continued in Washington, where he led efforts to make the federal government solvent so that it could be a dependable ally to the American people.

The man who approached me to write this book at the behest of a group of Sabo friends wanted to lift up something more.

"I'm hung up on leadership," Bill Kelly said. "I know no one more intent than Martin was on making the system work better for all the right reasons."[21]

At age eighty-two in 2022, Kelly was ailing with the cancer that would take his life on July 31, 2023. Like his friend Sabo, Kelly had a lifelong love affair with representative democracy. As Sabo did at the end of his life, Kelly was watching with dismay as elected officials often appeared to put short-term electoral advantage ahead of the long-term interests of the state and nation.

Winning the next election was never Sabo's ultimate goal, Kelly said. Good governance was. The temptations of political expediency—the demonizing of opponents, the twisting of facts into half-truths and even lies, the shilling for campaign donors—were to be avoided because they undermined good governance.

"Martin's view came out of his North Dakota experience, growing up in a small town. You give a damn about the whole thing. Not just your own career or your own glory. It's, 'How does the whole place function? What can you do to make that better?' That's what he educated us about," Kelly said.

That's what leadership in American government should be about.

ACKNOWLEDGMENTS

THIS BOOK OWES ITS ORIGIN TO THE DEEP ADMIRATION A small group of friends had for Martin Sabo. Bill Kelly, Tom Berg, Edward Dirkswager, Eileen Baumgartner, Jim Solem, and Joe Graba met regularly for years. Their meetings inspired Tom Berg's book about the Minnesota Legislature's accomplishments in the 1970s, *Minnesota's Miracle: Learning from the Government that Worked* (University of Minnesota Press, 2012). Sabo often joined the group and participated in the preparation of Berg's important volume. After Sabo's death in 2016, the meetings continued, and conversation turned to the possibility of a more fulsome telling of his story. Given my own respect for Sabo, I happily accepted the group's assignment in 2022. Each member of that group made considerable contributions to bringing this book to fruition, serving as funders, counselors, editors, and vital sources along the way. I consider this book their work as much as mine.

I discovered that people who knew Martin Sabo were eager to share their stories with me. In a few cases people who heard from others about my project contacted me to volunteer their memories. That's rare in the experience of a political journalist.

Sabo daughters, Karin Mantor and Julie Sabo, were generous in sharing family lore and papers and, in Julie's case, accompanying me to interview Anna Marie Sabo Heubers, Martin's sister and a resident of a care facility in Plymouth, Minnesota. Gary Rust, Martin's childhood friend who today lives in Fortuna, North Dakota, painted a vivid verbal picture of life in Alkabo in the 1940s and 1950s. Allan and Margaret Bostelmann told me about young Sylvia Lee, Margaret's sister and Sabo's wife of fifty-three years.

Augsburg College of the 1950s came into view for me in conversations with Jim and Elaine Pederson, Joanne Stiles Laird, Vicki Skor Pearson, Grace Kemmer Sulerud, and Garry Hesser. Winston Chrislock described the special bond that developed between his father, professor Carl Chrislock, and the shy young student from North Dakota. Lyall Schwarzkopf, who knew Sabo as a Riverside Avenue neighbor before becoming his legislative colleague, also shared information about Augsburg, where his father-in-law was a professor. Vivian Jenkins Nelsen, who joined the Augsburg faculty in 1969 and became a nationally known diversity consultant, described Augsburg's commitment to civil rights.

A host of people who watched Sabo's legislative career shared their memories. At the risk of unintentional omission, for which I apologize, I thank Jack Davies, Pat Davies, John Haynes, Patrick Mendis, Robert Vanasek, Joan Anderson Growe, Harry "Tex" Sieben, Michael Sieben, Ted Kolderie, Paul Gilje, Richard Moe, James Nobles, Roger Moe, Wyman Spano, Henry Savelkoul, Ted Suss, Richard Cohen, Wes Skoglund, Russ Stanton, Gerry Knickerbocker, Andrew Kozak, and Phyllis Kahn. Bill Pound, the longtime leader of the National Conference of State Legislatures, invited me to his home in Colorado and briefed me on Sabo's importance to that organization's start. I was greatly helped by the privately published memoir of the late Gerald Christenson, a gift he gave me during the final months of his life with the message that he expected I might find it useful one day. So true, Jerry!

Memories of Sabo's congressional career were supplied by Michael Erlandson, Leon Panetta, John Kasich, Vin Weber, Tim Penny, George Latimer, Sheletta Brundidge, and Greg Ortale—and, at the naming ceremony for the Martin Olav Sabo Post Office, by Ilhan Omar, Betty McCollum, and Amy Klobuchar. Thanks to them all.

I am honored to work again with the publishing and marketing professionals at Minnesota Historical Society Press, who on three previous occasions have brought my books to fruition. Ann Regan, a legendary editor at the press, retired not long after giving this project her blessing—a crucial first step. Ryan Hemmer, Shannon Pennefeather, and freelancer Deborah Schoenholz provided much-appreciated editing.

My first and most valuable editor—and partner in all things—is my husband, Martin Vos. He's a thorough and thoughtful copy editor, an ever-ready sounding board, and a consistent source of support for this and my previous books. I'm very lucky and enormously grateful.

NOTES

See bibliography for full citation details. Also see the acknowledgments to learn more about interviewees and others who contributed to the narrative.

Notes to Chapter One: Alkabo's Son

Quotes from friends and family in Chapter 1 are taken from the following interviews: Anna Marie Huesers; Julie Sabo; Vicki Skor Pearson; Karin Sabo Mantor and Julie Sabo; and Gary Rust.

1. Dura, "Alkaba N.D."
2. "Map," Kulturminnesøk, accessed January 17, 2025, https://tinyurl.com/vbpn5kv5; Hasle, "The Migration of Tradition."
3. "Homestead Act (1862)," Milestone Documents, National Archives website, accessed January 17, 2025, https://www.archives.gov/milestone-documents/homestead-act.
4. Leininger, *Portraits of Prairie Pioneers*, 195–99.
5. Leininger, *Portraits of Prairie Pioneers*, 195; Julie Sabo interview.
6. Leininger, *Portraits of Prairie Pioneers*, 196.
7. "Writing Rock State Historic Site," State Historical Society of North Dakota, accessed January 26, 2025, https://www.history.nd.gov/historicsites/writingrock/.
8. Michael Truman, "Alkabo School," *The View from Here* (blog), April 5, 2018, http://everybodyhastobesomewhere.blogspot.com/2018/04/alkabo-school.html.

9. "Martin Olav Sabo: A Journey through Forty-Six Years in the Minnesota House and the United States Congress," oral history interview, September 14, 2015, Martin Olav Sabo Papers, Minnesota Historical Society, St. Paul.

10. "Our History," Association of Free Lutheran Churches, accessed January 26, 2025, https://www.aflc.org/about-us/history-of-the-aflc.

11. "Home Page," Metigoche Ministries, accessed January 26, 2025, https://metigosheministries.com/.

12. Szczur, "Norwegian Settlement in North Dakota," 93–94.

13. "The Birth of the Nonpartisan League," Bank of North Dakota, accessed January 26, 2025, https://tinyurl.com/3bas4pep.

14. Leininger, *Portraits of Prairie Pioneers*, 197.

15. "Lesson 3: Building Communities, Topic 1: Youth Organizations, Section 1: YCL," North Dakota Studies, State Historical Society of North Dakota, accessed January 27, 2025, https://tinyurl.com/52bcrax4.

16. "Lesson 3: Building Communities, Topic 4: Communications, Section 2: Radio," North Dakota Studies, State Historical Society of North Dakota, accessed January 27, 2025, https://tinyurl.com/hbbctcnc.

17. Oral history interview, Sabo Papers, 5; Leininger, *Portraits of Prairie Pioneers*, 197.

18. "Year of First State Driver License Law and First Driver Examination," Department of Transportation, Federal Highway Administration, accessed January 27, 2025, https://www.fhwa.dot.gov/ohim/summary95/dl230.pdf.

19. Oral history interview, Sabo Papers.

20. Leininger, *Portraits of Prairie Pioneers*, 197.

Notes to Chapter Two: Pivot to the City

1. Oral history interview, Sabo Papers.

2. "Top 100 Biggest US Cities by Population," Biggest Cities, accessed January 27, 2025, https://www.biggestuscities.com.

3. Chrislock, *From Fjord to Freeway*, 229.

4. Chrislock, *From Fjord to Freeway*, 162.

5. Chrislock, *From Fjord to Freeway*, 140–62, 170.

6. Holt, "Bernhard Christensen," 3. Chrislock, *From Fjord to Freeway*, 173, reports the year of Christensen joining the faculty as 1930.

7. Joanne Stiles Laird interview; "Augsburgian 1957," 11, Augsburg University Archives, accessed January 30, 2025, https://archives.augsburg.edu/islandora/object/AUGrepository%3A3681#page/5/mode/2up/search/1957.

8. Chrislock, *From Fjord to Freeway*, 224.

9. Holt, "Bernhard Christensen," 3.

10. Pamela Miller, "Carl Chrislock, Augsburg Professor and Historian," *Minneapolis Star Tribune*, September 29, 2001; see also Adamo, "Martin Olav Sabo for Congress."

11. Holt, "Bernhard Christensen," 3. Christensen and his wife, Gracia, frequently opened the on-campus president's house for Bible study, prayer groups, and hospitality. Carl Chrislock, *The Progressive Era in Minnesota, 1899–1918* (Minnesota Historical Society, 1971).

12. Chrislock, *From Fjord to Freeway*, 232; oral history interview, Sabo Papers, 6.

13. Vicki Skor Pearson interview.

14. Grace Kemmer Sulerud interview.

15. Chrislock, *From Fjord to Freeway*, 173, 228.

16. Oral history interview, Sabo Papers, 6.

17. Jim Pederson interview.

18. Oral history interview, Sabo Papers.

19. Winston Chrislock interview.

20. "Augsburgian 1956," 82, https://archives.augsburg.edu/islandora/object/AUGrepository%3A1581#page/1/mode/2up; "Augsburgian 1957," 74, 79.

21. State of Minnesota Legislative Manual, 1959–60, 337–43, Minnesota Legislative Reference Library, https://www.lrl.mn.gov/mngov/bluebooks, and Legislative Party Control Chart, 1901–present, Minnesota Legislative Reference Library, https://www.lrl.mn.gov/history/caucus_table.

22. "College Head Named to Relations Council," *Minneapolis Star*, November 1, 1947; "Human Relations Study to Give Community 'Image,'" *Minneapolis Morning Tribune*, March 30, 1948, 3; see also Nathanson, *Minneapolis in the Twentieth Century*, ch. 4.

23. Pederson interview.

24. For more, see Fraser, *She's No Lady*.

25. Pederson interview.

26. Oral history interview, Sabo Papers, 7.

27. "Hennepin DFL Refuses to Endorse Veteran Legislator," *Minneapolis Sunday Tribune*, April 3, 1960, 30; "Hagland Plans Race Despite Snub," *Minneapolis Star*, March 30, 1960, 6D; "Rigging Denied in DFL Caucus," *Minneapolis Star*, March 31, 1960, 1W.

28. Wallace Mitchell and Ted Smebakken, "Know your Minnesota Legislators," *Minneapolis Star*, December 6, 1960, 17.

29. Chrislock interview.

30. Oral history interview, Sabo Papers.

31. State of Minnesota Legislative Manual, 1961–62, 471, 483, Minnesota Legislative Reference Library, https://www.lrl.mn.gov/mngov/bluebooks.

Notes to Chapter Three: A Torch Passes, Slowly

1. Mark Shepard and Patrick McCormack, "Regular Sessions of the Minnesota Legislature," Minnesota State Legislature, updated July 2010, https://www.house.mn.gov/hrd/pubs/ss/ssregses.pdf.

2. "Sessions of the Minnesota State Legislature and the Minnesota Territorial Legislature, 1849–present," Minnesota Legislative Reference Library, https://www.lrl.mn.gov/history/sessions; "State Constitutional Amendments Considered," Minnesota Legislative Reference Library, https://www.lrl.mn.gov/mngov/constitutionalamendments.

3. "Number of Seats in the Minnesota Legislature," Minnesota Legislative Reference Library, https://www.lrl.mn.gov/history/seats; see also Alexis C. Stangl and Matt Gehring, "History of Minnesota Legislative Redistricting," Minnesota State Legislature, November 2018, https://www.gis.lcc.mn.gov/html/history_of_legislative_redistricting.pdf.

4. *Smith v. Holm*, 220 Minn. 486, 19 N.W.2d 914 (1945); Stangl and Gehring, "History of Minnesota Legislative Redistricting," 2; see also M. W. Halloran, "Legality of Legislature Now an Issue," *Minneapolis Star-Journal*, August 24, 1945, 1.

5. *Magraw v. Donovan*, 163 F. Supp. 184 (D. Minn. 1958), decided July 10, 1958.

6. Wallace Mitchell, "Key Figures in the Minnesota Legislature," *Minneapolis Star*, January 4, 1961, 1C.

7. Charles Raymond Adrian, "The Nonpartisan Legislature in Minnesota," PhD thesis, University of Minnesota, 1950, 231, https://www.leg.mn.gov/docs/NonMNpub/oclc19607893.pdf.

8. "Voters' Guide," *Minneapolis Tribune*, October 28, 1964, 3–4.

9. Oral history interview, Sabo Papers, 7.

10. Oral history interview, Sabo Papers, 8.

11. 1962 General Election Results, State of Minnesota Legislative Manual, 1963–64, 528, Minnesota Legislative Reference Library, https://www.lrl.mn.gov/archive/sessions/electionresults/1962-11-06-g-man.pdf.

12. "Remembering Inez (Olson) Schwarzkopf, '59" Augsburg University, June 30, 2023, https://www.augsburg.edu/giving/2023/06/30/remembering-inez-olson-schwarzkopf-59/.

13. See Andersen, *A Man's Reach*.

14. Oral history interview, Sabo Papers, 9.

15. "Rev. Sylvan Lee, Father-in-Law of Sabo, Dies," *Minneapolis Star Tribune*, February 24, 1998, B4.

16. "Sylvia Ann (Lee) Sabo," obituary, *Minneapolis Star Tribune*, November 6, 2022; "Martin Sabo, Sylvia Lee are Married," *Minneapolis Tribune*, July 4, 1963, 9.

17. *Baker v. Carr*, 369 U.S. 186 (1962).

18. *Reynolds v. Sims*, 377 U.S. 533, 558 (1964); *Wesberry v. Sanders*, 376 U.S. 1 (1964).

19. *Honsey v. Donovan*, 236 F. Supp. 8 (D. Minn. 1964), decided December 4, 1964.

20. Larry Fitzmaurice, "State Reapportioning Act Held Unconstitutional,"

Minneapolis Star, December 4, 1964, 1A; Maurice Hobbs, "DFL Readies Bill on Reapportionment," *Minneapolis Star*, March 23, 1965, 7D; Bob Weber, "Reapportionment Bill Vetoed; Rolvaag Calls It 'Intolerable,'" *Minneapolis Star*, May 24, 1965, 1A.

21. "Message of Governor Karl. F. Rolvaag Vetoing Senate File 2," Minnesota State Legislature, accessed February 2, 2025, https://www.leg.state.mn.us/archive/vetoes/1966_sp1veto_SF2.pdf.

22. Bob Ylvisaker, "House Unit Approves 4 Area Sewage Bills," *Minneapolis Tribune*, April 29, 1965, 22.

23. Ted Kolderie interview.

24. "Senators Balk on Metro Bill Vote," *Minneapolis Star*, May 16, 1967, 1; "Group Tasked with Reforming Met Council Offers Lawmakers Six Options," *Minnesota Star Tribune*, February 1, 2024.

25. Gilje, *How Could You Do This?*, ch. 2 and 3; Kolderie, *Thinking Out the How*, 86–89.

26. Oral history interview, Sabo Papers, 8.

27. Durenberger with Sturdevant, *When Republicans Were Progressive*, 77–83.

28. Oral history interview, Sabo Papers, 8.

29. Bob Weber, "3% Sales Tax Bill Passed by House," *Minneapolis Star*, May 20, 1967, 1A.

Notes to Chapter Four: Minority Leader

1. "Conservatives in City Tighten Hold on House," *Minneapolis Tribune*, November 6, 1986, 4; "Incumbents Lead Hennepin House Races," *Minneapolis Tribune*, September 11, 1986, 13.

2. Gordon Slovut, "DFLers Start Search for New House Leaders," *Minneapolis Star*, November 7, 1968, 1B.

3. George McCormick, "State Legislators Check Prospects for Leadership Posts," *Minneapolis Tribune*, November 10, 1968, 29.

4. George McCormick, "DFL Gains in Legislature, but Loses Leaders," *Minneapolis Tribune*, November 7, 1968, 23; see also George McCormick, "Sabo Appears Gaining Ground in DFL Leadership Bid," *Minneapolis Tribune*, November 22, 1968, 19.

5 George McCormick, "DFL Gains in Legislature, but Loses Leaders," *Minneapolis Tribune*, November 7, 1968, 23.

6. "House DFLers Elect Sabo of Minneapolis Caucus Leader," *Minneapolis Tribune*, November 24, 1968, 6B.

7. "Pre-Legislative Prayer Is Planned," *Minneapolis Star*, January 4, 1969, 10A.

8. Anduin Wilhide, "Trinity Lutheran Congregation: Getting by with a Little Help from Friends," Augsburg Digi-Tours, accessed February 3, 2025, https://tinyurl.com/2tyubk8f.

9. Gerry Nelson, Associated Press, "New Finery Awaits Legislators," *Minneapolis Star*, December 31, 1968, 7B; oral history interview, Sabo Papers, 10.

10. Berg, *Minnesota's Miracle*, 15; see also oral history interview, Sabo Papers, 10.

11. Ted Smebakken, "LeVander Told: Give Full Budget Details," *Minneapolis Star*, February 6, 1969, 22B; Ted Smebakken, "Sabo to Talk Money with LeVander Aide," *Minneapolis Star*, February 6, 1969, 1B; Ted Smebakken, "Sabo: 'Hole' Still in Budget," *Minneapolis Star*, February 7, 1969, 14A; Ted Smebakken, "Sabo Charges LeVander Lacked Candor," *Minneapolis Star*, March 13, 1969, 7C; Jim Shoop, "LeVander May Seek More Taxes," *Minneapolis Star*, March 13, 1969, 1A.

12. Ted Smebakken, "Business Tax Breaks Cause 'Mess'—DFLer," *Minneapolis Star*, April 9, 1969, 1A.

13. Ted Smebakken, "Panel Clears Tax-Relief Shift over Protest," *Minneapolis Star*, April 3, 1969, 4D; United Press International, "Tax Package Awaits Senate," *St. Cloud Times*, May 21, 1969, 1A.

14. "The 1969 State Legislature: 'Uninspiring,'" *Minneapolis Tribune*, May 26, 1969, 6; Gerry Nelson, Associated Press, "For Coming Elections, LeVander, Some DFLers Gain Points," *Minneapolis Star*, May 26, 1969, 18A.

15. Tom Berg interview.

16. Wes Skoglund interview.

17. "Legislator Confirms Fee Paid by Bus Line," *Minneapolis Star*, March 7, 1969, 13A.

18. "Governor Leaving 'His Mess,' Foe Says," *Minneapolis Star*, January 27, 1970, 3; "Minnesota Poll: Shift toward GOP Indicated," *Minneapolis Tribune*, November 1, 1970, 1.

19. "Court Backs Conservatives in State Senate Dispute," *Minneapolis Tribune*, January 14, 1971, 1.

20. Oral history interview, Sabo Papers, 12.

21. "DFLers in House Seek Rules Changes," *Minneapolis Star*, December 11, 1970, 22.

22. "House Recesses after Adopting Permanent Rules," *Winona Daily News*, January 8, 1971, 1; Berg, *Minnesota's Miracle*, 27.

Notes to Chapter Five: It's a Miracle!

1. Berg, *Minnesota's Miracle*, 34–37.

2. John Earl Haynes interview.

3. Eileen Baumgartner, interview, 2008, Bill Clinton Presidential History Project; Eileen Baumgartner interview, March 13, 2023.

4. Berg, *Minnesota's Miracle*, 36; Haynes interview.

5. Bernie Shellum, "Gov. Anderson Asks Tax Increase of $762 Million," *Minneapolis Tribune*, January 28, 1971, 1A, 2A.

6. "Conservatives Offer Anderson Little Hope on Budget," *Minneapolis*

Star, January 28, 1971, 2A; "Business, Labor Split on Tax Plan," *Minneapolis Tribune*, April 8, 1971, 2B.

7. For example, see Sabo's comments here: Peter Ackerberg, "Majority Tax Plan Vote Near," *Minneapolis Star*, May 13, 1971, 4.

8. "The State Budget Process," Minnesota House Research, November 2024, https://www.house.mn.gov/hrd/issinfo/gvst_sbp.aspx?src=14.

9. Peter Ackerberg, "Majority Tax Plan Vote Near," *Minneapolis Star*, May 13, 1971.

10. Joe Graba interview.

11. Gerry Nelson, Associated Press, "House, Senate Approve First Black Regent for University," *Winona Daily News*, May 14, 1971, 7.

12. Graba interview.

13. Oral history interview, Sabo Papers, 15.

14. Peter Ackerberg, "Sabo May Urge Tax Veto," *Minneapolis Star*, May 10, 1971, 1; Haynes interview.

15. Finlay Lewis and Steve Dornfeld, "Special Session Set to Write Tax Bill," *Minneapolis Tribune*, May 23, 1971, 1A.

16. Deborah Howell, "Governor Reverses, Signs Money Bills," *Minneapolis Star*, June 8, 1971, 4A.

17. Steven Dornfeld, "Freshman Senator Stages 'Polka Protest' at the Capitol," *Minneapolis Tribune*, June 9, 1971, 1B.

18. Associated Press, "Senate Leaders See Tax Plan Progress," *Fergus Falls Daily Journal*, June 9, 1971, 1; "Touring Lindstrom Is Told Public Backs Tax-Bill Veto," *Minneapolis Tribune*, August 13, 1971, 2B.

19. Gerry Nelson, "Tax Philosophy Being Fought Out," *Minneapolis Star*, August 13, 1971, 32.

20. Associated Press, "Tax Picture at a Glance," *Fergus Falls Daily Journal*, July 31, 1971, 1.

21. "Angry Anderson Vetoes Tax Bill," *Minneapolis Star*, August 3, 1971, 1.

22. Haynes interview.

23. Peter Ackerberg, "Tax Compromise More Likely," *Minneapolis Star*, September 23, 1971, 6C.

24. Pat Dalton, "The Local Government Aid (LGA) Program: A History," Minnesota House Research, October 2020, https://www.house.mn.gov/hrd/pubs/lgahist.pdf; "Local Government Aid Certification for Cities," Minnesota Department of Revenue, 2024, accessed February 4, 2025, https://www.revenue.state.mn.us/site-search?site_search_text=Local+Government+Aid+Certification; "Local Government Aid 101," League of Minnesota Cities, August 2023, https://tinyurl.com/2p8a772m.

25. Associated Press, "Tax Question Heating Up," *Winona Daily News*, September 10, 1971, 2.

26. Berg, *Minnesota's Miracle*, 42.

27. Finlay Lewis, "State Tax Bill Passes, Is Sent to Governor," *Minneapolis Tribune*, October 28, 1971, 1A.

28. Oral history interview, Sabo Papers, 11.

29. Advisory Commission on Intergovernmental Relations, *Federalism in 1971*, 6.

30. Patrick Mendis interview.

31. "Sabo to Head Legislative Group," *Minneapolis Tribune*, August 20, 1974, 10B.

32. Bill Pound interview.

33. Deborah Howell, "Sabo's View May Decide Redistricting Plan's Fate," *Minneapolis Star*, October 28, 1971, 8C.

34. "Senate to Ask Court to Study Redistricting," *Minneapolis Tribune*, November 3, 1971, 1B.

35. "Cut-Legislature Ruling Creates Capitol Furor, New-Session Talk," *Minneapolis Star*, December 4, 1971, 1A.

36. "Number of Legislators and Length of Terms in Years," National Conference of State Legislatures, accessed February 5, 2025, https://www.ncsl.org/resources/details/number-of-legislators-and-length-of-terms-in-years.

37. Deborah Howell, "Special Redistricting Session Sought as Parties File Plans," *Minneapolis Star*, December 30, 1972, 1B.

38. *Minnesota State Senate v. Beens*, 406 U.S. 187 (1972), decided April 29, 1972, https://supreme.justia.com/cases/federal/us/406/187/.

39. Deborah Howell, "Redistricting May Help Both Parties," *Minneapolis Star*, June 2, 1972, 1A.

Notes to Chapter Six: The Key Turns

1. Richard Moe interview.

2. Bernie Shellum, "Moe Is Elected DFL Chairman by 134–106 Vote," *Minneapolis Tribune*, December 7, 1969, 10B.

3. Minnesota DFLers changed the name of their party leaders from "chairman" to "chair" and "chairwoman" to "associate chair" in 1975: Wikipedia, accessed February 5, 2025, https://tinyurl.com/yc6m5pb8.

4. Moe interview.

5. Moe interview.

6. Peter Ackerberg, "DFL to Go All-Out to Seize Control of 1972 Legislature," *Minneapolis Star*, December 30, 1971, 21; see also Ted Smebakken, "Party Activity on Upswing in Legislature," *Minneapolis Star*, January 15, 1969, 1B.

7. "Your Key to Open Government," Democratic-Farmer-Labor Party brochure, 1972, provided to the author by 1972 legislative candidate Robert Vanasek.

8. Robert Vanasek interview.

9. Vanasek interview.

10. "Anderson Says McGovern Has Made State Gains, Needs More," *Minneapolis Star*, October 13, 1972, 6.

11. Bernie Shellum and Steve Dornfeld, "DFL Endorses Homosexuals'

Right to Marry," *Minneapolis Tribune*, June 12, 1972, 1B; Berg, *Minnesota's Miracle*, 60; "Governor Spurns Three Planks in DFL Platform," *Minneapolis Star*, June 17, 1972, 16A.

12. Berg, *Minnesota's Miracle*, 63.

13. Graba interview.

14. Moe interview.

15. Scrapbook clipping, *New Prague Times*, supplied to author by Robert Vanasek.

16. Vanasek interview.

17. Berg, *Minnesota's Miracle*, 62–63.

18. Oral history interview, Sabo Papers, 9.

19. Growe interview; Phyllis Kahn interview.

20. Growe with Sturdevant, *Turnout*, 41.

21. "Table 2: Minnesota State General Election Statistics," Office of the Minnesota Secretary of State, accessed February 7, 2025, https://www.sos.state.mn.us/media/4395/minnesota-election-statistics-1950-to-2020.pdf; "Voting May Be Record in State," *Minneapolis Star*, November 8, 1972, 17A; "1972 United States Presidential Election in Minnesota," Wikipedia, accessed February 7, 2025, https://tinyurl.com/2ce4e4xw.

22. Peter Vaughn, "DFL Wins Senate, Is Ahead for House," *Minneapolis Star*, November 8, 1972, 1A; Steven Dornfeld, "DFL Takes Legislature for 1st Time," *Minneapolis Tribune*, November 9, 1972, 1A.

Notes to Chapter Seven: In Charge

1. "New Legislators with No Previous Legislative Experience," Minnesota Legislative Reference Library, https://www.lrl.mn.gov/legdb/freshmen.

2. Oral history interview, Sabo Papers, 12.

3. Graba interview.

4. "Lloyd L. Duxbury," obituary, *Minneapolis Star Tribune*, March 26, 2002.

5. Oral history interview, Sabo Papers; Berg, *Minnesota's Miracle*, 76.

6. "Sabo to Seek Speaker of House Post," *Minneapolis Tribune*, November 11, 1972, 21; Joan Anderson Growe interview; "Dirlam Elected Conservative Leader Despite Reform Opposition," *Minneapolis Tribune*, November 16, 1972, 8B.

7. "Dirlam Elected Conservative Leader Despite Reform Opposition," *Minneapolis Tribune*, November 16, 1972, 8B.

8. "Dirlam Elected Conservative Leader Despite Reform Opposition," *Minneapolis Tribune*, November 16, 1972, 8B.

9. Graba interview.

10. Vanasek interview.

11. Oral history interview, Sabo Papers, 12.

12. "House Rules Unit Backs Broad Changes," *Minneapolis Star*, January 3, 1973, 9A; "Minorities on Committees," *St. Cloud Times*, January 3, 1973, 4.

13. Associated Press "Government Openness Two-Edged Sword," *Winona Daily News*, January 5, 1973, 2.

14. Oral history interview, Sabo Papers, 12.

15. "House Adopts Liberalizing Set of Rules," *Minneapolis Star*, January 4, 1973, 4.

16. Oral history interview, Sabo Papers, 14.

17. Bill Kelly interview.

18. "Austin Woman to Head House Committee," *Minneapolis Star*, December 9, 1972, 11; "Lemke Is Easy Winner of District 2-B Seat," *Winona Daily News*, May 5, 1971, 3; legislator biographical information from "Minnesota Legislators Past and Present," Minnesota Legislative Reference Library, https://www.lrl.mn.gov/legdb/.

19. Oral history interview, Sabo Papers, 14.

20. Karin Sabo Mantor, email to author, January 14, 2024.

21. Kelly interview.

22. Mark Shepard and Patrick McCormack, "Regular Sessions of the Minnesota Legislature," Minnesota State Legislature, updated July 2010, https://www.house.mn.gov/hrd/pubs/ss/ssregses.pdf ; "Constitutional Amendments," *Fergus Falls Daily Journal*, October 14, 1972, 4.

23. Shepard and McCormack, "Regular Sessions of the Minnesota Legislature."

24. "Legislators Agree on Workload Committee," *Minneapolis Tribune*, December 20, 1972, 5C.

25. Susan B. Fox., "Annual versus Biennial Legislative Sessions," Montana Legislative Council, January 8, 2014, https://tinyurl.com/4txcmdyr.

26. Oral history interview, Sabo Papers.

27. Lori Sturdevant, "Legislators Come and Sometimes Go Too Soon," *Minneapolis Star Tribune*, July 19, 2015, OP1.

28. "Voters Guide," *Minneapolis Tribune*, October 28, 1964, 3.

29. 1913 Minn. Laws Ch. 389, Office of the Revisor of Statutes, https://www.revisor.mn.gov/laws/1913/0/General+Laws/Chapter/389/pdf; "Party Control of the Minnesota House of Representatives, 1951–Present," Minnesota Legislative Reference Library, https://www.lrl.mn.gov/history/caucus?body=h.

30. Jim Talle, "DFL Plans Early Changes," *Minneapolis Star*, November 9, 1972, 1; Governor Wendell R. Anderson, "State of the State Address," January 3, 1973, 2, https://www.leg.mn.gov/docs/pre2003/other/i691.pdf; "The State of the State," editorial, *Minneapolis Star*, January 4, 1973, 6.

31. "Senate Passes Party Designation for Legislators," *Minneapolis Tribune*, February 13, 1973, 1B; "Party Designation Goes to Governor," *Minneapolis Tribune*, February 15, 1973, 4B.

32. Gerald Knickerbocker interview; "Should Legislature Lose Party Labels?," *Minneapolis Star Tribune*, March 19, 2018, 10.

33. "Sabo Defends His Publicly Financed, Out-of-Town, '74 Trips as Legitimate," *Minneapolis Tribune*, April 6, 1975, 1.

34. State of Minnesota Legislative Manuals, 1971–72, p. 124, and 1975–76, p. 226, Minnesota Legislative Reference Library, https://www.lrl.mn.gov/mngov/bluebooks; "Nobles Shoes Will Be Hard to Fill," *Minneapolis Star Tribune*, August 25, 2021, 6A; Dennis Anderson, "His Work Lives on for Minnesota," *Minneapolis Star Tribune*, July 18, 2021, C14; Baumgartner interview, 2008.

35. Berg, *Minnesota's Miracle*, 99–101.

36. Edward Dirkswager interview.

37. Moe interview.

38. Oral history interview, Sabo Papers, 14.

39. "'73 Legislature Ready to Show 2 New Faces," *Minneapolis Star*, January 1, 1973, 1.

40. Kelly interview; "Remodel," *Minneapolis Tribune*, January 14, 1974, 11A.

41. "Contract for New Offices in House Awarded," *Austin Daily Herald*, October 2, 1973, 2.

42. Stephen Alnes, "Our New Legislature: Policy and Operations," *Minneapolis Star*, February 26, 1974, 7; Edward Dirkswager, email to author, January 23, 2024.

43. "Number of Bills Introduced and Laws Passed in the Minnesota Legislature, 1849–Present," Minnesota Legislative Reference Library, https://www.lrl.mn.gov/history/bills.

44. Steven Dornfeld interview; Dirkswager interview.

45. Berg, *Minnesota's Miracle*, 97; Paul Gilje interview; Karin Sabo Mantor, email to author, January 14, 2024.

46. Berg, *Minnesota's Miracle*, 103.

47. Growe with Sturdevant, *Turnout*, 48–50.

48. Growe with Sturdevant, *Turnout*, 53–54.

49. Governor Wendell R. Anderson, "State of the State Address," January 3, 1973; "Political Scene by Dave Hoium," *St. Cloud Times*, April 23, 1973, 19.

50. "Legislature Passes Lobby, Campaign Bill," *Minneapolis Tribune*, March 28, 1974, 2B.

51. "Campaign Finance Reform: Then and Now," PBS, accessed February 8, 2025, https://www.pbs.org/johngardner/chapters/6a.html.

52. "Three State Legislative Units Likely to Merge," *St. Cloud Times*, August 15, 1974, 12.

Notes to Chapter Eight: A Speaker for Everyone

1. Oral history interview, Sabo Papers, 14–15.

2. "Proclamation of Pardon," *New York Times*, September 9, 1974, 1.

3. Berg, *Minnesota's Miracle*, 96–98.

4. "Governor Rejects Pay Increase for Legislators," *Minneapolis Star*, April 3, 1974, 1, 6.

5. "Anderson Vetoes Pay Raise," *Minneapolis Tribune*, April 4, 1974, 1A.

6. "Compensation of Minnesota Legislators, 1858–Present" Minnesota Legislative Reference Library, https://www.lrl.mn.gov/history/salary.

7. Joan Anderson Growe, "Minnesota General Election Results, 1974," 33–35, https://www.lrl.mn.gov/archive/sessions/electionresults/1974-11-05-g-sec.pdf. One of the two Minneapolis Republicans still in the Minnesota House in 1975 was future governor Arne Carlson.

8. "Speaker of the House Is Unopposed," *Minneapolis Star*, October 31, 1974, 51.

9. Graba interview.

10. Kelly interview.

11. "DFL Leaders Predict Large Gains in Minnesota House," *Minneapolis Tribune*, November 4, 1974, 1; "Legislature: DFL Gains," *Minneapolis Star*, November 6, 1974, 7A.

12. "Sabo Expects a Less Busy 1975 Legislative Session," *Minneapolis Star*, November 9, 1974, 9A.

13. "GOP Hurt Most by Lack of Republicans at the Polls," *Minneapolis Tribune*, November 6, 1974, 1; State of Minnesota Legislative Manuals, 1971–72, 1975–76, Minnesota Legislative Reference Library, https://www.lrl.mn.gov/mngov/bluebooks.

14. The first female state senator in the modern era was Nancy Brataas, elected in a special election in February 1975 to fill a vacancy created when Senate Republican leader Harold Krieger resigned to take a judicial appointment: "Brataas, Nancy," Minnesota Legislative Reference Library, https://www.lrl.mn.gov/legdb/fulldetail?ID=10074. Brataas was the second woman elected to the Minnesota Senate. The first, Laura Naplin, served from 1927 to 1934.

15. Jack Davies interview; see also "2 DFL Legislators Lose to Party-Backed Women," *Minneapolis Star*, September 11, 1974, 16B.

16. Baumgartner interview, 2023.

17. Christenson, *A Minnesota Citizen*, 154–57.

18. "Minnesota News," *Austin Daily Herald*, December 13, 1973, 5; Kelly interview.

19. "Minnesota Horizons: A Brief History," Minnesota Legislative Reference Library, https://www.leg.mn.gov/leg/minnesota/2003/history.

20. "Merritt Quits as PCA Chief," *Minneapolis Star*, May 2, 1975, 1; Kelly interview.

21. Berg, *Minnesota's Miracle*, 113–14.

22. "Anderson's Address Covers National Problems," *La Crosse (WI) Tribune*, January 8, 1975, 17.

23. Oral history interview, Sabo Papers, 14.

24. Pavlak, Raymond L. "Ray," Minnesota Legislative Reference Library, https://www.lrl.mn.gov/legdb/fulldetail?ID=10511.

25. Kelly interview.

26. Ted Suss interview.

27. Michael Erlandson interview.

28. Baumgartner interview.

29. Dirkswager interview.

30. James Solem interview; "Minn. Stat. 462A.05, subdiv. 14," Office of the Revisor of Statutes, https://www.revisor.mn.gov/statutes/cite/462A.05.

31. "Second Inaugural Address of Governor Wendell R. Anderson," January 8, 1975, Minnesota Legislative Reference Library, https://www.leg.mn.gov/docs/pre2003/other/1099.pdf; "Passage of Health Insurance Bill Unlikely," *Minneapolis Tribune*, April 3, 1975, 1A; Berg, *Minnesota's Miracle*, 143–45.

32. "About MCHA," Minnesota Premium Security Plan, Minnesota Comprehensive Health Association, https://mchamn.com/about-mcha/.

33. "History," Office of the Legislative Auditor, https://www.auditor.leg.state.mn.us/g-hist.htm.

34. 1973 Minn. Laws 1088–90; Sturdevant, *The Pillsburys of Minnesota*, 69–70.

35. "History," Office of the Legislative Auditor, https://www.auditor.leg.state.mn.us/g-hist.htm; James Nobles interview; "State Legislative Auditor to Retire after 36 Years," *Minneapolis Tribune*, December 5, 1976, 13B.

36. "Savelkoul Appointed," *Emmons Leader*, February 20, 1975, 1.

37. "Background," Program Evaluation Division, Office of the Legislative Auditor, https://www.auditor.leg.state.mn.us/ped/resmeth.htm.

38. "$172 Million Roads Bill Offered by House DFL," *Minneapolis Star*, April 24, 1975, 2B; "House Approves Tax Relief, Freezes Teacher Benefits," *Minneapolis Tribune*, May 13, 1975, 1; "Wednesday Busy Day for Legislature," *Austin Daily Herald*, April 24, 1975, 3; Berg, *Minnesota's Miracle*, 134.

39. Dirkswager interview.

40. Nobles interview.

41. "Second Panel Takes Up Study of General Revenue for Roads," *Albert Lea Tribune*, April 22, 1975, 3; "Drinking-Age Bill Passes Test in House," *Minneapolis Star*, February 28, 1976, 7.

42. Betty Wilson, "Legislative Smoking: She Huffs, He Puffs," *Minneapolis Star*, January 4, 1975, 1; Representative Phyllis Kahn, speaking at a Minnesota House memorial for Martin Sabo, House floor session, March 14, 2016, "Martin Sabo Remembered on MN House Floor—Full Tribute," YouTube, https://www.youtube.com/watch?v=PrWYreR3A08; Berg, *Minnesota's Miracle*, 143.

43. Berg, *Minnesota's Miracle*, 143.

44. Jack Coffman, "House DFLers Try Out New Muscle," *Minneapolis Tribune*, January 21, 1975, 2B.

45. Gerry Nelson, Associated Press, "Minnesota House Gives Approval to Tax Bill," *Fergus Falls Daily Journal*, May 1, 1975.

46. Betty Wilson, "Special Session Chances Growing," *Minneapolis Star*, May 15, 1975, 16B; "Second Inaugural Address of Governor Wendell R. Anderson," January 8, 1975, 16; "Minnesota House Gives Approval to Tax Bill," *Fergus Falls Daily Journal*, May 1, 1975, 1.

47. "Tax Bills Hinged on Relief Plans," *Minneapolis Star*, May 9, 1975, 1.

48. Dirkswager interview.

49. Baumgartner interview.

50. "Tax Plans Debated," *Fergus Falls Daily Journal*, May 13, 1975, 4; see also Berg, *Minnesota's Miracle*, 128.

51. "Conferees Still Working on Tax Bill," *Albert Lea Tribune*, May 18, 1975, 1; "Tax Bill Tops Logjam of Issues," May 16, 1975, 1.

52. "Property Tax Relief Approved," *Minneapolis Tribune*, May 20, 1975, 1.

53. Jim Shoop, "Politics," *Minneapolis Star*, May 23, 1975, 6A.

Notes to Chapter Nine: Dominoes Fall

1. "Carter Chooses Mondale, Pledges Presidency of 'Vigor and Vision,'" *Minneapolis Tribune*, July 16, 1976, 1; "Anderson Will Take Senate Seat," *Minneapolis Star*, November 10, 1976, 1A.

2. Betty Wilson and Eric Pianin, "Mondale: Political Futures on the Line," *Minneapolis Star*, August 9, 1976, 4A.

3. An exception was the single three-year term of Lucius Hubbard, 1883–86, to accommodate a state constitutional change that moved gubernatorial elections from odd- to even-numbered years: see "Gov. Lucius Frederick Hubbard," National Governors Association, accessed February 8, 2025, https://www.nga.org/governor/lucius-frederick-hubbard/.

4. Milton, *For the Good of the Order*, 456.

5. "55% Oppose Anderson's Naming Himself to the Senate," *Minneapolis Tribune*, October 10, 1976, 1.

6. "More Than Half of Those Surveyed Think Anderson Is Doing a Good Job," *Minneapolis Tribune*, June 11, 1976, 2.

7. Christenson, *A Minnesota Citizen*, 171.

8. Steven Dornfeld, "Labor Leaders Urge Anderson for Senate," *Minneapolis Tribune*, November 6, 1976, 1A, 6A.

9. "State Bloc Is Big at One More Convention," *Minneapolis Tribune*, September 3, 1976, 1A.

10. Suss interview.

11. "Haugerud to Challenge Irvin Anderson for House Majority Post," *Minneapolis Tribune*, November 6, 1976.

12. "Irvin Anderson Reelected Leader of House DFLers," *Minneapolis Star*, November 9, 1976, 5D.

13. Wilson, *Rudy! The People's Governor*, 70–77.

14. "Perpich Has Hot Exchange on Radio," *Minneapolis Star*, April 26, 1977, 1B.

15. "Chopping Starts on Perpich Plans," *Minneapolis Tribune*, January 27, 1977, 11.

16. "Special Session Considered," *St. Cloud Times*, May 24, 1977, 1.

17. Rudy Perpich, "Tax Relief Needed," *Minneapolis Star*, November 5, 1977, 6.

18. Bill Kelly, "Tax System Fair," *Minneapolis Star*, November 5, 1977, 6.

19. "Rep. Fraser to Seek Senate Seat of HHH, Will Not Run for House," *Minneapolis Star*, January 24, 1978, 1.

20. Milton, *For the Good of the Order*, 471–75.

21. "Coleman Joins Perpich's Lonely Call for Cut in Taxes," *Minneapolis Star*, December 14, 1977, 30A.

22. "Muriel Accepts Senate Post," *Minneapolis Star*, January 25, 1978, 1. The story of the early relationship between Hubert Humphrey II and Muriel Buck is well told in Samuel G. Freedman, *Into the Bright Sunshine: Young Hubert Humphrey and the Fight for Civil Rights* (Oxford University Press, 2023).

23. "Sabo Meets with Carter," *Fergus Falls Daily Journal*, February 24, 1977, 8.

24. Sturdevant, *Her Honor*, 104.

25. "Sabo Says He's Candidate for Fraser's House Seat," *Minneapolis Star*, January 25, 1978, 17A.

26. Karin Sabo Mantor, letter provided to the author.

27. Oral history interview, Sabo Papers, 17.

28. Graba interview.

29. Margaret Bostelmann interview.

30. "Accord Awaited on Major Bills," *Minneapolis Tribune*, March 14, 1978, 2B.

31. "Senate Race Looks Very Close," *Minneapolis Tribune*, March 19, 1978, 1.

32. Betty Wilson, "Key Legislators Worry Treasury Is Being Drained," *Minneapolis Star*, March 15, 1978, 10B.

33. "Conferees Ratify Bill to Cut State Taxes," *Minneapolis Tribune*, March 23, 1978, 1A.

34. "Session: All Eyes on Taxes," *Minneapolis Star*, March 24, 1978, 7A.

35. Henry Savelkoul interview.

36. "Legislators Wind Up 1978 Session," *Minneapolis Star*, March 24, 1978, 8A.

37. "Legislators Wind Up 1978 Session," *Minneapolis Star*, March 24, 1978, 8A.

38. Steven Dornfeld and Steve Brandt, "The Changing Legislature," *Minneapolis Tribune*, February 5–9, 1978, 1.

39. "Legislature," *Minneapolis Tribune*, February 6, 1978, 8; "DFL Legislators Propose Shift to Full-Time Legislature," *Minneapolis Star Tribune*, April 30, 2022.

Notes to Chapter Ten: The Way to Washington

1. Robert Whereatt, "2 DFLers Vie for Fraser Seat," *Minneapolis Star*, April 13, 1978, 1.

2. "History Gives GOP an Edge in 11th Ward," *Minneapolis Star*, October 20, 1973, 13.

3. Lois Gibson, letter to DFL convention delegates, Sabo family archives, April 1978. The city's library board was abolished when city libraries merged

with those operated by Hennepin County in 2007. The Minneapolis Park and Recreation Board is alive and well in 2025.

4. Gibson, letter to delegates.

5. "Issue of Fraser's Successor Ignored," *Minneapolis Star*, April 3, 1978, 19A.

6. Martin Sabo, text of April 29, 1978, convention remarks, Sabo family archive.

7. "Endorsement Skirts Caucus Organization," *Minneapolis Tribune*, April 29, 1978, 8.

8. "Sabo Endorsed by DFL in Fifth," *Minneapolis Tribune*, April 30, 1978, 1.

9. "Redrawn District Unsettled Firm Support," *Minneapolis Star Tribune*, May 11, 1992, 6; "Sabo Fights Off Surprise Challenge for DFL Party Endorsement in District," *Minneapolis Star Tribune*, May 11, 1992, 1.

10. State of Minnesota Legislative Manual, 1993–94, 361, Minnesota Legislative Reference Library, https://www.lrl.mn.gov/mngov/bluebooks.

11. For more about the Fraser–Short contest, see Nathanson, *Don Fraser*, 105–21.

12. Sabo's opponents were Willis Trueblood and Lester Betts, both first-time candidates who did not mount active campaigns. Sabo received 81 percent of the vote. Joan Anderson Growe, "Minnesota Election Results, 1978," 4, https://www.lrl.mn.gov/archive/sessions/electionresults/1978-09-12-p-sec.pdf.

13. "IR Gives Nod to Till in Fifth District," *Minneapolis Tribune*, April 23, 1978, 3B; "Campaigns," *Minneapolis Tribune*, October 31, 1978, 4.

14. "IR Hoping Till Can Conquer DFL, Sabo in 5th District," *Minneapolis Tribune*, September 30, 1978, 1.

15. "61 Legislators Campaigning, Drawing Pay," *Minneapolis Tribune*, August 3, 1978, 1.

16. "Population Notes," Minnesota Department of Energy, Planning, and Development, April 1983, https://mn.gov/admin/assets/median-income-of-minnesota-families-increases-msdc-april1983_tcm36-249195.pdf; "Salaries of Members of the United States Congress," Wikipedia, accessed February 22, 2025, https://en.wikipedia.org/wiki/Salaries_of_members_of_the_United_States_Congress.

17. "Economic Recovery Tax Act of 1981," Wikipedia, accessed February 22, 2025, https://tinyurl.com/2uua868d; Robert Whereatt, "Sabo, Till Disagree on Tax Cutting," *Minneapolis Star*, October 26, 1978, 5.

18. "6 of 8 U.S. Congressmen Are Seeking Reelection," *Minneapolis Tribune*, October 31, 1978, 12.

19. For details about Proposition 13 and its aftermath, see "Proposition 13: Its Impact on California and Implications," California Budget and Policy Center, April 1997, https://tinyurl.com/2p9wcyfj.

20. "Ya, Shure, Yew Betchew," *Minneapolis Star*, December 30, 1978, 5.

21. Suss interview.

22. Richard Cohen interview.

23. Russell Stanton interview.

24. "Spanish Heading for Defeat on Range," *Minneapolis Tribune*, September 13, 1978, 7A.

25. Cohen interview.

26. Skoglund interview.

27. Jim Parsons, "IR Hoping Till Can Conquer DFL, Sabo in 5th District," *Minneapolis Tribune*, September 30, 1978, 1A.

28. Jim Parsons, "Congress," *Minneapolis Tribune*, November 8, 1968, 20A.

29. "Here Are the Star's Choices for Congress," editorial endorsement, *Minneapolis Star*, October 24, 1978, 8; "Frenzel, Vento and Sabo for Congress," editorial endorsement, *Minneapolis Tribune*, October 28, 1978, 10.

30. "Martin Olav Sabo for Congress," *Echo* 85, no. 9 (November 3, 1978), provided by Augsburg University president Paul Pribbenow, 2024.

31. "Minnesota's Vote Leaders," *Minneapolis Tribune*, November 8, 1978, 1A.

32. "A House Divided to Be Run by Diplomats, Not Democrats," *Minneapolis Star*, November 10, 1978, 8.

33. Cohen interview.

Notes to Chapter Eleven: Congressman Sabo

1. "Rep. Martin Sabo Speaks with Senior Brademas Fellow Linda Douglass," John Brademas Center for the Study of Congress, "Reflections with Martin Sabo," December 6, 2006, YouTube, https://tinyurl.com/bddc37bw.

2. "Mondale Assistant Will Join Sabo Staff," *Minneapolis Tribune*, December 20, 1978, 1B; Baumgartner interview, 2023.

3. Oral history interview, Sabo Papers, 18.

4. Baumgartner interview, 2008, 6–8.

5. "Sabo Is Nominated for Membership on Appropriations Panel," *Minneapolis Tribune*, January 17, 1979, 2B.

6. "Sabo Named to Housing, Transportation Panels," *Minneapolis Tribune*, January 31, 1979, 5B; Baumgartner interview, 2008, 7.

7. Baumgartner interview, 2023.

8. Bostelmann interview.

9. Oral history interview, Sabo Papers, 21.

10. Sabo and Douglass, Brademas Center interview.

11. Erlandson interview; "Barney Frank," Britannica, accessed February 10, 2025, https://www.britannica.com/biography/Barney-Frank.

12. Bostelmann interview.

13. Erlandson interview.

14. "Martin Sabo, Vice Chair," Minnesota Ballpark Authority, accessed February 10, 2025, https://ballparkauthority.com/mobile/Martin_Sabo.html.

15. "Following the Party *Base*line," *Minneapolis Star Tribune*, June 22, 2001, A14.

16. "Martin Sabo? Who Did the Twins Trade for Him?," *Minneapolis Star Tribune*, June 18, 1982.

17. Sabo and Douglass, Brademas Center interview.

18. "Sabo Sits Out Last Ballgame on Hill," *Minneapolis Star and Tribune*, July 1, 2006, A4.

19. Sabo and Douglass, Brademas Center interview.

20. Baumgartner interview, 2008.

21. Steve Berg, "Sabo Set for Long Haul in House," *Minneapolis Star and Tribune*, February 14, 1983, 6A.

22. Steve Berg, "Sabo Set for Long Haul in House," *Minneapolis Star and Tribune*, February 14, 1983, 6A.

23. Vin Weber interview.

24. Oral history interview, Sabo Papers, 18.

25. For a roster of House appropriations committees and subcommittees, see US Congress House Committee on Appropriations, *A Concise History*.

26. Baumgartner interview, 2008, 8–9; Erlandson interview.

27. State of Minnesota Legislative Manual, 1993–94, 361, Minnesota Legislative Reference Library, https://www.lrl.mn.gov/mngov/bluebooks.

28. Baumgartner interview, 2008, 19.

29. "State Delegation Gears Up for New Session," *Minneapolis Star Tribune*, January 3, 1993, 17A.

30. Baumgartner interview, 2008, 21.

31. "Sabo Elected Chair of Budget Committee by House Democrats," *Minneapolis Star Tribune*, January 7, 1993, 1A; Erlandson interview.

32. "1992 United States Presidential Election," Wikipedia, accessed February 10, 2025, https://en.wikipedia.org/wiki/1992_United_States_presidential_election; "Federal Debt: Total Public Debt as Percent of Gross Domestic Product," Federal Reserve Bank of St. Louis, accessed February 10, 2025, https://fred.stlouisfed.org/series/GFDEGDQ188S.

33. "Budget," *Minneapolis Star Tribune*, March 19, 1993, 13A; Baumgartner interview, 2008, 10.

34. "Sabo Quietly Kept House in Order for Clinton Plan," *Minneapolis Star Tribune*, March 22, 1993, 1.

35. Leon Panetta interview.

36. "Omnibus Budget Reconciliation Act of 1993," Wikipedia, accessed February 10, 2025, https://en.wikipedia.org/wiki/Omnibus_Budget_Reconciliation_Act_of_1993.

37. Erlandson interview.

38. Tim Penny interview.

39. "Penny's Budget-Cut Plan Fails," *Minneapolis Star Tribune*, November 23, 1993, 1A.

40. John Kasich, "Sabo at the Budget Helm," *Minneapolis Star Tribune*, August 4, 1993, 14.

41. John Kasich interview.

42. Baumgartner interview, 2008, 14, 24. An example of one such "Dear Colleague" letter is here: https://tinyurl.com/kvdszdk4.

43. "GOP Deficit Fix: Tried—But True?," *Minneapolis Star Tribune*, October 2, 1994, 15, 22.

44. Baumgartner interview, 2008, 27.

45. Sabo and Douglass, Brademas Center interview.

46. Oral history interview, Sabo Papers, 20; "Blue Dog Coalition," Wikipedia, accessed February 10, 2025, https://en.wikipedia.org/wiki/Blue_Dog_Coalition.

47. "Budget: Compromise Hours, Or Days, Away?," *Sacramento (CA) Bee*, December 18, 1995, 12M; "Blue Dog Democrats Sink their Teeth into Budget," *Fort Worth (TX) Star Telegram*, November 26, 1995, 8.

48. "Eyeball to Eyeball Standoff Shows Depth of Budget Impasse," *Minneapolis Star Tribune*, November 15, 1995, 14; "Minnesotans in House Cautiously Welcome New Plan," *Minneapolis Star Tribune*, December 8, 1995, 11; "GOP Leaders Open to Talks on Scaling Back Tax Cut," *Minneapolis Star Tribune*, December 4, 1995, 4; "Push To Balance First, Cut Taxes Later Gains Momentum," *Minneapolis Star Tribune*, December 21, 1995, 17.

49. Baumgartner interview, 2008, 28; "1995–1996 United States Federal Government Shutdowns," Wikipedia, accessed February 10, 2025, https://en.wikipedia.org/wiki/1995%E2%80%931996_United_States_federal_government_shutdowns. For a history of the Blue Dog coalition, see "History," Blue Dog Coalition, accessed February 10, 2025, https://bluedogcaucus-golden.house.gov/about/history.

50. "Sabo Leaves Successor a Sizeable Legacy to Fill," *Minneapolis Star Tribune*, March 27, 2006, 4.

51. Oral history interview, Sabo Papers, 19.

52. Erlandson interview.

53. "Sabo to the Road Rescue Again? Transit Bill Includes $37.2 Million He Sought," *Minneapolis Star Tribune*, October 27, 1997, 9.

54. "Martin Olav Sabo Bridge," Wikipedia, accessed February 11, 2025, https://en.wikipedia.org/wiki/Martin_Olav_Sabo_Bridge.

55. "Transportation Bill OKed by House Panel Includes $1 Billion for State," *Minneapolis Star Tribune*, September 11, 1997, 15; Penny interview.

56. "ITU Press and Public Information Services," International Telecommunication Union (ITU), accessed February 11, 2025, https://www.itu.int/newsarchive/press/PP98/index.html.

57. Greg Ortale interview.

58. "Martin Sabo on the Wage Gap and His Income Equity Proposal," *Midday*, April 23, 1998, Minnesota Public Radio, https://archive.mpr.org/stories/1998/04/23/martin-sabo-on-the-wage-gap-and-his-income-equity-proposal.

59. Jessica Thompson, "Sabo Tries Again," *Minneapolis Star Tribune*, August 1, 2001, 4; oral history interview, Sabo Papers, 22.

60. "Corporate Gilt," *Minneapolis Star Tribune*, September 9, 2001, 32; Sam Pizzigati, "The Income Equity Act: Another Try!," Inequality.org, March 4, 2015, https://inequality.org/great-divide/income-equity-act-great-idea/.

Notes to Chapter Twelve: The Liberal Decentralist

1. "I Hope that I've Made a Difference," *Minneapolis Star Tribune*, March 19, 2006, 1B.

2. Erlandson interview; "I Hope that I've Made a Difference," *Minneapolis Star Tribune*, March 19, 2006, 1B.

3. Tom Scheck, "Former Party Chief Now Bucks the Party Process," Minnesota Public Radio News, July 6, 2006, https://www.mprnews.org/story/2006/07/06/erlandsonfiles.

4. Erlandson interview. See list of House appropriations committee members through history: US Congress House Committee on Appropriations, *A Concise History*.

5. Bill Salisbury, "Martin Olav Sabo, Longtime Minnesota Representative, Has Died," *St. Paul Pioneer Press*, March 13, 2016; "Sabo Center for Democracy and Citizenship," Augsburg University, accessed February 10, 2025, https://www.augsburg.edu/sabo/about/#history.

6. Oral history interview, Sabo Papers, 3, 17, 23.

7. "The 'Minnesota Miracle' recollections of the 1970–1971 Minnesota Legislative Sessions," videotaped conversation, Public Education Funding Reform: The "Minnesota Miracle of 1971," January 8, 2007, Minnesota Historical Society, https://tinyurl.com/4ttxpcb2.

8. Oral history interview, Sabo Papers, 21.

9. "National Fix the Debt Group Gets Help from Boschwitz, Sabo, Penny," *St. Paul Pioneer Press*, January 14, 2013.

10. Sabo and Douglass, Brademas Center interview.

11. Oral history interview, Sabo Papers, 22.

12. Eric Black, "Why Liberal Martin Sabo Is Allying with the Deficit Hawks," *MinnPost*, February 1, 2013.

13. Karin Mantor interview.

14. Erlandson interview.

15. "State Loses a Legislative Giant," *Minneapolis Star Tribune*, March 14, 2016, 1; "Martin Olav Sabo, Longtime Minnesota Representative, Has Died," *St. Paul Pioneer Press*, March 14, 2016.

16. "Martin Olav Sabo, Congressman Known for Civility in Partisan Times, Dies at 78," *New York Times*, March 13, 2016; "It Was an Honor to Know Him," *Minneapolis Star Tribune*, March 21, 2016, A12.

17. "Sabo Gave His All to Strengthen Democracy," *Minneapolis Star Tribune*, March 15, 2016, 6.

18. Sheletta Brundidge interview.

19. For more about Sheletta Brundidge, see "Sheletta Brundidge Can Do It All!," Sheletta Makes Me Laugh, accessed February 10, 2025, https://www.shelettamakesmelaugh.com/about. Among those killed with Mickey Leland in Ethiopia in August 1989 was his chief of staff Patrice Johnson, daughter of Twin Cities civil rights leader Josie Johnson: "Leland Chief of Staff Patrice Johnson Remembered as Likeable Achiever," *Minneapolis Star Tribune*, August 14, 1989, 9.

20. "Please Remember in Your Prayers Martin Olav Sabo," March 14, 2016, University of St. Thomas Newsroom, accessed February 11, 2025, https://news.stthomas.edu/please-remember-prayers-martin-olav-sabo/. Photo and text of the courthouse plaque supplied by federal courts communications officer Rebeccah Parks, October 29, 2024.

21. Bill Kelly interview, March 2, 2023.

BIBLIOGRAPHY

Archives

Minnesota Historical Society, St. Paul. Martin Olav Sabo Papers.

Minnesota Legislative Reference Library, St. Paul.

Sabo Family Archives.

Interviews by the Author

Baumgartner, Eileen. March 13, 2023.

Berg, Tom. August 16, 2023.

Bostelmann, Margaret. October 30, 2023.

Brundidge, Sheletta. October 12, 2023.

Chrislock, Winston. April 4, 2023.

Cohen, Richard. May 15, 2024.

Davies, Jack. November 1, 2022.

Dirkswager, Edward. January 19, 2024.

Dornfeld, Steven. January 10, 2024.

Erlandson, Michael. April 26, 2024.

Gilje, Paul. October 19, 2023.

Graba, Joe. October 2, 2023.

Growe, Joan Anderson. September 25, 2023.

Haynes, John Earl. September 18, 2023.

Huesers, Anna Marie. August 18, 2022.

Kahn, Phyllis. November 8, 2023.

Kasich, John. July 3, 2024.

Kelly, Bill. October 5, 2022; March 2, 2023.

Knickerbocker, Gerald. October 20, 2023.

Kolderie, Ted. January 9, 2024.

Laird, Joanne Stiles. February 16, 2023.

Mantor, Karin. July 25, 2024.

Mantor, Karin Sabo, and Julie Sabo. January 9, 2023.

Mendis, Patrick. September 21, 2023.

Moe, Richard. October 20, 2023; December 21, 2023.

Nobles, James. January 29, 2024.

Ortale, Greg. July 23, 2024.

Panetta, Leon. July 1, 2024.

Pearson, Vicki Skor. February 16, 2023.

Pederson, Jim. August 12, 2022.

Penny, Tim. July 22, 2024.

Pound, Bill. July 3, 2023.

Rust, Gary. February 25, 2023.

Sabo, Julie. January 9, 2023.

Savelkoul, Henry. April 30, 2024.

Skoglund, Wes. May 30, 2024.

Solem, James. February 1, 2024.
Stanton, Russell. March 25, 2024.
Sulerud, Grace Kemmer. March 1, 2023.
Suss, Ted. April 26, 2024.
Vanasek, Robert. September 22, 2023.
Weber, Vin. June 24, 2024.

Other Interviews

Baumgartner, Eileen, oral history. 2008. Bill Clinton Presidential History Project. University of Virginia Miller Center, Charlottesville, VA. https://millercenter.org/the-presidency/presidential-oral-histories/eileen-baumgartner-oral-history.

"Martin Olav Sabo: A Journey through Forty-Six Years in the Minnesota House and the United States Congress," oral history interview. September 14, 2015. Martin Olav Sabo Papers, Minnesota Historical Society, St. Paul.

"Rep. Martin Sabo Speaks with Senior Brademas Fellow Linda Douglass." December 6, 2006. John Brademas Center for the Study of Congress, "Reflections with Martin Sabo." YouTube, accessed February 22, 2025, https://tinyurl.com/bddc37bw.

Newspapers

Albert Lea Tribune
Austin Daily Herald
Emmons Leader
Fergus Falls Daily Journal
Fort Worth (TX) Star Telegram
La Crosse (WI) Tribune
Minneapolis Morning Tribune
Minneapolis Star
Minneapolis Star and Tribune
Minneapolis Star-Journal
Minneapolis Star Tribune
Minneapolis Sunday Tribune
Minneapolis Tribune
MinnPost
New Prague Times
New York Times
Sacramento (CA) Bee
St. Cloud Times
St. Paul Pioneer Press
Winona Daily News

Published Works

Adamo, Phil. "Martin Olav Sabo for Congress." Hold Fast to What Is Good: A History of Augsburg University in 10 Objects. Minneapolis, 2019. https://web.augsburg.edu/alumni/Adamo-Martin%20Olav%20Sabo%20for%20Congress.pdf.

Advisory Commission on Intergovernmental Relations. *Federalism in 1971: The Crisis Continues.* Thirteenth Annual Report, Report M-73, February 1972.

Andersen, Elmer L. *A Man's Reach.* Edited by Lori Sturdevant. University of Minnesota Press, 2000.

Berg, Tom. *Minnesota's Miracle: Learning from the Government That Worked.* University of Minnesota Press, 2012.

Chrislock, Carl H. *From Fjord to Freeway: 100 Years, Augsburg College*. Augsburg College, 1969.

Christenson, Gerald W. *A Minnesota Citizen: Stories from the Life and Times of Jerry Christenson*. Published by author, 2005.

Dura, Jack. "Alkabo, N.D." *Dakota Datebook*. December 19, 2016, Prairie Public Television. https://news.prairiepublic.org/show/dakota-datebook-archive/2022-06-10/alkabo-n-d.

Durenberger, Dave, with Lori Sturdevant. *When Republicans Were Progressive*. Minnesota Historical Society Press, 2018.

Fraser, Arvonne Skelton. *She's No Lady: Politics, Family, and International Feminism*. Edited by Lori Sturdevant. Nodin Press, 2007.

Gilje, Paul. *How Could You Do This? 50 Years of Property-Tax-Base Sharing in Minnesota*. Center for Policy Design Press, 2021.

Growe, Joan Anderson, with Lori Sturdevant. *Turnout: Making Minnesota the State that Votes*. Minnesota Historical Society Press, 2020.

Holt, Bradley P. "Bernhard Christensen: An Informal Sketch." *Till & Keep* (a journal on vocation) (Spring 2010). https://web.augsburg.edu/acfl/tillandkeep/tk10.pdf.

Joranger, Terje Mikael Hasle. "The Migration of Tradition: Land Tenure and Culture in the U.S. Upper Midwest." *European Journal of American Studies* 3, no. 3 (2008).

Kolderie, Ted. *Thinking Out the How*. Beaver's Pond Press, 2017.

Leininger, Elaine. *Portraits of Prairie Pioneers and the Early Years of Alkabo*. 6th printing. Published by author, 2001.

Milton, John Watson. *For the Good of the Order: Nick Coleman and the High Tide of Liberal Politics in Minnesota, 1971–1981*. Ramsey County Historical Society, 2012.

Nathanson, Iric. *Don Fraser: Minnesota's Quiet Crusader*. Nodin Press, 2018.

Nathanson, Iric. *Minneapolis in the Twentieth Century: The Growth of an American City*. Minnesota Historical Society Press, 2010.

Sturdevant, Lori. *Her Honor: Rosalie Wahl and the Minnesota Women's Movement*. Minnesota Historical Society Press, 2014.

Sturdevant, Lori. *The Pillsburys of Minnesota*. Nodin Press, 2011.

Szczur, Walter J. "Norwegian Settlement in North Dakota." Master's thesis, University of Montana, 1949. https://scholarworks.umt.edu/cgi/viewcontent.cgi?article=6376&context=etd.

US Congress House Committee on Appropriations. *A Concise History of the U.S. House of Representatives Committee on Appropriations*. US Government Printing Office, 2010. https://democrats-appropriations.house.gov/sites/evo-subsites/democrats-appropriations.house.gov/files/House_Approps_Concise_History.pdf.

Wilson, Betty. *Rudy! The People's Governor*. Nodin Press, 2005.

IMAGE CREDITS

Page 5	Homestead Act of 1862: 37th US Congress, public domain, via Wikimedia Commons
Page 6	Homestead Act stamp: Fred Hultstrand, public domain, via Wikimedia Commons
Page 10	Alkabo, ND: Andrew Filer, In memoriam afiler, CC BY-SA 2.0, via Wikimedia Commons
Page 28	Adlai Stevenson campaign pin: NPR, public domain, via Wikimedia Commons
Page 40	Edward Chilgren: photograph by Kenneth M. Wright Studios, MNHS collections
Page 46	Karl Rolvaag: MNHS collections
Page 58	Hubert Humphrey 1968: Kheel Center for Labor-Management Documentation and Archives, Cornell University Library, CC BY 2.0, via Wikimedia Commons
Page 70	Harold LeVander: MNHS collections
Page 76	Wendell Anderson: MNHS collections
Page 100	George McGovern with Anderson, Humphrey, and Mondale: MNHS collections
Page 105	Martin Sabo and Helen McMillan: MNHS collections
Page 107	Joan Growe: MNHS collections
Page 150	Phyllis Kahn: MNHS collections
Page 156	Jimmy Carter and Walter Mondale: *US News and World Report*, public domain
Page 162	Martin Sabo reelected speaker: photograph by Kent Kobersteen, MNHS collections
Page 184	Martin Sabo at 1978 convention: photograph by Steve Schlueter, MNHS collections
Page 197	Nicholas Coleman and Martin Sabo: MNHS collections
Page 220	Martin Sabo Bridge: Kris Laynon, CC 2.0, via Wikimedia Commons

INDEX

NOTE: Page numbers in *italics* indicate images in the text.

abortion, 67, 180, 182, 186
Ackerberg, Peter, 96
ADA (Americans for Democratic Action), 180, 201
Adams, James, 36, 44, 51, 59, 137–38
Adams, Salisbury, 45
adjournment date, 120–21, 154–55
Affordable Care Act, 146
affordable housing, 144–46, 225
age of House members, 37, 110, 122
Agranoff, Robert, 96
Agriculture committee, 117
Alkabo, ND: Alkabo School, 9–14, 18–19; building a new house, 12; church and school, 12–15; electrical services to, 16–17; gravel road intersection, *10*; high school graduations, 20; and Minneapolis, MN, 21–22; population of, 3–4; Sabo family's homestead claim, 6–9
Alnes, Stephen, 127
American Lutheran Church, 47–48
Americans for Democratic Action (ADA), 180, 201
American Society of Legislative Clerks and Secretaries, 89–90
Andersen, Elmer L., 37, 42, 45
Anderson, Irvin, 113–14, 117, 126, 162–64, 193, 197
Anderson, Kathleen Clarke, 200
Anderson, Wendell: budget proposal, 75–79; Christenson on, 159–60; election of 1970, 70–72, 95–96; election of 1972, 109; election of 1974, 136–37; election of 1978, 174, 191, 194, 196; employees' pension bill, 133–35; health insurance, 145; homosexual marriage question, 101; legislative requests, 155; Loaned Executive Action Program (LEAP), 146; party designation, 123; photograph of, 76, *100*; presidential election of 1972, 100; property tax relief, 152; and redistricting, 90–91; sales tax bill, 57; "same-day" registration provision, 130; Senate self-appointment, 157–60; State of the State address, 115; tax/school funding issue, 81–85; veto of the House's tax bill, 81–84; youthful members of state's lawmaking body, 37
annual sessions, 121–22, 132, 176–77
Appropriations committee, 54, 201, 208–9, 218–19
Association of Minnesota Counties, 129

attack ads, 1, 198
Augsburg College (now Augsburg University), 21–31; accreditation, 22, 26; and Anna Marie Sabo, 20; Augsburg Young Democrats club, 28–29; and Chrislock, 22, 26–29, 30; and civil rights, 31; evolution of, 21–26; Lutheran Free Church, 13; rules about behavior, 25–26; Trinity Lutheran, 63

Backstrom, Charles, 35
Baglien, Dave, 18–19
Bailey, Charles, 139
Baker v. Carr, 48
balanced budgets, 79, 208, 211, 218, 226
ballot labels, 41–42, 122–23
Bang, Otto, 45
baseball, 17–18, 205–6
Baumgartner, Eileen: on Clinton budget, 211; committee assignments, 201–2; Deficit Reduction Act of 1993, 215; election of 1992, 209–10; gender diversity, 138; government shutdowns, 218; House Research, 124, 143–44; on Obey, 207; Republican tax plan, 216; Sabo's congressional staff, 200; state planning agency, 77; tax conference committee, 152–54
Berg, Steve, 205–7
Berg, Tom: campaign finance reform, 130–31; committee assignments, 143; Duxbury on Sabo's speakership, 112; election of 1970, 67–70; employees' pension bill, 133; majority leader contest, 163; *Minnesota's Miracle*, 112, 128–29, 133; Sabo's reaction to news stories, 128–29; and Vanasek, 99
Berglin, Linda, 107, 118, 172
Bieging, David, 199, 201
biennial budgets, 79, 177
Bismarck, ND, 16
Blackmun, Harry, 49
Blatz, Jerome, 153
Bloomington, MN, 51–52
Blue Dog Democrats, 217–18
Board of Regents, University of Minnesota, 80–81
Bolling, Richard, 201–2
Boschwitz, Rudy, 174, 196, 226
Bostelmann, Margaret, 173, 203, 234
Boundary Waters Canoe Area, 169, 186
Bradley, Methuselah, 182–83
Brandt, Steve, 176
Bredevin, Peder, 7
Brennan, William, 48
brochure prepared by the state DFL party, 97–98
Brown, Bob, 134
Brundidge, Sheletta, 228–29
Budget committee, 209, 210–15, 217–18
"bull pens," 42, 64, 126
Burdick, Edward, 89–90, 151
Burnsville, MN, 52

Cain, Ruth, 101
California, 190, 201
California Supreme Court, 86
campaign(s): for 1960 election, 34–36; for 1974 election, 136; for 1992 election, 209; campaign finance reform, 129–31; campaign gifts, 131; clean campaigning, 102–3; legislative campaigns, 198; role of state political parties, 96
Campaign to Fix the Debt, 226
candidate recruitment, 33, 41, 69, 95–96, 135, 198
Candid Comment (radio show), 165
Capitol remodeling project, 63–64, 126–27

Capitol reporters, 79, 111, 115, 128–29, 141, 145, 153
Carlson, Arne, 179–80, 248n7
Carlson, Bernard, 117–18, 142
Carter, Jimmy, *156*, 157, 170
caucus leaders, 60–62, 64, 102, 104, 139, 162–63, 198, 209
caucus steering committees, 102, 113, 192–93
caucus-to-convention system, 183–85
"The Changing Legislature" series, 176–77
Chilgren, Edwin J., 40, *40*, 42
Chmielewski, Florian, 83
Chrislock, Carl, 22, 26–29, 30
Chrislock, Winston, 29, 30, 35
Christensen, Bernhard, 24–25, 26, 31
Christenson, Gerald W., 76–77, 125, 138–40, 159–60
Christenson, Theodore, 158
Christianson, Harlan, 28, 30
Cina, Fred, 40, 56, 60–61, 67
"circuit breaker," 152–55
Citizens League, 52–53, 71
civil rights, 31, 101
Clark, Janet, 137–38
Clay, Charles, 52
Clean Indoor Air Act, 150–51
Clinton, Hillary Rodham, 214, 227
Clinton, William J. "Bill," 209–10, 211–12, 217–18
Coffman, Jack, 151
Cohen, Richard, 192–93, 196–98
Coleman, Nicholas: and Anderson, 82; caucus leadership, 71–72; election of 1970, 95–96; employees' pension bill, 133; Office of Senate Counsel, 124; party designation, 123; and Perpich, 165; photograph of, *197*; as Senate candidate to replace Humphrey, 169–70, 174; state aid to cities, 86; state taxes, 128; tax conference committee, 152–55
committee assignments, 42–43, 72, 116–19, 141–44, 200–202
committee structure, 114–15
compensation for legislative leaders, 74, 104, 134–35, 136, 178
congressional elections: of 1960, 34–36; of 1962, 43–46; of 1966, 49–51; of 1968, 59–61; of 1970, 94–97; of 1972, 94–109; of 1974, 132, 135–37, 140; of 1978, 179–98; of 1992, 209; of 1994, 215–17
"Contract with America" reform package, 215
Conzemius, George, 152–54
corporate taxes, 221–22
Council on Human Relations, 31
crime control bill, 216
Crime Prevention and Corrections committee, 118
Crosby, ND, 11, 20
Crosby High School, 13

D'Aquila, Carl, 165–66
Davies, Jack, 37, 138
Davies, Pat, 43
Dayton, Mark, 224
"Dear Colleague" letters, 215
defense spending, 208–9
Defense subcommittee, 208–9
Deficit Reduction Act of 1993, 212–15
Democratic-Farmer-Labor (DFL) Party: Anderson's self-appointment, 157–60; ballot labels, 122–23; candidates in the 1970 election, 69–70; candidates in the 1978 election, 191–93, 194–95; caucus leaders, 60–61; convention of 1960, 34; convention of 1978, 183–85; creation of, 182; election of 1970, 94–97; election of 1972, 108–9; election

of 1974, 135–37; endorsement, 34–35, 51, 59, 183–85; Fifth District DFL endorsing convention, 173–75; House DFL Policy Research, 124–25; as legislative majority, 161–64; majority leader, 113; merger in 1944, 30–31, 41; Minnesota massacre, 196–98; "openness in government" campaign, 97–98, 114–16, 126, 129; precinct caucuses, 32; Republicans in DFL-dominated House, 140–41; rules change proposals, 72–74; rules package, 115–16; sales taxes, 55, 79–80; split within, 62; state convention in 1972, 101
Democratic National Convention in 1976, 157–58
Democrats: and baseball, 205–6; Blue Dog Democrats, 217–18; budget bill, 212–13; budget resolution, 212; congressional election of 1994, 216; "Dear Colleague" letters, 215; government shutdowns, 218; partisan divide in state lawmaking, 122; voters, 108
Department of Homeland Security, 219
Devitt, Edward, 91–93
Diana E. Murphy Federal Courthouse, 231
Dicks, Norm, 214
Dirkswager, Edward: caucus press releases, 128; House DFL Policy Research, 124–25; housing and health care, 144–46; Office of the Legislative Auditor, 147–48; oral history project, 227; Sabo's relationship building, 149; tax conference committee, 152–53; time spent at the Capitol by House members, 127
Dirlam, Aubrey, 64, 72–74, 113, 114–15, 133, 135, 140
Dlugosch, Jim, 144–45
Dome Club, 173
door-knocking, 28–29, 34–35, 44–45, 50–51, 69, 102, 181, 186, 195, 198
Dornfeld, Steven, 128, 160, 176
Doyle, Mike, 206
Drew, John, 192–93
drivers' licenses, 19–20
DuBois, B. F. "Pat," 56, 60
Duluth, MN, 61, 86
Durenberger, David, 174, 194, 196
Duxbury, Lloyd, 54, 72, 111–12, 172

Eagan, MN, 52
Eagleton, Thomas, 99–100
Eagleton Institute for Young Legislators, 88
earned income tax credit, 212
Echo (newspaper), 196
Education committee, 143
Eisenhower, Dwight, 16
Eken, Willis, 69, 117
Elkhorn Township, 6–7
Ellison, Keith, 224
employees' pension bill, 133–35
Erdahl, Arlen, 45, 108, 137
Erlandson, Michael: budget bill, 213; Department of Homeland Security, 219; election of 1992, 209–11; Martin Olav Sabo Post Office, 229–30; relationship building, 204; Sabo's retirement decision, 223–24; Sabo's tax policy, 143; saying goodbye, 227
expense payments, 187–88

Fairview Hospital, 28, 30, 46–47
Fairway Grocery, 30
Falls of St. Anthony, 22
Fargo, ND, 13
Faricy, Ray, 69, 99, 163
federal courts, 39, 48–50, 91
federal spending, 190, 202

Feinstein, Sue, 195
feminism/feminist organizations, 104–5, 182
Fifth District, 31, 171–75, 180–81, 183–84, 186–87, 189, 195, 196, 208, 209
financial security for retirees and the disabled, 226–27
"fiscal disparities" bill, 53
fiscal policy, 211–15
Fischer, Hank, 106
Fister, Ola Ellingson, 4, 7
Fitzgerald, Dick, 52
Flakne, Gary, 45
floor debates, 56, 67, 72, 80, 113, 115, 141, 151, 162
Foley, Tom, 213
Ford, Bill, 201
Ford, Gerald, 133
Forsythe, Mary, 107
Fourteenth Amendment, 48
Fox, William, 128
Frank, Barney, 204
Fraser, Arvonne Skelton, 32–33, 182
Fraser, Donald, 32–34, 169, 171–72, 174, 180, 185–87, 191, 194
Frazier, Lynn J., 15
Frederikson, Larry, 145
Freeman, Orville, 31, 33, 40, 42, 91, 158
Frenzel, Bill, 45, 52–53, 196, 207
From Fjord to Freeway (Chrislock), 22, 26
Fudro, Stan, 117
Future Teachers of America club, 29

Gearty, Ed, 54, 133
gender diversity, 137–38
General Land Office, 4–6
General Legislation committee, 117
Gibson, Lois, 180–83, 228
Gingrich, Newt, 212, 215, 218
Gore, Al, 213
Government Operations committee, 118, 143, 147, 149
government shutdowns, 82–83, 218
Graba, Joe: and campaigning, 102; committee assignments, 117, 143; counting votes, 81; election of 1970, 69; election of 1972, 108; oral history project, 227; and redistricting, 102; on Sabo as the floor leader, 111, 114; on Sabo's campaigning, 136; on Sabo's career success, 80, 173; Sabo's congressional staff, 200; and Vanasek, 99
Graham, Dick, 221
Great Depression, 9, 24, 54
Greater Minnesota, 60–62, 95, 186, 194
Green, Zollie, 59
Greenwood, Hal, 80–81
Growe, Joan Anderson, 104–6, *107*, 129–30, 137
gubernatorial tenure in Minnesota, 158
guns, 186
Gustafson, Earl, 62

Haga, Kari Velde (maternal grandmother), 9
Haga, Martin (maternal grandfather), 9
Hagland, Carl, 33–34, 36
Hall, Lawrence, 172
Hartl, Albert, 80
Hatfield, Rolland, 66, 86
Hauge, Hans Nielsen, 13
Haugerud, Neil, 162–64
Haynes, John Earl, 77–78, 81, 85, 200, 201–2
Head, Douglas, 44, 70–71
Health and Welfare committee, 51, 118
health insurance, 144–46, 214

Heaney, Gerald, 91–93
Helland, John, 124
Hemenway, Ray, 32–34
Hennepin County, MN, 50
Hetland, James, 52
Heusers, Anna Marie, 228
Hibbing, MN, 165
high-risk insurance pool, 146
Hillside School, 14
Hjelmeland, Norway, 4
Hoium, David, 130
Holmquist, Stanley, 82–83, 86–87, 92
home-improvement loan program, 145
Homestead Act of 1862, 4–7, *5*
Honsey, Milton, 49
House appropriations subcommittees, 212
House DFL Policy Research, 124–25
House districts, 50, 92–93, 95, 135
House Journal, 73
House Research, 64, 124–25, 143–44, 149
House rules, 72–74
House Ways and Means committee, 201
Housing and Urban Affairs subcommittee, 202
Howell, Deborah, 90–91, 170
Hoyer, Steny, 224
Huesers, Lloyd, 20
Humphrey, George, 68, 71–72
Humphrey, Hubert: Americans for Democratic Action (ADA), 180; and Bolling, 201; death of, 168–71; and the DFL, 30–32; face-to-face candidate recruitment, 96; photograph of, *58*, *100*; presidential election of 1968, 59–60, 62; presidential election of 1972, 99–100; reclaims US Senate seat, 70
Humphrey, Hubert H. "Skip" III, 129
Humphrey, Muriel, 169–70, 174, 185–86
Hurner, Robert, 95

Income Equity Act, 221–22
income taxes, 54–55, 78–79, 87, 166–68, 169, 175, 188–90, 212
Independent-Republicans, 163, 174, 193
interfaith prayer service, 62–63

Johnson, Arv, 128
Johnson, Carl, 143
Johnson, Doug, 118
Johnson, John, 137
Johnson, Josie, 80–81
Johnson, Lyndon, 60, 71, 99
Johnson, Robert, 56
Johnson, Verne, 52–53
Jones, Phil, 139
Jopp, Ralph, 150
Judd, Walter, 31, 52, 172, 187
Judiciary committee, 118

K–12 education budget, 66, 71
K–12 Education committee, 54
Kahn, Phyllis, 106–7, *150*, 150–51, 172
Kandiyohi County, MN, 46–48
Karth, Joe, 77
Kasich, John, 213–15, 217
Keith, A. M. "Sandy," 185–86
Kelly, William "Bill": Capitol remodeling project, 126; Christenson's plan, 139; Clean Indoor Air Act, 151; committee assignments, 117, 142–43; election of 1970, 69; election of 1978, 196; leadership in American government, 232; majority leader contest, 163; Minnesota Horizons, 140; Office of the Legislative Auditor, 147; on Sabo's campaigning, 136; on socializing, 119; tax conference

committee, 152–54; tax policy, 167–68, 175; and Vanasek, 99
Kelm, Elmer, 159
Kelm, Tom, 159
Kennedy, John F., 37, 42
Kennedy, Robert F., 62
Kenny, Kevin, 145–46
King, Martin Luther Jr., 62–63
Klobuchar, Amy, 231
Knickerbocker, Gerald, 123
Knoblach, Jim, 123
Kolderie, Ted, 52
Kozak, Andrew, 159

Lahammer, Gene, 128
Laird, Joanne Stiles, 25
Lake Metigoshe, 14
Larson, Earl, 91, 92–93
Latz, Robert, 43
League of Minnesota Cities, 129
League of Women Voters, 106
LEAP (Loaned Executive Action Program), 146
Lee, L. J., 62
Lee, Sylvan and Agnes Dahl, 47
Legislative Audit Commission, 146–48
legislative days, 38, 120–21
legislative districts, 48, 90–93
legislative pay, 133–35, 188
Leininger, Elaine, 8, 16, 20
Leland, Mickey, 229
Leland Fellows, 229
Lemke, Dick, 118
LeVander, Harold, 55–57, 65–67, 70, *70*, 75–77, 174, 185
LGA (Local Government Aid), 85–86
licensure requirements, 19–20
Lindstrom, Ernest, 74, 84, 113, 116
Loaned Executive Action Program (LEAP), 146
Local and Urban Affairs committee, 143
Local Government Aid (LGA), 85–86
local governments: Office of the Legislative Auditor, 147; open-meeting requirements, 129; property taxes, 54–55, 65–66; tax policy, 71, 190
Lockhart, Greer, 52
Ludeman, Cal, 196
Luther, Sally, 104
Lutheran Free Church, 13–14, 20, 21, 23, 29, 47–48. *See also* Augsburg College (now Augsburg University)
Luther League meetings, 20
Luther Seminary, 25

Mann, George, 117
Mantor, Karin Margaret (née Sabo) (daughter), 51, 104, 119, 172–73, 202–3, 227–28
Martin Olav Sabo Bridge, 219, *220*
Martin Olav Sabo Post Office, 229–31
mass transit operations, 220
McArthur, Ernee, 107
McCarthy, Eugene, 31, 62
McCollum, Betty, 231
McCutcheon, William, 169
McGovern, George, 99–101, *100*, 108, 191
McMillan, Helen, *105*, 106–7, 118
Medicare, 212–14, 226–27
Mendis, Patrick, 89
Menke, Dick, 98–99
Menning, Marion "Mike," 174
Metropolitan and Urban Affairs committee, 51
Metropolitan Council, 51–53
Metro Transit in the Twin Cities, 220
military spending, 215–16
Minge, David, 217
minimum wage, 226
Minneapolis, MN: and Alkabo, ND, 21–22; civil rights, 31;

congressional election, 1974, 135; Diana E. Murphy Federal Courthouse, 231; and redistricting, 49, 61; Sabo moved home to, 224–25; Seward neighborhood, 144–45, 203; state aid to cities, 86. *See also* Augsburg College (now Augsburg University); Humphrey, Hubert

Minneapolis Star (newspaper): ballot labels question, 123; door-knocking, 35; election of 1972, 108–9; McGovern's candidacy, 100; "pro-con" essays in, 167; and redistricting, 90–91; Sabo's congressional bid, 172, 195; Sabo's full given name, 191; Till's tax proposal, 189

Minneapolis Star Tribune (newspaper): and baseball, 205–6; budget resolution, 212; Kasich letter to the editor, 214–15; Republican tax plan, 216; Sabo's retirement decision, 223; tribute to Sabo, 228; Twin Cities transit projects, 219

Minneapolis Tribune (newspaper): "The Changing Legislature" series, 176–77; election of 1972, 109; election of 1978, 195, 196; election of DFL caucus leaders, 60–62; employees' pension bill, 134; feminist organizations, 182; homosexual marriage question, 101; majority leader contest, 163; Minnesota Poll, 158–59; National Conference of State Legislatures (NCSL), 161; session of 1969, 67; on Stanton, 193; voters' guide, 41, 122, 136, 190; weekly expense payments, 187–88

Minnesota: civil rights, 31; gubernatorial tenure in, 158; legal drinking age, 149–50; legislative districts, 90–93; NCSL delegates, 161; state aid to cities, 85–86; statewide voter registration system, 129–30; tax policy, 54, 81–87, 143–44, 151–55, 168; women in, 104–5

A Minnesota Citizen (Christenson), 159–60

Minnesota Comprehensive Health Association (MCHA), 146

Minnesota Constitution, 38, 44, 93

Minnesota Federation of Teachers, 86

Minnesota Horizons, 139–40

Minnesota Legislative Reference Library, 64

Minnesota Legislature: ballot labels, 41–42; biennial sessions, 120; budget proposal, 75–79; calendar, 38, 120–21; campaign finance reform, 129–31; Capitol remodeling project, 63–64, 126–27; constitutional amendments, 38, 44; and Duxbury, 111–12; election of 1974, 135–37, 140; employees' pension bill, 133–35; Liberal majority, 95, 110; majority leader contest, 161–64; Metropolitan Council, 51–53; modernization of, 176–78; nonpartisan elections, 41–42; older workforce, 37–38; party designation, 41–42, 122–23, 132, 176; professionalization, 123–24; and redistricting, 38–39, 43–45, 48–50, 91–92; Sabo's departure from, 175–76; Sabo's legacy, 232; speakership in, 110–12, 113–14, 136, 140, 172; state demographer, 139; state operations, 127; statutes, 1973 session, 127–28; tax/school funding issue, 81–87; women in, 37, 104–6, 110, 137–38; workload, 38; Young Turks, 43–46

Minnesota massacre, 196–98
Minnesota Miracle, 88, 151, 166, 200
Minnesota Poll, 158–59, 174
Minnesota Real Estate Taxpayers Association, 86
Minnesota's Miracle (Berg), 112, 128–29, 133
Minnesota State Finance Department, 127
Minnesota State Planning Agency, 125
Minnesota Supreme Court, 39
Minnesota Women's Political Caucus, 182
Minnetonka, MN, 104–6
minority caucus members, 114–16
Minot State Teachers College, 20
Moe, Don, 118, 125
Moe, Richard: and campaigning, 103; congressional campaign message, 191; DFL convention delegates, 101; election of 1970, 94–96; election of 1972, 98, 108; McGovern's candidacy, 100; and redistricting, 91, 93; Sabo's congressional staff, 200
Moe, Roger, 125, 200
Mondale, Walter F.: Anderson's self-appointment, 157–60; and Bieging, 199, 201; election of 1970, 96; election of 1972, 108; and Moe, 191; photograph of, *100*; presidential election of 1972, 100; Sabo's committee assignments, 219; youthful members of state's lawmaking body, 37
municipal overburden, 86

National Conference of State Legislative Leaders, 88–89, 131
National Conference of State Legislatures (NCSL), 89–90, 160–61, 200
National Legislative Conference, 88–89, 121, 123–24, 131, 146
National Security subcommittee, 219
National Society of State Legislatures, 89, 131
NCSL (National Conference of State Legislatures), 89–90, 160–61, 200
Nebraska, 122
Nelson, Gerry, 67, 80, 137, 151
Nelson, Gordon, 68
Newcome, Tom, 126
New Deal, 12
New Hampshire, 92
New Prague, MN, 98
New Prague Country Club, 103
New Prague Times (newspaper), 103
newspaper endorsement, 195–96
New York Times (newspaper), 228
Niebauer-Stall, Lisa, 184–85, 209
Nixon, Richard, 42, 60, 69–70, 99, 108, 130–31, 133
Nobles, James, 124, 147–48, 149
Nonpartisan League, 15–16
nonpartisan legislative elections, 41–42, 122
Norby, Ingeborg, 11
Norby, Julius, 11
North Central Association of Colleges and Schools, 26
North State Advisors, 159
Norton, Fred, 62
Norwegian-Danish Evangelical Lutheran Church in America, 23
Norwegian immigration to North Dakota, 4–8, 15
Norwegian Lutheran Church in America, 47

Oak Grove Seminary, 15
Oberstar, James, 201
Obey, David, 206–7
Occupational Safety and Health Act, 166

O'Connell, Tom, 182–83
Office of Senate Counsel, 124
Office of the Legislative Auditor, 146–48
Oftedal, Sven, 13, 22–23
Ogdahl, Harmon, 52
Oliva, Tony, 205
Olmsted County, MN, 50
Olson, Floyd B., 54
Omar, Ilhan, 229, 231
one-dollar checkoff provision, 130–31
O'Neill, Joseph, 63
O'Neill, Thomas P. "Tip," 197, 201
One Minnesota Conference, 139
"one person, one vote" rule, 48–51, 90
open-meeting requirements, 129
"openness in government" campaign, 96–98, 114–16, 126, 129
Opperman, Vance, 221
organized labor, 34, 113, 160, 164
Ortale, Greg, 220–21
Otter Tail County, MN, 50
Overgaard, Paul, 45

PAF (Public Affairs Federation), 29
Palmer, Richard, 71
Panetta, Leon, 209, 211–12
Parsons, Jim, 195
party designation, 31, 41–42, 122–23, 132, 176
party endorsement, 34–35, 41, 92, 171, 181–83
Paul, Ron, 206
Pavlak, Raymond, 142
Pearson, Vicki Skor, 27
Pederson, Dwight, 30
Pederson, Jim, 28, 30–34, 45, 95
Pelosi, Nancy, 224
Penny, Tim, 214, 220, 226
Penny-Kasich budget proposal, 214–15
Perot, Ross, 211
Perpich, A. J. "Tony," 152
Perpich, Rudy: and Anderson, 163–64; Anderson's self-appointment, 157; appointing a senator to replace Humphrey, 168–71; congressional election calendar, 174; election of 1978, 191, 194, 196; numbers in the Senate, 71; and Sabo, 164–66; taconite taxation, 165–66; tax policy, 166–68, 175
Peterson, Collin, 217
Peterson, Dennis, 30
Peterson, P. Kenneth, 31
Petrafeso, Pete, 175
Pianin, Eric, 158
Pillsbury, John S., 146–47, 158
Pleasant, Ray, 110
Plenipotentiary Conference of the International Telecommunications Union, 221
Porkbusters group, 220
post office–naming bill, 229
Pound, Bill, 90
presidential elections: of 1968, 59–60, 62; of 1972, 99–100, 108; of 1976, 157; of 1992, 211
Prifrel, Joseph, 60
primaries: 1960 election, 36; 1978 election, 183–86, 194–95; 1992 election, 185
private offices, 64, 126, 176–77
professionalization, 123–24
The Progressive Era in Minnesota, 1899–1918 (Chrislock), 27
pro-lifers, 182–83
Property Tax Refund Program, 155
property tax relief, 54–57, 65, 70–71, 76–79, 87, 151–55, 166–67, 188, 190
Proposition 13, 190
Public Affairs Federation (PAF), 29
public financing of campaigns, 130–31

public opinion polling, 125, 193
public school funding, 76–77

Quie, Al, 174, 196
Quirin, E. W., 60

Ramberg, Leonard, 52
Rauenhorst, George, 80–81
Reagan, Ronald, 83–84, 189, 216
redistricting, 38–39, 43–45, 48–50, 90–93, 102, 184
Reinhardt, Hazel, 139
Republicans: and baseball, 205–6; budget bill, 212–15; budget resolution, 212; congressional election, 1974, 135–37, 140; "Contract with America" reform package, 215; in DFL-dominated House, 140–41; and DFL merger, 30–31, 41; election of 1962, 44–45; federal taxation, 188–89; government shutdowns, 218; House majority in 1971, 71; Minnesota massacre, 196; Minnesota's legal drinking age, 149–50; partisan divide in state lawmaking, 122; primary of 1978, 185–86; property tax bill, 155; rules package, 115–16; sales taxes, 55; and taxes, 215–17; Tomlinson bill, 130; trifecta control, 67; Watergate scandal, 133
revival movement, 13
Reynolds v. Sims, 48–49
Rice, James, 115, 192–93
Richfield, MN, 24
Riemerman, William, 152–53
Riokedal, Maria Jonsdottir, 4
Rockenstein, Walter, 180
Roe, David, 101
Roll Call (newspaper), 205
Rolvaag, Karl, 45–46, *46*, 49–50, 55, 185–86
Roosevelt, Franklin D., 15, 17
Rosenmeier, Gordon, 53
Rotunda Club, 173
Rules committee, 72–74, 114–16, 117, 150–51, 162–63
Rural Electrification Act, 17
rural legislators, 38–39, 61
Rust, Gary, 17–18

Sabo, Anna Marie (sister), 8, 11, 12–15, 19–20
Sabo, Bjorn (Ben) (father), 4–10, 11–12, 13–16, 18, 19
Sabo, Elling (uncle), 4–7, 19
Sabo, Julie Ann (daughter), 9, 14, 17, 51, 104, 119, 171–73, 202–3, 228
Sabo, Klara Haga (mother), 8, 9, 11–12, 13–15, 18, 19, 171, 228
Sabo, Martin Olav: Anderson-Haugerud contest, 163–64; Anderson's self-appointment, 157–60; at Augsburg College, 21–22, 26–30; and Baglien, 18–19; baseball, love of, 17–18, 205–6; bid for speaker, 112; bill to increase Minnesota's legal drinking age, 149–50; and Blue Dog Democrats, 217–18; Budget committee, 209–10; candidate recruitment, 68–69; changes at the Capitol, 62–65, 126–27; and Chrislock, 26–29; and Christenson, 138–39; church and school, 14–15; civility in public affairs, 231; Clean Indoor Air Act, 150–51; and Coleman, 72; committee assignments, 42–43, 51–52, 54–57, 72–74, 141–44, 206–9; committee rosters, 116–19; congressional candidate in 1978, 179–98; congressional elections of 1992, 183–85, 209–10; congressional elections of 1994, 215–17;

congressional service, 199–222; congressional staff, 199–200; counting votes, 80–81, 210; "Dear Colleague" letters, 215; death of, 227–28; departure from the House, 175–76; DFL state convention in 1978, *184*; and diversity, 138; and Duxbury, 111–12; early life of, 11–20; elected for a second term as House speaker, 140–41; election of 1968, 59–60; election of 1972, 94–109; election of 1974, 135–37; end of legislative apprenticeship, 51; fiscal policy, 211–15; House Research, 124–25, 149; housing and health care, 144–46; Income Equity Act, 221–22; income taxes, 166–68, 169, 175; institutional changes, 121–22; Irvin Anderson on leadership team, 113–14; legacy of, 231–32; Legislative Audit Commission, 146–48; legislative candidate in 1960, 32–36; legislative candidate in 1966, 50–51; legislative candidate in 1978, 171–73; legislative pay, 133–35; liberal decentralist label, 225; Martin Olav Sabo Post Office, 229–31; Metropolitan Council, 51–53; minority caucus in 1963, 46; minority leader, 60–62, 65–67; National Legislative Conference meetings, 131; national legislative organizations, 88–90; openness in government, 96–97, 129; party designation, 41, 122–23; and Perpich, 164–66; political style of, 1–2, 160–61; politics, early interest in, 15–17; and professionalization, 123–25; property tax relief, 151–55; and redistricting, 90–93; relationship building, 40, 148–49, 204; relocation to Washington, 202–4; reporters, relationship with, 128–29; responsibilities given to as a young person, 19–20; retirement decision, 223–24; Rules committee, 72–74, 114–16; and Savelkoul, 141; sewage disposal legislation, 51–52; speakership, 110–13, 132; state aid to cities, 85–86; state and federal governments, thinking about, 225–27; and Sylvia, 46–48; Taxes committee, 54–57, 142–43; tax/school funding issue, 81–87; and transportation, 218–21; Twin Cities transit projects, 219–21; Young Turks, 46; youthful members of state's lawmaking body, 37

Sabo, Sylvia (née Lee) (wife), 46–48, 51, 63, 128, 171–73, 202–4, 210, 224, 228, 230

Sabo Center for Democracy and Citizenship, 225

St. John's Lutheran Church, Sioux Falls, SD, 47

St. John's University, 139

St. Louis County, MN, 50

St. Olaf College, Northfield, MN, 23, 47–48

St. Paul, MN, 61, 77, 86

St. Paul Pioneer Press (newspaper), 109

St. Paul Technical College, 139

Salchert, John, 60–62

sales taxes, 54–57, 65, 79, 87, 167, 190

"same-day" registration provision, 130

Savelkoul, Henry, 140–41, 147, 161, 176

school property taxes, 55, 71, 78, 82

Schwarzkopf, Incz (Olson), 45

Schwarzkopf, Lyall, 45–46, 69, 91

Searle, Rod, 126, 135, 140, 188, 197

second wave of feminism, 104–5

Senate districts, 34–36, 49–50, 91–93, 95

seniority, 116–17, 142, 201, 207
September 11, 2001, 219
settlers in North Dakota, 4–8, 15
Seward neighborhood, Minneapolis, 144–45, 203
Shoop, Jim, 155
Short, Robert, 174, 185–86, 194–95, 196, 205
Sieben, Harry "Tex" Jr., 69, 99, 118, 143
Skabo, Myrtle, 16
Skoglund, Wes, 68–69, 194, 196
Smith, Georgia M., 106
Smith, Jay, 39
smoking, 150–51
Social Security, 226–27
soft power, 116
Solem, James, 144–45
Southwest State University, 166
space subcommittee, 126
Spannaus, Warren, 94–95
speakership in the Minnesota House, 110–12, 113–14, 136, 140, 172
Spear, Allan, 59
special sessions, 38, 44, 57, 82–83, 92, 120
spending cuts, 212–13, 218
spending limits, 131
spending subcommittees, 211
Spratt, John, 210
Stangland, Arlan, 113
Stanton, Russell, 192–93, 196
Stark, Matthew, 106
state budgets, 65–67, 75–79
state demographer, 139
State Office Building, 63, 126–27, 143
state operations, 127
state Senate, 31, 41, 54, 92
state taxes, 78–79, 103, 128, 142–44
statewide voter registration system, 130
steering and policy committee, 200–201
Stevenson, Adlai, 16, 28
Stone Arch Bridge, 219
Stranik, Richard, 107
Strossen, Nadine, 182
subcommittee appointments, 202
Sulerud, Grace Kemmer, 27
Sullivan, John, 193
supply-side economics, 189
Suss, Ted, 143, 161, 191–92, 196
Sverdrup, Georg, 13, 22–24
Swift County, MN, 50
swing districts, 100–101, 192, 198

taconite taxation, 165–66
Talle, Jim, 123
tax-base sharing, 52
tax conference committee, 151–55
Taxes committee, 54–57, 142, 200
tax increases, 87, 211–14, 216
tax law changes of 1967, 65
tax policy, 54–57, 76–79, 81–87, 143–44, 151–55, 166–68, 175, 177, 188–90
tax revenue, 78–79
television ad campaigns, 187
Thomas, Clarence, 184
Thompson, Jessica, 222
Thrane, LoAnne, 80–81
Ticen, Thomas, 61, 72
Till, Michael, 186–89, 195
Tomlinson, John, 129–30
Transportation committee, 117–18
transportation subcommittee, 202, 208–9, 218–21
Trinity Lutheran, 63
Trump, Donald, 227
Turner, John, 145–46
Twin Cities metropolitan area, 51–53
Twin Cities transit projects, 219–21

unallotment, 79
United Norwegian Lutheran Church in America, 13

University of Minnesota, 30, 80–81, 166
University of St. Thomas, 231
US Advisory Commission on Intergovernmental Relations, 88
US Eighth Circuit Court of Appeals, 91
US House: committee assignments, 114–16, 200–202; newcomers in, 110, 137–40; new leadership, 113–14; relationship building, 202–4; Rules committee, 114–16; Sabo's approach to the work, 206–9; speakership, 162–63; tax conference committee, 152–55; tax policy, 167–68. *See also* congressional elections
US Senate: Anderson's self-appointment, 157–60; appointing a senator to replace Humphrey, 168–71, 174; campaign finance reform, 129–31; election of 1972, 108; numbers of, 71; Office of Senate Counsel, 124; sales tax bill, 56–57; tax conference committee, 151–55
US Supreme Court, 48–50, 92–93, 131

Vanasek, Robert, 97–99, 103, 108, 114, 192
Vanderpoel, Peter, 52
Vento, Bruce, 118
Veterans Affairs committee, 117
Vietnam War, 59–60, 62–63, 71–72, 99, 208
voter-eligibility age, 34, 108

Wartburg Seminary, Dubuque, IA, 47
Washington County, MN, 50
Watergate babies, 191, 196
Watergate election, 135–37
Watergate scandal, 131, 132–34
Ways and Means committee, 209
Weaver, Charles, 53
Weber, Vin, 207–8
Wellstone, Paul, 98
Wesberry v. Sanders, 48
Whereatt, Robert, 179, 189–90
Whitaker, Robert, 147
White, Richard, 68, 69
widows, appointing to complete elective terms, 170
Wilson, Betty, 150–51, 152, 158, 175
Winkler, Mark, 106
women, 104–6, 110, 118, 137–38, 170
Writing Rock Lutheran Church, 9, 13–14, 20

Yngve, John, 45
Young Citizens League, 16
Youngdahl, Reuben, 31
Young Turks, 43–46, 69

LORI STURDEVANT is a Minnesota journalist and author who focused on state and local government and politics during a forty-three-year career at the *Minnesota Star Tribune*. She is the author or editor of thirteen books about notable Minnesotans and is a three-time winner of the Minnesota Book Award. She and her husband, Martin Vos, live in St. Paul; they have three grown children and two grandchildren.

Martin Sabo: The Making of the Modern Legislature was designed and set in type by Judy Gilats in St. Paul, Minnesota. The text typeface is Garamond ATF Text Medium and the display typeface is Bebas Neue Pro.